Write
to Learn

Write to Learn

THIRD EDITION

DONALD M. MURRAY

Holt, Rinehart and Winston, Inc.

Fort Worth   Chicago   San Francisco   Philadelphia
Montreal   Toronto   London   Sydney   Tokyo

For Minnie Mae.
Without her there would be no books.

Publisher Charlyce Jones Owen
Acquisitions Editor Michael A. Rosenberg
Design Supervisor/Cover John Ritland
Cover Illustration John Hulsey
Product Management Printers Representatives, Inc.

Library of Congress Cataloging-in-Publication Data

Murray, Don, 1917–
  Write to learn.

  Includes index.
  Summary: Offers step-by-step instructions for
developing effective writing skills.
    1. English language—Rhetoric. 1. English
language—Rhetoric I. Title.
PE1408.M79 1990   808'.042   89-29876

ISBN: 0-03-033123-4

Address Editorial Correspondence to: 301 Commerce Street, Suite 3700, Fort Worth, Texas 76102

Address Orders to: 6277 Sea Harbor Drive, Orlando, Florida 32887
1-800-782-4479, or 1-800-433-0001 (in Florida)

Printed in the United States of America

0 1 2 3 090 9 8 7 6 5 4 3 2 1

Holt, Rinehart and Winston, Inc.
The Dryden Press
Saunders College Publishing

Preface to the Third Edition

I wrote *Write to Learn* to reveal the writer at work and to celebrate how the writer learns by writing.

Art is what someone else—quite possibly after you are dead—says you have done. Craft is what you do. This book attempts to remove the mystery from the writer's craft so that the reader can see and use the writer's methods to make writing that is true, effective, and graceful.

Those who do not write often think writing is something done after the work is over—the sprig of parsley tossed in the vicinity of the chop. Writers know that is not true. Writing is how we explore our world and discover its meaning. We write to learn.

Writing Process

Writing isn't magic, but then magic isn't magic either. Magicians know their craft, and writers must also know their craft.

Process is the most effective way I discovered to learn my craft. I take the entire writing act from before the blank page when there is no idea for—or even of—writing until a draft is completed, edited, and published, then break it down into its sequential parts.

My concept of the writing process is based on many sources. Beginning in junior-high school, I started noting what writers say about writing. A book, *Shoptalk—Learning to Write with Writers*, which reprints my favorite quotations from the thousands I have collected, was recently published by Heinemann. Although there are differences in how we write in varied genres for different audiences, I have discovered remarkable similarities in studying science writers, novelists, business writers, critics, poets, journalists, technical writers, playwrights, historians, scholars, movie and TV writers, memo writers, and essayists.

The basic writing process as I see it has been greatly affected by two sources: my observations of the thousands of students who have solved their writing problems by adapting to their own needs the techniques used by professional writers, and my observations of the publishing writers with whom I work as a writing coach.

Most of all, the writing process I describe is my own. *Nulla dies sine linea.* Never a day without a line. I write every day and observe my own writing. The process in the book is what I do—with the variations I discuss in the book.

Writers at Work

In these pages, you watch the evolving writing process of a publishing writer. You also see five Freshman English students at work. You will see false starts, failures, the bad writing that is necessary to produce writing that works. You will observe me trying the techniques I suggest you try, and unlike in most books on writing, you will not see only the final, published piece of work, polished, edited, all cleaned up with no evidence of the work that produced the final copy. You will be beside me at the writing desk as I snarl and grumble my way toward my own meaning, failing and, I hope, learning from my failures.

What Happened to Grandma?

This text was first conceived as a book that would show one writer exploring a single territory. The result was a personal essay on my grandmother, the dominant parent of my childhood. I liked the essay and I still do. I also admit to a personal fascination in seeing a writer play with the same material over and over and over again. I wish it were some other writer but this is the only one handy.

But there are two problems:

▶ Some students—and their instructors—get bored with grandmother.
▶ This device limits the writing to one genre—the personal essay.

Therefore, in the third edition, I will show that handy writer, myself, working on different writing tasks at each stage of the writing process and then integrate the entire writing process by using grandmother in an abbreviated form in the last chapter. This was not an idea forced on me. It was my own suggestion after listening to the reactions of users of the first two editions.

Increased Demonstrations of Form

This edition shows the professional writers and the student writers at work on a variety of forms. The text begins with description, the genre I believe is underrated and is the most effective genre for the beginning writer to begin to understand the writer's craft. It proceeds to the reflective narrative, a term I use to refine the personal-experience essay so it avoids the complaint many instructors have with that form and connects student writing more effectively with academic writing.

The text moves through the genres that connect directly with academic and most professional or postacademic writing: analysis, argument, and reports on research. The last chapter includes brief, practical suggestions for those students who want to explore other forms of nonfiction, fiction, poetry, and drama.

Other Changes in the Third Edition _____

Besides the changes in the professional and student case histories, I have made many other improvements based on my own writing and teaching experience since the publication of the second edition as well as the response of students and teachers who have used *Write to Learn.*

Primary Process Techniques

One of the virtues of this text—in my opinion—is the inventory of techniques available at each stage of the writing process, but the abundance of this material can be confusing. In the third edition, a single technique will be emphasized at each stage of the writing process and later the others will be described.

Finding the Line

The primary technique for the focus chapter is new. It has come from my experience in writing a newspaper column. I realized that I began writing *after* I found a line, a fragment of language, and I realized that was the focusing point in almost all of my writing in every form. This method is described in detail with examples.

Fastwriting and Layering

The chapter on development begins with a new emphasis on fastwriting and the introduction of a technique I call layering that has helped me in my own writing and that I have used with students, teachers, and professional writers. It is also described in detail and demonstrated.

The Voice of the Text

The third edition develops and clarifies the concept that each text has a voice and although the writer has a personal voice, it is important for the writer to tune that voice to the writing task and the reader.

Writing on a Computer

The second and now the third edition of this book were written on a computer. Since most writers, and now an increasing number of students, are using computers, I have added material on writing on a computer.

Self-Teaching by Commentary

I have found it important to write about my own writing so that I can learn what I do well and how I do it and what I don't do so well and how I may do it better. I have used this method with students and professionals with excellent results. I am including a section that students can use on their own or that teachers may assign.

Writing for Yourself—and Others

I emphasize the importance of writing for yourself—and then extending to the audience of the reader. I have included new material on this act of distancing that is central to effective writing.

Personal Experience and Academic Writing

The work I have done in the past few years, especially in developing the concept of the reflective narrative, has allowed me to draw a closer relationship between the personal writing we usually find is the most effective starting place for the beginning writer and the great variety of academic and professional writing students will do in school and on the job.

The Lead as Promise

In the second edition of *Write to Learn* I developed the idea that the lead or the first lines of a piece of writing make a promise to the reader. I have incorporated that concept in the third edition of *Write to Learn*.

Qualities of an Effective First Draft

Most students—and many of their instructors—do not know how to react to the first draft, a text that often has raw but undeveloped potential. I have included material that tells the writer how to read and evaluate the experiment in meaning that is a first draft.

Clear Thinking—Clear Writing

The introduction to the chapter on clarity presents a new—for me—case for the relationship between clear thinking and clear writing, a relationship that is obvious *after* you have understood it.

The Master Checklist

The earlier editions of this text had extensive checklists for three readings of the next-to-final draft. That was a bit much for many readers. I still present the possibility of three readings, but have combined the checklists into one master list that is more focused and more practical for the student.

Using Tradition

Many students see themselves as writing against the traditions of language, style, and form. I make the case for first using the tradition that is, after all, the experiments of earlier writers that were so successful they became traditional.

Using the Third Edition with *Read to Write* _____

Although *Write to Learn* is designed to be used alone or with other readers, *Read to Write* was written after *Write to Learn* and each text supports the other. They have the same process design, a similar attitude toward the act of writing, and examples of writing in each text support and extend the other.

Using *Write to Learn* _____

Before Writing

The third edition can be scanned as an introduction to writing. In using it that way, I would read the first chapter, then the introductions to each of the following chapters and the primary techniques in Chapters 2 through 6.

An effective way to introduce the writing process is to take six 3 by 5 cards and perform the primary techniques in Chapters 2 through 7: brainstorming, seeking the revealing specific, finding the line, making the promise, fastwriting. Take only four to five minutes with each stage and move on. You can share with a neighbor but, if so, each person should take only two minutes to listen and respond.

I have timed this exercise, giving each assignment, going four minutes [with four minutes for conferences if I do those], announcing the end of each sequence arbitrarily, keeping everyone moving. No time to be discouraged. It's a silly game, see what you do. If I write, I share my writing, and they see how badly a professional can write.

At the end, we go around and share our last card. I am always astonished at some of the writing that is produced. The class or workshop hears voices that are inspiring and everyone gets a feel for the writing process.

It is important to use small cards. They are forgiving. When I go to 4 by 6, 5 by 8, or regular paper, I lose a few people. With the small cards, we can have six four-minute writing periods in less than half an hour.

This exercise shouldn't work as well as it does. It is arbitrary, superficial, ridiculous, and astonishing in what it unleashes. I have done variations of this with students from grades one through graduate school, with teachers, and with professional writers, and I have done it myself several hundred times, and most everyone gets a start on a piece of worthwhile writing.

It is also possible to do one or two stages of this exercise at the beginning of a series of three or six classes, taking that time to assign each chapter in the book and discuss them.

During Writing

As you can see, I can't talk about using my text for more than a paragraph without getting the reader writing. I start my day writing and I started my classes writing first, especially in the beginning.

This text—and any other—will be best understood by the person who is in the act of writing. Until you are trying to find what you have to say and how you can say it, you don't understand the territory.

Write to Learn is designed to be used by students who are writing. It is a desk book, a resource that attempts in every part of its design—not just in the questions and answers at the end of most chapters—to anticipate the concerns of the beginning writer and to respond to them.

After Writing

The text is meant to be especially valuable after the student has finished writing. Now the beginner can join the community of writers, see what other writers might have done, reinforce what worked, find new experiments for the next assignment, put the particular writing process just completed into a larger context.

The Instructor's Manual

I have written an Instructor's Manual for the third edition of *Write to Learn* that is based on my own experience as a teacher and the experiences of instructors who have used the first edition in many different types of institutions and courses with students of many levels of accomplishment. It is specific, practical, and designed to help beginning and experienced instructors in realistic teaching situations. It may be obtained from the English editor, Holt, Rinehart and Winston, Inc., 301 Commerce Street, Fort Worth, Texas 76102.

Make My Book Yours _____

Pay close attention to your drafts; learn from your own learning. As a writer, you should be self-taught. What I have attempted to show in this book is how one writer after fifty years of publication is still learning to write. But you have to take this book away from me and make it your own.

Richard Hugo was a fine poet and teacher who told his students, "You'll never be a poet until you realize that everything I say today and this quarter is wrong. It may be right for me, but it is wrong for you. Every moment, I am, without wanting or trying to, telling you to write like me. But I hope you learn to write like you. In a sense, I hope I don't teach you how to write but how to teach yourself how to write. At all times keep your crap detector on. If I say something that helps, good. If what I say is of no help, let it go. Don't start arguments. They are futile and take us away from our purpose. As Yeats noted, your important arguments are with yourself. If you don't agree with me don't listen."

Good advice. In the end, the writer at eighteen or eighty is alone with the writer's own experience and the writer's own language. The writer, in that loneliness, keeps learning to write.

I learned by writing each edition of *Write to Learn*, and I will go on learning in writing the next one. "One thing that is always with the writer—no matter how long he has written or how good he is—is the continuing process of learning how to write," says Flannery O'Connor. "As soon as the writer 'learns to write,' as soon as he knows what he is going to find, and discovers a way to say what he knew all along, or worse still, a way to say nothing, he is finished."

You'll have to keep setting your own standards, putting the bar high enough so it trembles but does not fall when you jump over it. If your standards are too high, you will choke and not write; if your standards are too low, you will not learn and you will not be read. Those standards are always changing, and it is your job to keep inching the bar up, deciding what you can attempt this day at your desk.

Good luck.

Acknowledgments ——————————————————————————

It is traditional when acknowledging all those who have helped you with a book to place the name of one's spouse at the end. It would be totally inappropriate in this case. My wife, Minnie Mae, has been my closest colleague and strongest supporter on this writing project, as she has on every other one.

The lineage of this book goes back to the late Mortimer B. Howell of Tilton School and Junior College, who turned my life around when he taught me Freshman English. When I first taught Freshman English, he gave me my own Freshman English papers, which he had saved—a humbling gift. At the University of New Hampshire, I have learned from and with many colleagues. Among those who deserve special mention is Lester A. Fisher. Our early shouted arguments in the corridors about the teaching of writing settled down to a relationship that underlies all my teaching and constantly reminds me of the importance of respect for the individual student. Thomas A. Carnicelli first got me involved in directing Freshman English, and he has been a constructive, tough-minded critic of my work through the years. Thomas R. Newkirk's scholarship and wise counsel have helped me keep my work in perspective. I've shared almost daily discussions of writing and the teaching of writing with Donald Graves. We have learned about writing and the teaching of writing together. I am also indebted to Brock Dethier, who is one of many master teachers of writing I've been able to work with on the staffs of Freshman English and Advanced Composition courses at the University of New Hampshire. We have all shared our teaching and our learning, and I am indebted to all of them for contributing so much to my education. I've learned most from the thousands of students with whom I had weekly writing conferences during my twenty-four years teaching at the University of New Hampshire.

I've also been fortunate in those away from Durham who have taught me about writing and the teaching of writing. A few who must be mentioned include Christopher Scanlan of the Washington Bureau of Knight-Ridder Newspapers; Carol Berkenkotter of Michigan Technological University; John and Tilly Warnock of the University of Wyoming; Driek Zirinsky of Boise State University; and dozens of others who have influenced my thinking.

I am indebted to the fifty students and twenty teachers from Idaho in the Whittenberger Foundation–State Department of Education Summer Program who read and attacked the first draft of this book and who are responsible for many improvements in the text.

I must also pay tribute to the officers of the Conference on College Composition and Communication, whose work has made it possible for those of us interested in studying writing to get together and exchange our views in print and in person.

I was greatly helped with the third edition by many candid, helpful readers including Allison Chestnut, Jones County Junior College; Michael Donaghe, Eastern New Mexico University; Charles R. Duke, Clarion University; Roger George, Bellevue Community College; Linda Hunter, St. Olaf College; Pat Mathias, Des Moines Area Community College; John Nelson, St. Mary of the Plains College.

I owe special thanks to the editor of the first edition, Nedah Abbott, and to Charlyce Jones Owen, who has given the same level of support to the writing of the second and third editions. Michael Rosenberg was an effective midwife to my final labors. Jeanette Ninas Johnson supervised the editorial production of this book with craft and efficiency. Catherine Buckner, the copy editor, caught my mistakes, and Bob Kopelman supervised the design of this book so the graphic art supported my words and my meaning.

Contents

3. Explore Your Subject: COLLECT

4. Explore Your Subject: FOCUS

5. Explore Your Subject: ORDER

6. Explore Your Subject: DEVELOP

7. Explore Your Subject: CLARIFY

Chapter 1

༄ Find Your Way to Write

I must keep to my own style, and go on in my own way; and though I may never succeed again in that, I am convinced that I should totally fail in any other.

JANE AUSTIN

To be nobody-but-yourself—in a world which is doing its best, night and day, to make you everybody else—means to fight the hardest battle which any human being can fight; and never stop fighting.

e. e. cummings

There is no one right way. Each of us finds a way that works for him. But there is a wrong way. The wrong way is to finish your writing day with no more words on paper than when you began. Writers write.

ROBERT PARKER

When most people think of writing, they see words on a page, all neatly ordered, marching toward a meaning. When writers think of writing, they see a blank page, and they see what was before the blank page.

You are reading the finished process of writing. But before there was this page, I stacked up 500 sheets of 8½ by 11, twenty-weight blank paper. I was attracted to its blankness—and terrified by it. I didn't know if I had anything to say.

Before I could find words to put on the paper I had to go back. Staring out the window, beyond the pile of blank paper, I heard my Uncle Will reciting poems as he carried me in his arms late at night. My grandmother, stern matriarch of our clan, stood approving in the shadows. Do I remember it, or was it something that was told me? No matter, I hear his voice, see Grandma's approving smile, and hear the music of those Scottish poems.

Looking out the window of my office, I see myself, a small boy in bed, a lonely boy in a house of grownups with problems he couldn't understand. And I remember the stories that boy told himself about football, and fights in the street, and traveling across the ocean, and girls. There were more and more stories about girls.

Writing Is Discovering

What has this got to do with this book? Everything. That's where it started. The boy learned to read and to write, and the excitement in writing was that he didn't know exactly what he was going to say when he wrote. There were always surprises on the page. Sometimes the surprises were large, sometimes small, but there was always something unexpected. In writing, two and two may add up to five, or twelve, or seventy-seven.

This book is based on more than forty years, no, close to fifty years of published writing. I was first published in a newspaper printed on a strange gelatin substance in Miss Chapman's fourth grade class at the Massachusetts Field School in Wollaston, Massachusetts, which, I am told, has been turned into condominiums. This book is also based on years of teaching writing, teaching teachers about writing, and teaching professional writers to write. I had outlined and reoutlined this text, carefully planning what I would write, but the first pages are different from what I expected. I intended to be impersonal, to talk about other writers, and I found myself talking about myself, because I think you need to know that this book, and all books, start with an individual human being's thoughts and feelings. Much of the most important writing takes place before words begin to appear on blank paper.

Am I upset that my planning seems to have gone down the drain, that I am writing what I do not expect to write? Just the opposite. That planning got me started and it's all being used subconsciously, but if I thought I knew that I would write, I wouldn't have agreed to do the book. Writers write to learn, to explore, to discover, to hear themselves saying what they do not expect to say.

Words are the symbols for what we learn. They allow us to play with information, to make connections and patterns, to put together and take apart and put together again, to see what experience means. In other words, to think. According to Robert Bolt, "Writing a play is thinking, not thinking about thinking." Writing, in fact, is the most disciplined form of thinking. It allows us to be precise, to stand back and examine what we have thought, to see what our words really mean, to see if they stand up to our own critical eye, make sense, and will be understood by someone else.

Why Write? _____

Sometimes we write just for ourselves, to record what we have seen or felt or thought. Sometimes we write to celebrate experience. Many times we write just to find out what it all means, for by writing we can stand back from ourselves and see significance in what is close to us.

Most of the time, however, writing is a private act with a public result. We write alone to discover meaning. But once that meaning is discovered, once we understand what we have to say, then we want or need to share it with other people.

Sometimes that need precedes the impulse to write. We receive an assignment and have to write a paper, an examination, a memo for the boss, a news story. We may have to report an experiment, turn in a poem, write a skit, send out fund-raising publicity, create a job résumé, complain about being badgered for a bill we've already paid. There are hundreds of writing tasks we may have to perform. We may have to write speeches, books, brochures, letters of sympathy, case histories on patients. But whatever writing we do, if it is to be done well, we have to go back to gather information and make sense of it.

We can't write writing. Some readers think professinals who turn out political speeches or company reports can use language to weave a meaning without information. I've been hired as a corporate and a political ghostwriter and know we can't. First we have to understand what the candidate is trying to do, or why the company has made a profit or a loss. We have to do research and attempt to build a meaning from the product of our research that a reader can understand.

The writer may write to inform, to explain, to entertain, to persuade, but whatever the purpose, there should be, first of all, the satisfaction of the writer's own learning, the joy and surprise of finding out what you have to say.

There are many side benefits to writing. Writing allows you to discover that you have a voice, a way of speaking that is individual and effective. It allows you to share with others and even to influence others.

Writing can bring attention to you or to your ideas. It can add to your job skills, and it can improve your grades. Writing can give you power, for we live in a complicated technological society, and those people who can collect information, order it into significant meaning, and then communicate it to others will influence the course of events within the town or nation, school or university, company or corporation. Information is power.

If you have the ability to find specific, accurate information and fit it together in a meaningful pattern through language, you will have the pleasure of making something that was not there before, of finding significance where others find confusion, of bringing order to chaos. If you can do this clearly and gracefully, you will have readers, for people are hungry for specific information ordered into meaning.

First of all, we write for ourselves, then for others. This is true of science writing, business writing, academic writing, argument, essay, and report. We write first to understand and, if that understanding is clear to us, it may also be clear to others.

My attention turns from my uncle carrying me to my grandmother standing by the door of the living room. She approves more by not frowning than by smiling. I study the set of that stern mouth and begin to wonder how much her glance still governs me. If I write about her, I may find out.

I hope you will learn about writing when you read this book, but I know that when that pile of blank paper on my desk is filled with words I will have learned a great deal simply by writing about writing.

How We Write ⎯⎯⎯⎯⎯⎯⎯⎯⎯⎯⎯⎯⎯⎯⎯⎯⎯⎯⎯

Effective writing appears effortless. The words flow across the page, and we hear as well as see them. We listen to the voice of the writer and have the illusion that the individual writer is speaking across time and space to each of us. It seems like magic.

But most of the time it isn't spontaneous. It was carefully made to appear natural. A few moments ago the previous paragraph was typed, then edited by me in this way:

~~When we read~~ effective writing ~~it~~ appears effortless. The words flow across

the page, and we hear ~~them~~ as well as see them. ~~The music comes through,~~

~~and we hear~~ the voice of the writer. ~~We~~ have the illusion that ~~the~~ writer is

We listen to ~~~~ *and* *an individual*

speaking to us ~~one individual speaking~~ across time and space ~~to another~~

each of

~~individual.~~ It seems magic.

Writing is made. Writing is a logical, understandable process that we use to move information around so that it makes sense. We use words as the symbols for that information, and we follow a rational sequence in moving the words around to make our evolving meaning come clear. But it is as hard to imagine how writing is made from reading a finished page by a professional writer as it is to imagine a field of wheat from eating a slice of bread.

Good writing does not reveal its making. The problems are solved, the scaffolding has been removed, the discarded building materials have been hauled away. This book, however, will take you back to the beginning, to the moment of terror that every writer feels when there is a blank page or even before there is a blank page, when there is an assignment to write and the writer feels empty, without anything to say.

The writer never overcomes that feeling. Some writers get headaches, others get stomach aches; I get both. But I have learned, as all writers learn, that there are ways to work that will eventually fill the blank page with words that will make a meaning clear to the writer and the reader.

Writing Is a Process _____

Writing is, above all, a process. It is a logical sequence of activities that can be understood by everyone. You don't put on your overcoat, your pants, and then your underwear. We follow logical patterns in dressing, cooking, tuning a car engine, producing a draft. When we write, some steps precede others most of the time.

Of course, writing is much more complicated than getting dressed in the morning. The writing process is one of the most complicated of human activities. It varies according to the writing task. When we write of something we clearly understand to an audience we know, in a familiar form, we write differently from when we use writing to discover meaning, to reach a strange audience, or to explore a new form or subject.

Writing also varies with our thinking style. Some of us think out loud, and others work quietly. Some are long-distance runners, writing steadily and evenly day after day. Others of us are sprinters, and spend a lot of time sitting around between sudden spurts of writing. Some of us use a logic that is apparent, moving from A to B to C. Others use a logic that is less apparent, leaping to C and working back to B and then A. Or going to D, then B, E, F, C, G, A.

Most of us do not write—or think—the same way all the time. It varies according to the problems we have to solve, what we know about the subject, and how we feel. Our feelings are very important. Writing is a thinking activity, but our feelings create the environment in which we think. Terror, for example, can paralyze, so we have to know how to handle the feelings of terror before the blank page, or we would never write. Writing reveals us, and we know it. Yet we also know that we write best—just as we play tennis best—if we feel confident. We have to learn to write with confidence.

All of these factors affect the writing process, but no matter how much it changes from person to person and from task to task, it is more similar than it is different. We usually follow the same process when we use language to make meaning of our experience.

A Model of the Writing Process _____

There are many models of the writing process. This book is built on one model. It is the way I write, the way many of my students write, the way many other writers write, much—but never all—of the time. It is a way of introducing you to the process approach to writing, but you should pay as much attention to your own writing when the writing goes well as to my model. You should know how you made writing lead you to a meaning that others could understand. You should know what you did, how you did it, the order in which you did it, and how you felt before, during, and after you did it. You should develop your own models of the writing process so that when the writing doesn't go well, you'll have those positive experiences to look back on. By following your own effective writing process you may be able to write well again.

Let us look closely at my model of the writing process. We have to start with what happens inside the writer's brain. Ernest Hemingway was once asked where he wrote, and he is supposed to have answered, "In my head." If we could open up a writer's head during the act of writing we might see an electrochemical process that looks like this:

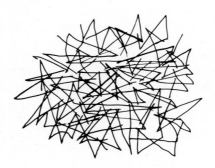

The Parts of the Process _____

If we could untangle that spaghetti we might find the following five primary activities taking place:

Collecting

The brain is constantly collecting and recollecting specific information that comes from all of the senses—seeing, hearing, smelling, tasting, touching. Some people believe that every piece of information delivered to the brain remains there in storage waiting to be called up, if only we know how. Writing is one of the best ways to recollect. We do not think we remember, but when we write we discover what we know.

Focusing

We focus on a single piece of information or several pieces that interest us to make sense of the confused jumble of information delivered to the brain. During the writing process, we pay particular attention to those scraps of information that begin to have particular meaning for us. The poet Maxine Kumin says that the writer looks for information that "informs." This information may be a code word that has private meaning for us, a specific detail, or a combination of words and details that catches our attention.

Ordering

As we focus on pieces of information, our brain keeps trying to connect the information that interests us with other information, so a meaning evolves. We keep lining up information and language, the way a baby builds with blocks, to see what it may mean. We discover the structure of what we may have to say.

Drafting

Once the potential order can be seen, we start writing. We talk to ourselves as we write, using our voices to tell us what we have to say. This talk becomes writing that we hear as we see it. And as this talk is recorded, we begin to know what we have to say and how we may be able to say it.

Clarifying

When our message is filled out in a draft, our brain reads it to see what has been said, if it is worth saying, and how well it is said. The writer reading the writer's own drafts is constantly trying to understand what the writer learned, thought, felt. The brain tries to understand, working at the text to make it more sensible, sharper, more understandable. Our brain goes through a constant process of tuning and adjusting to clarify what is being written.

The Parts Interact _____

All these activities take place simultaneously. It is indeed a complicated process.

▶ We clarify by ordering and reordering the information we are collecting and recollecting.
▶ We collect information by drafting what we have to say, reordering it trying to make it clear, and collecting new information to fill the holes we discover.
▶ We focus on a specific piece of information and then as we draft what we have to say about it we discover how it relates to other material. And as we collect that material, we have to order and reorder to make it clear.
▶ We start drafting, not knowing what we are going to say, and find we are

collecting material, and the order in which it begins to arrange itself on the page makes our focus clear.

I could go on making statement after statement about the writing process that would be true on a particular project at a particular time. Another way of looking at the primary activities in the writing process, to show how they take place simultaneously and also interact with each other at the same time, can be seen in the following chart.

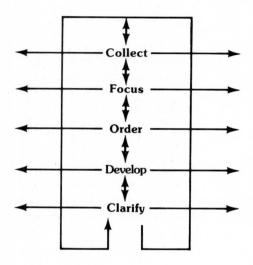

If we study those activities during the time that a piece of writing develops, we begin to see a pattern of emphasis. We see that the writer continues to collect during the entire writing process, but does much more collecting at the beginning. We also see that there is clarification going on from the very beginning, but that the emphasis on clarity comes toward the end of the writing process. There is a natural sequence of emphasis during the writing, a process most of us follow most of the time; it is illustrated by the following chart.

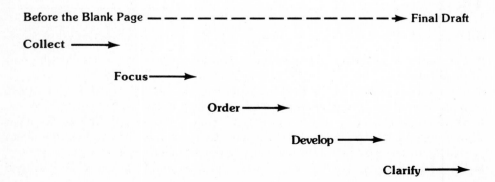

The writing process, however, is recursive. We move from an emphasis on collecting to focusing to ordering to drafting to clarifying, but it is not a neat, linear process. Often, when we focus, we find we have to go back and collect new information, and as we collect that information, we have to refocus.

As we move down through the writing process to ordering what we may say, we often have to go back and collect and refocus and reorder.

When we draft what we are saying, we may also have to go back to collect or focus or reorder or redraft.

And as we clarify what we have to say, we may have to go back to any part of the process, or to the beginning. We may have to collect more information, focus again, or reorder, or redraft.

The following diagram attempts to show the writing process at work, how the principal parts of this system interact so that we write and learn.

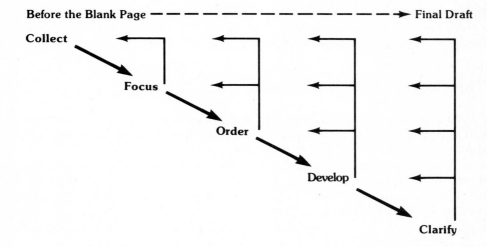

Before the Blank Page — — — — — — — — — — — — → Final Draft

Collect

Focus

Order

Develop

Clarify

How a Process Model Works

A mental picture of our writing process will help us solve many of the problems we run into in writing. If we don't have a model of the writing process, we are more likely to try solutions that don't work. We may, for example, try to revise and edit the language when the problem is a lack of specific, meaningful information. If the information is the problem, then we have to go back and research the subject. On the other hand, the problem may be communication, and an inexperienced writer may go back and look for more and more examples, when the writer needs to prune and shape the language.

A model of a process that worked for us in the past may allow us, at any point in the writing process, to look back and understand what we have done and what we have left to do. It gives us a map, a way to study our voyage toward meaning and plot an efficient course. The model also takes the unnecessary mystery away from writing and makes it possible for us to see, and therefore improve, our craft.

A common model of the writing process, which will, of course, allow variation, helps us understand how our classmates are writing. We can begin to see how they are making language work, how they are producing drafts that are evolving toward a clear, documented meaning. We can learn more easily from other writers when we can understand their writing process.

The process view of writing also allows us to help other writers. We can respond more intelligently and constructively to their questions about their work. We can help them see where they are in the writing process and, therefore, suggest strategies and techniques that may help them solve their writing problems.

An understanding of the writing process makes us more perceptive readers of published authors. We will begin to understand what has gone on backstage that makes the published performance possible. We may begin to learn from the master writers of our language, for we will see that their writing wasn't magic, that it was craft before it became art.

The Process Log or Daybook

As you move forward and backward and forward again through the writing process you may find it helpful—and fun—to keep a log or daybook to record where you have been and, even more important, where you may go.

You will find that you do not march through the writing process hup, two, three, four. While researching a piece, you may suddenly make a guess as to how the piece of writing will end—before you've even started it. While not consciously working on writing, you may see a possible order of arguments you may want to use, or hear—in your head—a sentence or two that captures the voice or style in which you hope to write. You may hear a quotation or spot a fact in your reading that you can use later. You may get an idea for the piece of writing you will do after you finish this one. It will help if you have a way to capture all these guesses and fragments. The act of writing them down will help you remember them, and will lead to more ideas and productive connections.

The most valuable writing tool I have is my daybook, and the name is important to me. For years I tried to keep a journal. I imagined I was Gide or Camus. I wasn't, and what I wrote was not perceptive but pompous, full of hot air, hilarious to read, and utterly useless to me as a writer. At other times I tried to keep a diary, but then I found myself recording trivia—the temperature, or whom I met, or what I ate. It made a rather boring life seem even more boring.

I don't know where I heard the term *daybook*, but a number of years ago I found myself using the term and writing every day—well, almost every day— in an 8 by 10 spiral notebook filled with greenish paper, narrow ruled, with a margin line down the left. This worked for me. I write in my lap, in the living room or on the porch, in the car or an airplane, in meetings at the university, in bed, or sitting down on a rock wall during a walk. A bound book doesn't work for me. I find a spiral book much more convenient, and since I write in all sorts of light, indoors and out, I find the greenish paper comfortable. I chose the size because it fits in the outside pocket of the bag I carry everywhere.

The organization is simple day-by-day chronology. When I change the subject, I write a code word in the margin. That way, I can look back through the book and collect all the notes I've made on a single project or concern.

I often write in the daybook the first fifteen minutes of the day before I eat breakfast. And then I have it near me all day long. If something occurs to me, I make a note during a television commercial, or in a meeting, or while walking, or in the car.

How I use my daybook varies from time to time. Since I now do most of my writing on a computer, my daybooks have pages or paragraphs I have printed out and pasted in the daybook so I can read, reconsider, play with that text in spare moments. All the writing in the daybook is a form of talking to myself, a way of thinking on paper. Much of my spontaneous writing can be tracked through years of daybooks where I have thought and rethought, planned and researched, drafted and redrafted its movement from interesting fragment to possible draft.

If you look through my daybook here are some of the things you would see:

- ▶ Questions that need to be answered
- ▶ Fragments of writing seeking a voice
- ▶ Leads, hundreds of leads
- ▶ Titles, hundreds of titles
- ▶ Notes from which I have made lectures, talks, or speeches
- ▶ Notes I have made at lectures, talks, or speeches of others; also notes I have made at poetry readings, hockey games, and concerts
- ▶ Outlines
- ▶ Ideas for stories, articles, poems, books, papers
- ▶ Diagrams showing how a piece might be organized or, more likely, showing the relationships between parts of an idea
- ▶ Drafts
- ▶ Observations
- ▶ Quotations from writers or artists
- ▶ Newspaper clippings
- ▶ Titles of books to be read
- ▶ Notes on what I have read
- ▶ Pictures I want to save
- ▶ Writing schedules
- ▶ Pasted-in copies of interesting letters I've received—or written
- ▶ Lists, lots of lists
- ▶ Pasted-in handouts I've developed for classes or workshops.

I don't have any one way to use the daybook. Anything that will stimulate or record my thinking, anything that will move toward writing goes into the daybook. When a notebook is filled—usually in about six weeks—I go through and harvest a page or two or three of the most interesting material for the beginning of the next daybook. When I'm ready to work seriously on a project, I go back through the daybooks for a year or more and photocopy those pages that relate to the subject I'm working on.

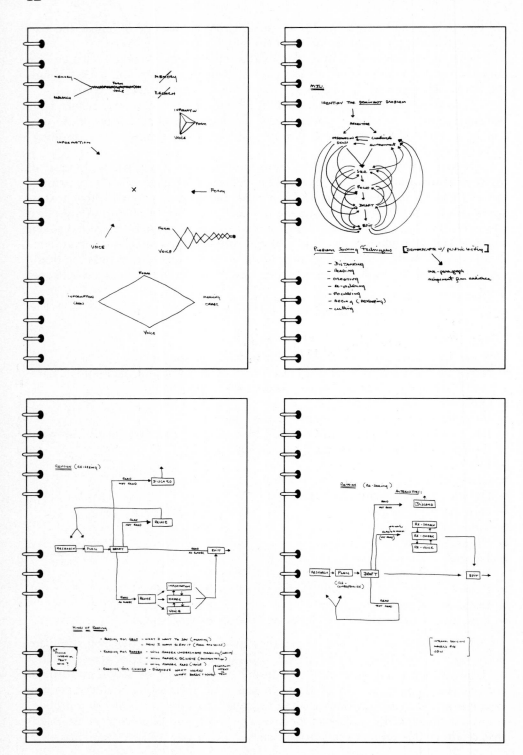

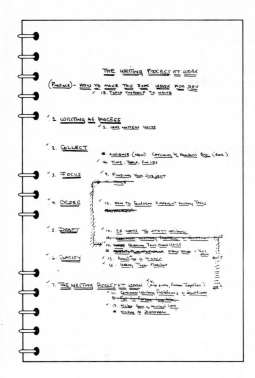

I feel like a person surprised when skinny dipping as I study these daybook pages exposing me writing. I hope they will help you understand that writing doesn't have to look like writing. On these pages I played with ideas, trying to encourage and capture surprise. All of these pages—and the more than 4000 in my other daybooks—reveal this writer at play, designing, listing, connecting, ordering and drafting. I hope you'll have as much fun in your daybooks.

The daybook stimulates my thinking, helps me make use of those small fragments of time that on many days is all the time I have to write. There is no sign of struggle. I'm not fighting writing, I'm playing with writing. If it isn't fun, if nothing is happening, I stop and wait until the magic begins. The daybook also keeps my writing muscles in condition; it lets me know what I'm concerned with making into writing; it increases my productivity.

If you decide to keep a daybook, make it your own. Don't try to follow anyone else's formula. And don't write it for another audience. It's a private place where you can think and where you can be dumb, stupid, sloppy, silly; where you can do all the bad writing and bad thinking that are essential for those moments of insight that produce good writing.

Make the Process Yours

The process log or daybook will help you make the process yours, will give you a chance to see how you write when the writing goes well. If you are to keep improving your writing, you need to build on the procedures you used that have worked.

This book will provide you with the process as I see it now, based on my own study of other writers, writing process research, what my students have taught me, and my own writing experience. This is a model that you should adapt and change to fit your own thinking style, writing habits, and writing tasks.

You should learn how to write from how you write, as well as from how others write. The end does justify the means in this case. What works—writing that is meaningful, clear, and graceful—is the measure by which any writing process must be judged. As this book is being printed and published I will go on writing, learning more about the writing process. And as you read it, and write, you will go on learning from this book and from your own experience.

Keep Putting the Process Back Together

When the process works, it is more than its parts. Michael Jordan driving toward the basket, rising, hanging in midair, oh so gently twirling the ball into the basket, is much more than a simple description of dribbling, jumping, and shooting. I heard Jascha Heifetz warm up by playing the scales, and it was much more than playing the scales. Writing is produced by a process, but effective writing is not the simple following of steps in that process.

The main reason for this is that writing does not so much work from parts to a whole as evolve from a constant interaction of parts and whole.

Too many people think that if you teach spelling, vocabulary, punctuation, grammatical usage, and rhetoric, you have taught writing. But writing starts with a guess, a global idea of what may be said, and then as the writer collects information and starts putting words on paper, the guess changes.

It is an incredibly complex, challenging, and difficult process. It wouldn't be any fun if it weren't. The global guess, at first vague and general, influences the writer's choice of facts, words, punctuation, spaces. Each fact, each word, each mark of punctuation, each space between words changes the guess or meaning of what is being said.

The writer constantly moves back and forth between part and whole, between word and meaning. Don't forget that as we study writing process. We will concentrate on one part of the process at a time, showing all sorts of techniques that may be used in that stage of writing. But when you are writing, keep trying to put it all together. Don't become so aware of the seam on the basketball that you can't shoot the basket, or so conscious of your manners you can't taste the food.

Disciplines for Writing

All this collecting—remembering, receiving, searching, and researching—produces the mass of material that is essential for effective writing. It also produces a need for discipline, a habit, a way of working that will allow the writer to turn a jungle of raw material into publishable copy.

"Everybody's different, everybody's habits are different," says Walker Percy. "I have to sit down at 9 o'clock in the morning and write for three hours or at least look at the paper for three hours. Sometimes I don't do *anything*. But unless you do that—punch the time clock—you won't *ever* do anything. On those days or mornings when you feel worst, when you think everything is hopeless, that nothing will happen—sometimes the best things happen."

Sounds simple, doesn't it? But it isn't. Getting the writing done day in and day out, despite interruptions, phone calls, obligations, duties, responsibilities, inertia, exhaustion, poor health, bad weather, invited and uninvited guests, too much drinking, too much eating, too little eating, wars, storms, births, deaths, marriages, divorces, travel, letters that come and letters that don't come, and a million other problems, is what separates the writer from the hope-to-be writer.

There are variations among writers, and a writer's discipline may change over a lifetime of work. But if you are to get the writing done this semester, and in the years ahead, you should pay some attention to the following counsel.

Time

We have two kinds of writing times—fragmentary and insulated. We obviously have much more fragmentary time than we have insulated time, and it is important that we make use of both kinds of time.

As I mentioned earlier in the book, 60 percent or more of my time is spent planning, and most of this work is done in small fragments of time that can be measured only in minutes, sometimes in seconds. This writing is done in my head and in my daybook. It isn't a question of hours but of minutes.

Try it yourself before class begins, waiting for a friend at the student union, during a commercial on television, waiting for the campus bus, during a coffee break at work, as a short break during studying; see how long it takes to brainstorm five titles, write a lead paragraph, draft a description, focus on a definition, sketch an anecdote, or even outline an article. I suspect you will find that when you thought you worked ten, or fifteen, or twenty minutes, you've worked two minutes, or four, or ninety seconds.

If you make good use of those fragments of time, you'll be able to write when you have a stretch of uninterrupted time. For most writers an hour is good, but not good enough. Two hours is plenty; three hours heroic. During those times, unplug the phone, lock the door; do not read, create interruptions, plan, edit, nap, or eat—just write.

The time of day is important. Most young writers start out writing late at night and end up writing in the morning—the early morning—when their mind is fresh and the world is less likely to intrude. Goethe said, "Use the day before the day. Early morning hours have gold in their mouth."

The time of day, however, is not as important as habit. Most productive writers—there are exceptions—establish a routine and write at the same time every day. They know it and the people around them know it. Alberto Moravia says, "When I sit down to write—that's between 9 and 12 every morning, and I have never, incidentally, written a line in the afternoon or at night—when I sit down at my table to write, I never know what it's going to be until I'm under way. I trust in inspiration, which sometimes comes and sometimes doesn't. But I don't sit back waiting for it. I work every day." And Flannery O'Connor explains, "Every morning between 9 and 12 I go to my room and sit before a piece of paper. Many times I just sit for three hours with no ideas coming to me, but I know one thing: if an idea does come between 9 and 12, I am there ready for it."

Do not try for long, exhausting writing sessions. Few writers are productive in that way. Most writers write regularly for one to three hours every day and those are full-time writers. You may have to try for an hour a day or half an hour. Philip Larkin says, "I don't think you can write a poem for more than two hours. After that you're going round in circles, and it's much better to leave it for twenty-four hours. . . . Some days it goes, and some days it doesn't go. But over weeks and months I am productive."

Once you have produced a draft, fragmentary time can serve you again. I find it better to edit in short bursts. If I edit more than fifteen minutes at a run I tend to be kind, far too kind. In these slivers of time, early and late in the day, I can cut, insert, reorder, and perhaps decide that I need another draft when I have a few hours of isolated time.

Place

It helps to have a place where you go to write. It should be a place where you can leave your work lying out and come back to it later, where you have your tools at hand and you have the climate that you prefer.

Ross MacDonald tells us, "I took my lifelong tenancy in the bare muffled room of the professional writer where I am sitting now, with my back to the window, writing longhand in a spiral notebook." I like to look up from my writing at a view. Other writers, such as Ross MacDonald, turn their backs to the view. I need music when I write; other writers have to have silence. Create a place of your own where you can shut the door and be by yourself.

That's the ideal most students can never achieve. Joyce Carol Oates says, however, "If you are a writer, you locate yourself behind a wall of silence and no matter what you are doing, driving a car or walking or doing housework, which I love, you can still be writing, because you have that space."

It isn't easy to create that internal space, and women writers in particular have difficulty achieving Virginia Woolf's "room of one's own." But it can be done, as Lois Duncan points out: "Now I keep a typewriter with a sheet of paper in it on the end of the kitchen table. When I have a five-minute lull and the children are playing quietly, I sit down and knock out a paragraph. I have learned that I can write, if necessary with a TV set blaring on one side of me and a child banging on a piano on the other. I've even typed out a story with a colicky baby draped across my lap. It is not ideal—but it is possible." Donald Graves has been able to write in a dormitory room with pneumatic drill construction going on next door or in a small summer cottage filled with family, friends, and dogs by using earphones and Beethoven at top volume.

You have to find ways to detach yourself from the world and go to that place where you can hear the writing. Depending on our personalities, those places may not be the ideal artist's cabin high in the Rockies. I wrote most of one novel in a park, either sitting in the car or at a picnic table far out of the range of my mother-in-law's voice. I like to write in coffee shops and diners where no one knows me, and where there is a stimulating but unobtrusive background life that I can observe or ignore.

When I was an undergraduate, my favorite writing places included the top row of the empty football stadium, a pleasing assortment of rocks on the Atlantic coast, a special table in the library, an empty classroom late at night. Find the places where you can hear your voice as it speaks from the page.

Then listen to what you have to say.

Computers and Other Writers' Tools _____

Every writer knows there is magic in tools. Writing comes out of the little blinking light on the computer screen, the ink, the pen, the typewriter, and the paper as much as the brain.

I have a closet full of once-favorite tools, and I travel with a supply of favorite pens and notebooks, the ones that have poems and stories in them.

Writing on a Computer

The computer, however, has become the greatest tool of all. When the Boston Globe switched over to computers years ago, they had a special program to persuade recalcitrant writers and editors to make the switch. They had more than 400 editorial workers, but they never had to use that program. Everyone switched.

Except for two poets and three fiction writers—four of the five in darkest middle age and one passing into that territory, every writer I know works on a computer. Electronics simply makes writing, rewriting, and editing faster and easier.

I was not an easy convert to computers and I can understand those who fear them. I am not handy with gadgets and I particularly dislike machines that feel they are smarter than I am. Yet when I got my first word processor, I was writing on it in twenty minutes.

Writers, after all, don't need to know how computers work. I don't know how a fountain pen, a telephone, the TV, my medium fi, or my station wagon works, but I can use them. What writers do on a computer is simple: We put down words, move them around, get rid of them. Even I can do that.

Here are some of the ways the computer has affected my writing:

• *Planning.* The computer encourages the most important planning activity: play. It allows me to list and reorder my list, one of the principal planning techniques I use. It encourages free writing that may lead me to the voice of a potential text. It makes it possible to record, connect, and reconnect fragments of information. It encourages all forms of outlining. This edition was outlined by my making a copy of the table of contents from the last edition, then making dozens of variations, taking items out, putting new ones in, moving stuff around to see where it best fitted. This section and the one that follows were built in this way: Early this morning I drafted and reordered all the headings such as planning, then, after a later, leisurely Sunday-morning breakfast with my wife and a visiting daughter, I have returned to fill in the holes under the headings, adding some new ones, cutting out others, moving the units of writing around.

• *Drafting* is easier. Much easier. I can write to see if I am ready to write. I can write from despair as well as confidence. I can write to see what happens. I can write poorly, and I can delete or wait to rework it later.

• *Speed.* The computer has multiplied my writing speed, and as you will see in Chapter 6, I have come to realize the importance of fast writing that allows the writer to outrun the censor and cause the accidents of language and meaning that lead to effective writing. The computer also allows me to type badly and capture the flood of inspiration, then to correct my errors when the flow of inspiration has slowed.

• *Experimenting* is as important to the writer as to the laboratory scientist. The computer encourages me to experiment with language, pattern, order, form, pace, length. I can, for example, take a poem and break it into short and long lines, into three, four, and five line stanzas as I did yesterday. It took me moments to experiment with the poem. It would have taken a whole day to do the same thing with pen or typewriter.

• *Reading* of my text is improved. My handwriting and my typing are so bad I have trouble reading what I write. The computer reveals my text to me clearly and gives me the essential distance so I can see what works and what needs work.

• ***Revising*** is a snap on the computer. For decades I crossed out, wrote in, moved around, cut, pasted, stapled, scotch taped, retyped, making an incredible mess of everything I wrote and rewrote. Now each change is made quickly—and clearly.

• ***Editing*** goes easily on a word processor, and in my software, there is even a program that checks the spelling. It doesn't do much for such words as the "there" that should be "their," but it saves this terrible speller from a great deal of embarrassment.

• ***Chunking*** is a term I use to describe something I often do when writing on a word processor. I often write six or eight paragraphs of rough draft, then reorder and polish before going on to another chunk of text.

• ***Layering*** is a method of writing I describe in detail in Chapter 6. The computer allows me to write over previous text, time and time again, making it better each time.

• ***Jumping*** around from text to text is possible because I have a hard disk that contains the five books I'm working on, my newsletter, my inventory of writers' quotes, my business correspondence, all my articles, poems, and columns, and I move among them in a matter of seconds. Often, when I'm working on one writing project, something will occur to me that fits another one and—zip—I can go there and—zip—return.

Learning to Use a Computer for Writing

Many of you—perhaps most—will have learned to use a computer in high school. If you haven't, take advantage of the programs offered at the computer centers on your campus and try using their computers for your writing. It is important in the society to which you are graduating that you be computer literate. That doesn't mean you have to be a programmer, but that you can use a computer.

Buying Your First Computer

If you are buying your first computer, most schools have a discount program. The major computer manufacturers all know that the computer and the software you first learn on will probably remain your favorite, and they want your business.

One thing to consider is the support you will have. Technology changes quickly. The first computer I had was the standard in the field when I bought it; three years later it was obsolete and the manufacturer was no longer making parts for it. Get a computer that is likely to be in business for a while and make sure that service is available.

I use one software program because it matches the newspaper I work with and another because I like it for the rest of my work. I chose the second one, however, because the university with which I am still connected is nine-tenths of a mile from my home office and the computer experts there use the same program. If you are working alone, it will be important to have experts to help you when you hit problems—and you will run into problems.

I'd spend the most I could afford for a computer with a hard disk and first-class software. I would delay buying a printer if money were a problem. You can work entirely on the screen. I never read or edit by hand, and you can find places to print what you have written until you can afford a printer.

What I Wish I Had Known

That the computer is dumb. It does nothing on its own. That it works on the basis of relatively simple commands and you can reveal those commands and go back and eliminate a command you didn't mean to give or forgot to take back—that is usually my problem.

If you can't touch-type, learn to. I started on a foreign keyboard, and I am a victim of years of hunt and peck. I have tried to learn touching, but it's too late for me. Make sure you learn because that skill will make all your writing on a computer or typewriter a thousand times easier than my clumsy system.

Back Up! *Back Up!! BACK UP !!!*

Back up what you write. Back up on the hard disk. Back up on another disk. Invest in a back-up program. Make a copy of everything you do every time you write. It takes only a minute. But I have lost a hard disk with all that I have described above on it. It was no problem because I had backed up everything.

Selecting Your Other Writing Tools

You can, of course, write without a computer. Will Shakespeare and others did quite well without a fancy-dancy software program. Make your own checklist in selecting your writing tools and make sure that you have tools with which you are not just comfortable but that give you fun.

Rehearsal tools especially will make it easy for you to plan what to write and prepare to write. I use a daybook as we have described earlier in the chapter and a fine-tipped, jet-black pen. They are almost always with me.

Next to my daybook, I keep lap desks handy in the living room, on the porch, in my office. The ones I have are built on a bean bag or fit across the arms of a chair. They make it possible for me set up shop anywhere at home or in a vacation cottage or motel.

But don't forget the writer really writes with brain and eye, memory and experience, form and language. No machine produces an insight, a perception, an idea, a concept, a theory; no machine orders and reorders random information into meaning; no machine documents or provides evidence; no machine produces the right word, the inspiring phrase, the clear-running sentence; no machine produces an individual voice that is heard by an individual reader.

Teach Yourself with a Commentary ————————————

I first had newspaper writers I was coaching write accounts of how they had written their best stories so their techniques could be shared with their colleagues. I wrote some as well and we found out that it also reinforced our writing skills, letting us know, first of all, how we wrote what we wrote well and then allowed us to define and solve our writing problems.

Later I tried it with students and found it was just as effective. I tell students to write their commentaries quickly and informally. The style and the tone should be that of a letter to a friend who is also writing.

My commentaries might include:

▶ It really helped to write the heads first in the text I did this morning. It wouldn't work in a poem or even in most of my columns, but it really helps in a text.

▶ I was surprised to find myself when writing a chapter of the novel, starting at the beginning of the chapter each day and writing over what I had written. I guess I've been doing that on a lot of poems. I wonder if it would work in nonfiction?

▶ This morning's writing really stunk. It ran off in all directions and the voice was uneven. Should I go back to the lead? Did I write too soon? Should I outline?

My commentaries cover many issues. Some of the most frequent concerns are:

▶ My *feelings* while I was writing. The affective—feelings—usually control the cognitive—thinking—in my life. It is important for me to know how I feel when I write well and what causes me to feel that way.

▶ The writing *techniques* I used when a draft went well. I keep discovering new ways to write and writing about them helps put them in the inventory in my head so that I can call on them when I need them.

▶ *Solutions* to writing problems. This book is filled with solutions to writing problems the same way that a chef has many pots, pans, knives, bowls, and gadgets that work to solve special cooking problems.

▶ Notes that connect my writing with *reading*. I learn from other writers if I make notes on how they write.

▶ *Process* notes help me understand what I do when the writing goes well so I can look back and repeat it when the writing doesn't go well.

Questions about Process and Discovery _____

• *I don't like what I'm finding out.*

Me too. If it's too uncomfortable, stop writing and move to something else. That often happens. We don't write what we know, we write to know—to learn. What we discover may not be what we want to discover—the football hero writing about what it's like to play big-time football may confront the fear of injury he's never admitted before.

• *A lot of the stuff I'm coming up with is personal, about me. Who would be interested in that?*

That's an individual decision. If it's too personal, you don't have to put it down and share it with anyone, but if you are willing to share it, the more specific and personal the information, the more readers will be interested.

- *Do I have to play "follow the leader" and march through the process exactly as you describe it?*

No. Follow the text; follow the language. It's helpful to have a plan or a way of working, but as John Fowles advises, "Follow the accident, fear the fixed plan— that is the rule." Writing should be an exciting, adventuresome activity. It should be full of surprises, unexpected opportunities, twists in the trail, surprising views, new challenges. If you have a way of working, then you can vary it and go back to it when you get in trouble. But a writing process should never make a writer march lockstep right by a good piece of writing.

- *What if I skip a step?*

Try it. I certainly skip steps from time to time. More than that, I start in different places, perhaps with order, perhaps with focus, sometimes with development. Whatever works is right. But when the writing doesn't work, it helps to go back to a procedure that has helped us make meaning in the past. There is, however, no one way to write.

- *Sometimes I know I have something to say. It's all there in my head and I just have to write it down. Is that wrong?*

It's wonderful. It means that you have rehearsed it, consciously and unconsciously saying it over and over to yourself, so you don't need to draft and revise to discover the meaning. This often happens when there is something important in our lives. We keep thinking about it, and we think in language, and when we come to write about it, it's all there.

- *My process is really different from yours. It's so different I'm not even sure it's a process. It seems more like a mess.*

If your writing is good, don't worry about it. If you hit a homerun every time you go up to the plate you shouldn't change your batting stance. The thing to do is to pick the best piece of writing you've done, and then remember the stages you followed in creating it. That's *your* writing process. This isn't based on a perfect piece of writing, it's based on your best piece of writing.

   If you run into writing tasks in which that process doesn't work, you may want to try a process suggested by one of your classmates, your teacher, or the text. You probably will not be able to follow another person's process exactly, but you'll learn ways of adapting your process to the writing job in front of you.

- *I don't have one writing process, I have different ones, depending on what I'm writing.*

Sounds good to me.

- *I don't believe you when you say that you don't know what you're going to write when you sit down at your desk.*

You won't believe it until it happens to you. But I didn't mean to say I know absolutely nothing. I have a hint or an idea, a pretty good guess, and later in the book we'll be showing how we develop those guesses. But there's always room for surprise. And the best pieces of writing are a lot different from what I expected. And the stuff I don't expect is usually the best stuff. John Galsworthy said, "I sink into my morning chair, a blotter on my knee, the last words or deed of some character in ink before my eyes, a pen in my hand, a pipe in my mouth, and nothing in my head. I sit. I don't intend; I don't expect; I don't even hope. Gradually my mind seems to leave the chair, and be where my character is acting or speaking, leg raised, waiting to come down, lips opened ready to say something." That's the way it feels to me. Not just in fiction, but in nonfiction as well, in writing texts, in writing this text, in writing this answer. I listen to the question, and then to my answer.

- *I'm worried about being too disciplined in my work habits. I might lose my spontaneity. I mean, I want to be really creative.*

John Kenneth Galbraith has said, ". . . when I'm greatly inspired, only four revisions are needed before . . . I put in that note of spontaneity." The spontaneity comes from the writing, not from thinking about writing. It arises from the spontaneous combustion of ideas and language as they meet on the page.

It is a romantic notion that creative people—scientists, engineers, artists, musicians, businessmen—get their best ideas staring out the window. They don't. The ideas come on the job from the job.

- *Should I try to find a clear chunk of time or a quiet place and wait to write?*

Yes, yes, and no. A clear chunk of time is to be treasured, as is a quiet place. Seek them, but don't wait to write. Write in bed, while watching TV, at the breakfast table, in the car, in a classroom waiting for the professor, in a bar, at a lunch counter, in a bathtub (not with a computer or electric typewriter), on a rock, in an airplane, in the library, on the pot. Write wherever you can so that you're in the habit of writing, and when you have a clear time and a quiet place you'll be ready to take advantage of them.

Process and Discovery Activities ——————————————

1. Turn on a tape recorder while you write, and talk out loud about what you're doing. Don't worry about talking in complete sentences. Just talk to yourself, the way you probably do talk without realizing it. "Let's see . . . mmm . . . I wonder if . . . perhaps I'd better go back . . . no, I guess I'll keep going on this draft . . . can't quit now . . . maybe I should get a Coke. No, stay here. Let's see, I've got to start this stronger, maybe use a better verb. I

can't write . . . I gotta write. Maybe it should be a beer. Let's see, let's try a sentence first. Don't worry about sentences, just a line. Get something down. Think I'll start with a fact, then see what that makes me write. Explain it. Make sure the reader knows what it means."

    After you've finished your draft, listen to the tape as you read your draft, then make notes on what you're doing so that you can discover how you write. It may be fun to have a friend or two do the same thing, and then you compare each other's versions. That way you can learn new tricks of the trade, and share yours.

2. Find a painter, composer, scientist, engineer, play director, journalist, or potter—some kind of creative person who will let you observe them while they work, so that you can see another process and discover its relationship to the writing process.

3. Think back on a skill that you know, and describe it in process terms. Then see if you can translate that skill—taking photographs, cooking a Chinese dinner, making a dress, repairing a motorcycle—into writing terms to see if it makes any sense to take the tricks of one skill and use them in another.

4. Work with your librarian to find books, such as, *Writers at Work—The Paris Review Interviews,* published by Viking, which reveal the creative process. Write your own description of the process as they describe it, and see how it may help reveal insights about the writing process. Follow your own interests and read interviews with actors or coaches, or successful business-men, or scientists, people who have found a way of making a breakthrough.

5. Perform a skill with which you're familiar, such as playing the guitar or climbing a rock face, and make yourself think how what you're doing might be applied to writing.

6. Start a process log or daybook, picking out a notebook that feels comfortable to you and is the right size so that you can have it with you almost all the time. Doodle in it, write in it, paste things in it, put down observations and thoughts, ideas and drafts for titles, leads, ends, middles. Make outlines and diagrams. Don't worry about neatness or correctness—this is a place to have fun. Talk to yourself, think to yourself, find out what you are seeing, hearing, feeling, thinking and what it means.

7. Find a classmate who will allow you to watch him or her write, noting down all the writer's habits, moves, behavior. Switch places and let the other person observe you. Interview each other to discover what the writer thinks he or she is doing while writing.

8. Take an interest of yours or a subject you are studying in another course and read biographies, autobiographies, diaries, letters, profiles, interviews to discover how that person has followed the trade—done the job—of being a painter, a prime minister, a physicist, a basketball star, a businessman, an inventor, a coach, a minister, a philosopher, a composer, a sociologist. See what connections you can find between what they do and what writers do.

9. Make a work schedule for the course, figuring out how you can write each day, breaking the assignments down into bite-sized chunks. Remember that habit helps and if you write at the same time, the same place, with the same

tools, you'll find it easier to maintain your discipline. Talk to joggers or executives or good students to find out how they manage their time.

10. Draw a picture of your writing process to see what it reveals of how you work *when the writing goes well*. Get classmates to do the same thing. See what tricks you can learn from one another.

Chapter 2

ﲪ Discover Your Subject

I write to find out what I'm thinking about.

    EDWARD ALBEE

How do I know what I think until I see what I say?

    E. M. FORSTER

For me the initial delight is in the surprise of remembering something
I didn't know I knew.

    ROBERT FROST

"I don't know what I have to say," cries the student.

"Good. You sound like a writer," answers the instructor. "Of course you don't know what to say—and you shouldn't. You find out what you have to say by saying it."

That's true, but little help to the student. Writers may not know what they are going to write, but they usually do have a pretty good idea of the territory they plan to explore in their search for meaning. The writer, as we have said, is an explorer always on the search for a new meaning. The subject is the territory the writer decides to explore; the meaning is what the writer finds during the exploration.

As a city boy, I was drawn to alien neighborhoods. I loved to escape the limits of my own world and walk the streets of Boston's North End, endlessly excited and fascinated by the life that burst out of the tenements and teemed over the sidewalk. There always seemed to be insult and laughter between the men leaning on the store fronts, standing on the street corners, sitting on the park benches. Young men preened for the young women who very obviously ignored them and those women, so brighty dressed, so mature, so young, were always seen against a moving backdrop of widows and nuns dressed in black. The store windows were hung with great provolones, salamis, animals with their fur pulled off, ice-filled trays with fish, and even what looked like octopus; pastry stores were piled with small cookies unlike any cookies I'd ever seen, and, over it all, was the music of people who yelled and hooted and whistled and laughed and grew angry, none of them tight-lipped like my relatives who fought with the weapons of silence: the unsaid, the turning away, the look, the rigid back. Here there were accusations and answers, arguments that echoed through the alleys and streets, jokes and insults, and young couples on street corners who accomplished more than I had attempted in the back row of the neighborhood movie house.

I hoped I would find out I was adopted and I was Italian. My feelings would pour out like Vesuvius. I would fight—and I would love, oh how I would love. I still like to visit Italy and to walk the streets that are as wonderful as Boston's North End. I could write articles about Italian food, about saving old neighborhoods, about the Venice I visited during World War II and the Venice I visited as a tourist a few years ago. I could write poems and stories. This is a territory I like to explore on foot and on paper.

You have to find your own territories, the mountains and alleys and oceans and neighborhoods you want to explore, the world of science or business or sports or politics or nature, wherever you are drawn to seek meaning.

And you have to learn in school how to explore the territories assigned to you by your teachers. Those territories may not be your personal choices but are areas of importance that may become interesting if you know how to find their mysteries and their meanings through writing.

The Elements of a Good Subject _____

The best subjects find you. We see someone behaving differently at a party than they do at school and that connects with a glimpse you have had of your father's behavior when he took you along on a fishing trip with his army buddies. We learn that more and more members of our society will be over eighty and wonder how that will affect our lives—jobs, taxes, politics, family obligations. We visit great-grandmother in a nursing home and she convinces you she really does want to die and you start to think differently about mercy killing. You see the coach in church and remember his drill on faking an injury when no time-outs are left.

Each day brings us possible subjects as we read and think and watch and act and watch ourselves acting. They come as questions to which we need answers, problems to which we can use solutions, situations that we need to study and explore, ideas that deserve mulling over, facts we need to absorb and understand. These subjects usually come when we least expect them, and we need to develop the habit of a mental notebook as well as a real notebook to record them.

When you are older, you may realize—as I have—that those subjects that haunted me before I was graduated from college, are the ones I'm still working on:

▶ Does school have to limit education?
▶ Does testing really tell you who is dumb? I had good reason to hope not.
▶ Should Grandmother have been allowed to die instead of being kept alive?
▶ Why did my mother, who said she believed in a God of love, hate people so much who believed in the same God in a different way?
▶ How can young men be trained to kill other young men so like themselves?
▶ How is it possible for some authors to make ideas and people come alive on the page?

Each of us has our own list of questions that we usually keep secret but puzzle over in the privacy of our minds. Then something we read, overhear, observe, remember, think, or experience connects with one of those fundamental questions, and we write to imagine an answer. As Theodore Morrison once wrote:

> A writer is a man walking down the street thinking how he would describe himself as a man walking down the street.... A novelist is someone who wonders why people act as they do, and he doesn't know, so he imagines an explanation, and that's his novel.

It is worth stopping a moment to consider that verb: *imagine*. It is closely related to image, a mental picture, and that is the way many of us first see an idea. We do not think of school as an education concept but as a place—a dreary, dark wood classroom with nailed down desks and chairs; a teacher—Miss Kelly, red faced, huge and angry; and a scene—a chubby little boy, myself, being jammed rear end down in a wastebasket and forced to spend a period looking at the class framed by my feet. From that image and others, we may construct an idea.

Information

However an idea for writing arrives, it either attracts, like a magnet, information we already have, or it forces us immediately to seek more information. The good subject is rooted in accurate, significant, revealing, and interesting detail. We need far more information than we can use so that we can pick and choose, connect and reconnect, as we make meaning. We need even more information than we know we have so there will be discovery as we write, not only discovery of meaning but discovery of revealing detail—what we didn't know we had stored in memory.

Opinion

The writer should have a point of view toward the subject. Editors want stories that have an edge, something that makes the reader want to read *this* story, something that makes the reader see the subject that is probably familiar in a new light. The writer cares about the subject. The subject, to the writer, is potentially good or bad, sad or happy, silly or important.

The writer should develop a strong opinion about the subject. That doesn't mean that the writer should be emotional about the subject—that may be appropriate or inappropriate—but that the writer becomes committed to the subject. The opinion the writer has when beginning to research, write, or even rewrite a subject, may change during the research or the writing—writing is thinking—but good writing will never happen when the writer is indifferent to the subject, simply doesn't give a hoot about that story or problem or book or person or idea. The reader won't care either.

To find a subject, the writer may work from the outside in, studying the world to see what creates a spark, or work inside out. In both cases, the writers may find it helpful to ask themselves questions that may reveal a territory to explore.

The following techniques are worth trying out. They may not work for you because they are in conflict with your thinking style. For example, I'm a visual thinker. I have to see my subject in pictures, images, diagrams, and charts. My wife and many of my readers are not. I have to translate for them. And when they want to communicate with me, they may have to translate their method of thinking into terms—pictures or charts—I can understand.

There is no right or wrong way to think. We need a great diversity of thinkers in our society, each identifying their own problems and solving them in their own way. But we find our own thinking style by trying on many styles.

We also may discover that a way of thinking with which we are comfortable simply doesn't do the job when we face a new thinking task, so we need some techniques to try on at that time. The next six sections of this chapter introduce some techniques that may help you discover subjects you wish to explore in writing or help you find a way to find your own subject within an area that has been assigned to you by a teacher.

Primary Technique for Finding a Subject: Brainstorming _____

One of the best ways to find out what you know is to *brainstorm*. When you brainstorm, you put down everything that comes into your head as fast as you can. You don't want to be critical; you do want to be illogical, irrational, even silly. You want to discover what is in your head. You want to be surprised.

After you have brainstormed, you should look at what you've written down to see what surprises you or what connects. These surprises and connections remind you of what you know and will make you aware of meanings you hadn't seen before.

It is important not to worry about how the brainstorming list is written. It is not a time to worry about spelling or penmanship or sentences; it is a time to write in a sort of private language of code words that stand for particular meanings in your own mind. If the phrases "night jump" appeared on my brainstorming list it would remind me of another jump in Tennessee when I tumbled through the sky before my chute opened, when I had the feeling that I could reach out and touch the stars. If I were going to use that in an essay, a story, or a poem I would have to develop it, but for the moment "night jump" is enough.

I brainstorm before I write important letters or a memo. I brainstorm class lectures and novels. I brainstorm articles and poems and textbooks such as this. I also brainstorm before I decide to buy a car or take a job or choose a vacation. Brainstorming shows me what I know, what I need to know, and what the connections are between what I know and don't know.

In this book, I am going to demonstrate most techniques I introduce with my own writing. For brainstorming and the other activities in this chapter, I'm going to reveal the work that led to the piece on my grandmother reprinted in the final chapter. You may want to turn to page 255 and read the final draft to better understand what I was doing here before I knew what I was going to say.

I've chosen a powerful subject, the grandmother who brought me up. No. I've not chosen that subject, it's chosen me. When, in the last chapter, I relived the experience of my uncle's carrying me I caught a glimpse of my grandmother in the corner of my eye. That image will not go away. I have to write about her.

Other subjects swirled through my mind as I used the techniques you will see on the pages ahead. Close to four decades after I marched into combat, I am beginning to be ready to write about it. That might be a subject. So might be my childhood in the Great Depression. I might write about being a policeman in the army, and later a police reporter who observed policemen close up. I might write about the summers I spent in the New Hampshire woods, and I might write about Lee, my daughter who died at twenty. But at this time, it was my grandmother who kept insisting herself upon my thoughts.

My parents, my uncle, and I all lived as children in her home. She suffered a stroke—what they called a "shock" then and a cardiovascular accident today—when I was eight years old, and she was paralyzed for the rest of her life, but she still ran our lives from her bed. I've written very little about her, but this book will teach me a great deal about her while teaching you how one professional writer worked to develop one subject.

As I look out of my office window at the New Hampshire woods filled with snow, I do not know my grandmother as well as I will when I finish this draft and edit it under the hot summer sky of Wyoming. I am a bit apprehensive. I am drawn to my grandmother because she was such a strong woman. The family made her a saint and wrapped her in legend, but she was not a saint; she did harm as well as good. I know I will understand her better when this book is done, but I do not know if I will like her better.

You should brainstorm beside me in the margin of the text. There's plenty of white space. If you do that, you'll understand better what I'm saying—and you may discover a subject you want to explore through writing. My list will probably be personal; I'm writing about my grandmother. Your list doesn't have to be. Brainstorm any topic, personal or impersonal, with which you have some experience to see if there's something you wish to explore.

Now to brainstorm:

- ▶ back-scratcher on my desk
- ▶ left hand
- ▶ transparent skin
- ▶ soft, unused hand, curled
- ▶ wispy white hair
- ▶ had been auburn as girl in Scotland
- ▶ scissors up nose of bull
- ▶ no sense of time
- ▶ thought I was going to fight Napoleon
- ▶ go in to see if she was alive
- ▶ shawl, dark green and black
- ▶ thin but heavy
- ▶ Black Watch?
- ▶ named for my uncle; named for his uncle
- ▶ washed out my mouth
- ▶ broke her arm
- ▶ wood stove
- ▶ kidney soup. Thick.
- ▶ grape jelly
- ▶ dumped hot jelly on me
- ▶ forcing mouth open to eat eggs
- ▶ dining room rug
- ▶ underside of dining room table

- ▶ didn't like my father
- ▶ Father thought her a lady, feared her
- ▶ Mother always scared of her
- ▶ paper route—seeing if Grandmother was alive
- ▶ bedpan
- ▶ lifting her up in bed
- ▶ her talking to Jesus
- ▶ ringing bell for help
- ▶ warning of bridge collapse
- ▶ Islay
- ▶ London as a girl
- ▶ marrying a widower in Glasgow hotel
- ▶ big house in North Grafton
- ▶ Newfoundland dog
- ▶ finding her on stairs
- ▶ trying to understand what she said. Family all around bed.
- ▶ canvas to carry her in
- ▶ Sunday dinners
- ▶ practical jokes. Cruelty.
- ▶ the uncles
- ▶ breaking robber's wrist
- ▶ maple trees outside her window
- ▶ her trunk
- ▶ my office in her closet
- ▶ playing imaginary games
- ▶ sitting in the gloaming
- ▶ tea

That took just under ten minutes. It's possible to brainstorm for a much longer time, but I find short spurts—fifteen minutes, ten minutes, five minutes—are more productive. You can also brainstorm together with another person, or a group of people. The important thing is not to censor what you say, not to judge it, not really to understand it—but to let it come.

This brainstorming list is printed simply as it came. I didn't prepare for it, except by living with my grandmother until I went off to school and in the army. I had to let it come.

How Brainstorming Leads to Writing

I don't know if it's a particularly good brainstorming list; that's not important. If I want to, I can brainstorm again and again. The important thing is that it's a start. It is a jumble, but it may be a productive jumble. It jumps back and forth in time. The last time I saw her alive I was in uniform and she thought I was off to fight Napoleon at Waterloo in 1814, as did her great-uncle for whom I was named. There are items from a house we left when I was four years old. Each of those things I mentioned are snapshots that I could develop if I wanted to. I could, for example, become again the boy who got up for his paper route at 4:30 in the morning (I had one alarm by the bed, one on a chair further away, and a third on the chest of drawers in the narrow little porch room where I slept). I thumbtacked *National Geographic* maps to the ceiling, and I used to lie in bed looking at Africa or Asia or the West, dreaming of escaping this dull, unhappy home. (Note how my mind slides off the subject. Brainstorming has triggered memories, and all sorts of things from my past are coming back in a rush. I must decide whether to keep remembering or whether I should let my mind go on getting away from my grandmother. I will force myself back on track.) I used to walk from my room through the dark hall into her room, lit with a small night-light, a yellow light that was on the floor and cast shadows across the bed and up on the ceiling. I would stand and watch the covers to see if she was still breathing. When I knew she was, I would go further down the hall to the bathroom. I started each day contemplating death.

Looking for Surprise

It is too early for me to write, however, and I look back at the list to see what surprised me. Whatever you are brainstorming—an academic paper or job-application letter—you should first go over the list to see what surprises you, to find out what discoveries you have made. Not too much on this list, but I am startled a bit by the abrupt "didn't like my father." I don't think I ever realized how she felt before, and writing it down makes it something I have to deal with. And "playing imaginary games" reminds me how good she was when I would tip a living-room chair over, put an old black electric fan in front of it, line up a couple of wooden chairs, and take her on an airplane trip back to Scotland. If I made a tent from a blanket, she would crawl in and visit me. If I painted the back steps with water, she would admire my work and step carefully over the wet paint. A piece of writing could start from those surprises.

Looking for Connections

Next, I look for connections. I see the legends that were built up about her: how a robber broke into the house when my grandfather was away, and she broke his wrist with a cane; how a bull attacked her on the way to school in Scotland, and she jabbed huge sewing scissors up his nostrils. This is how my brainstorm looks as I circle the surprises and make connections:

- ▶ back-scratcher on my desk
- ▶ left hand
- ▶ transparent skin
- ▶ soft, unused hand, curled
- ▶ wispy white hair
- ▶ had been auburn as girl in Scotland
- ▶ scissors up nose of bull
- ▶ broke her arm

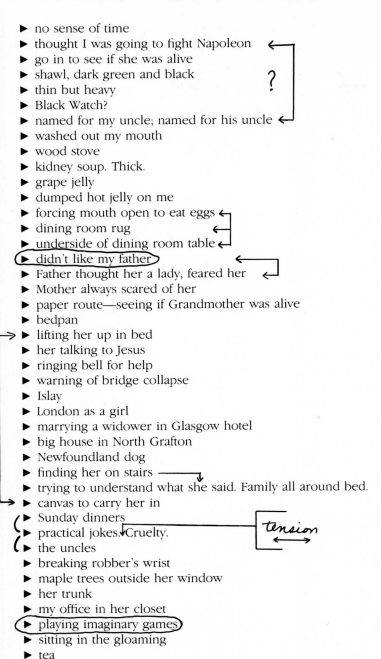

- no sense of time
- thought I was going to fight Napoleon
- go in to see if she was alive
- shawl, dark green and black
- thin but heavy
- Black Watch?
- named for my uncle; named for his uncle
- washed out my mouth
- wood stove
- kidney soup. Thick.
- grape jelly
- dumped hot jelly on me
- forcing mouth open to eat eggs
- dining room rug
- underside of dining room table
- didn't like my father
- Father thought her a lady, feared her
- Mother always scared of her
- paper route—seeing if Grandmother was alive
- bedpan
- lifting her up in bed
- her talking to Jesus
- ringing bell for help
- warning of bridge collapse
- Islay
- London as a girl
- marrying a widower in Glasgow hotel
- big house in North Grafton
- Newfoundland dog
- finding her on stairs
- trying to understand what she said. Family all around bed.
- canvas to carry her in
- Sunday dinners
- practical jokes. Cruelty.
- the uncles
- breaking robber's wrist
- maple trees outside her window
- her trunk
- my office in her closet
- playing imaginary games
- sitting in the gloaming
- tea

?

tension

Each time I go over this list I see more tensions, connections, and surprises in it. It sparks memories, feelings, contradictions—the raw materials for other pieces of writing I could work on.

At the moment, I am using brainstorming to explore my personal memory, but it is just as important a technique to use when you are deciding on what subject to explore in a term paper. Brainstorming will tell you the connections between memory or the connections between ideas. It is a way of developing theories, trends, concepts, a way of relating information. You can use brainstorming to develop a marketing plan for a new product, to start thinking about how to review a literary work, to plan a party, to decide what would be in a résumé for a job, to develop a legislative strategy, or to decide what to include in a report about a manufacturing plant that isn't making a profit. Brainstorming is a powerful thinking tool.

Additional Techniques for Finding a Subject: Mapping

Another form of brainstorming that may work when the traditional form doesn't is *mapping.* Many people think that brainstorming that works in lists is linear and tends to emphasize the kind of thinking that we do with the left side of our brain. The right side of the brain, supposedly, is less linear and doesn't work by listing. It circles the subject and makes unexpected leaps. It is certainly true that we think differently when we have more experience with a subject or an intellectual task. What we need is tools that we can use when a tool with which we are familiar doesn't work. One such valuable tool is mapping. In mapping, you put the subject or topic to be thought about in the center of the page, and then start drawing out lines from it when an idea occurs to you. These lines will branch off, and we can capture the fragments of information that we have in memory.

Again, I will demonstrate mapping by using it to see what it reminds me of about my grandmother, since she is the topic on which I am going to be writing.

How Mapping Leads to Writing

That map took only ten minutes, the same as the brainstorm, but it produced different information. One thing that is emphasized is her religion, and I've drawn arrows tying issues back to religion. For example, my mother had stones thrown at her going to school in Scotland because she was a Baptist and not a Presbyterian, and we didn't even have store-bought apple juice in our house in Massachusetts because that might become cider and give me a taste for booze. Again, I'm moving back and forth in history, but I have a lot more family in this outline. I've blacked out the name of one member of the family because I don't know if I want to get into that; that is private and might hurt family members who are still alive. You always have the choice of accepting or sharing what comes up from your subconscious. I remembered, while mapping, how delighted I was when I saw pictures of great black Watusi warriors in the *National Geographic*.

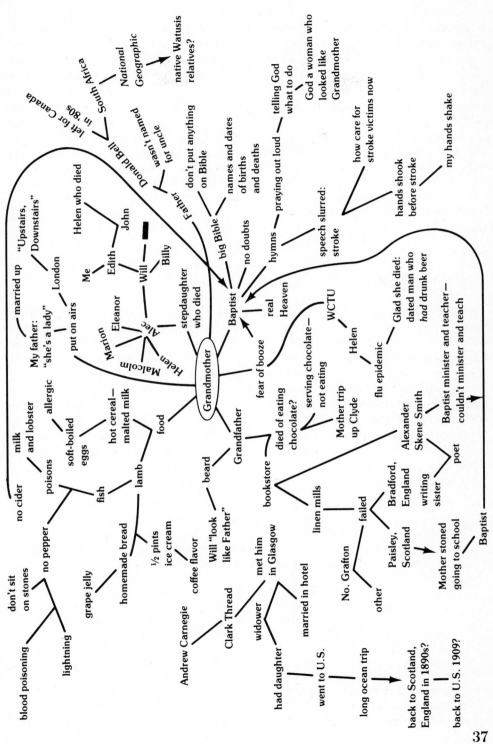

native Watusis
relatives?

National
Geographic

God a woman who
looked like
Grandmother

telling God
what to do

how care for
stroke victims now

my hands shake

left for Canada
in '80s

South Africa

Donald Bell

wasn't named
for uncle

don't put anything
on Bible

names and dates
of births
and deaths

hymns — praying out loud

hands shook
before stroke

Helen who died

John

London

married up "Upstairs,
Downstairs"

big Bible

no doubts

speech slurred:
stroke

"she's a lady"

My father:

Me

Edith

Will

Billy

put on airs

Eleanor

Marion

Alec

Helen

Malcolm

stepdaughter
who died

Baptist

real
Heaven

WCTU

Glad she died:
dated man who
had drunk beer

milk
and lobster

allergic

soft-boiled
eggs

hot cereal—
malted milk

food

fear of booze

serving chocolate—
not eating

Helen

flu epidemic

Alexander
Skene Smith

Baptist minister and teacher—
couldn't minister and teach

no cider

poisons

fish

lamb

beard

Grandfather

died of eating
chocolate?

Mother trip
up Clyde

poet

don't sit
on stones

no pepper

grape jelly

homemade bread

½ pints
ice cream

coffee flavor

Will "look
like Father"

bookstore

linen mills

failed

Bradford,
England

writing
sister

blood poisoning

lightning

Andrew Carnegie

Clark Thread

met him
in Glasgow

No. Grafton

other

Paisley,
Scotland

Mother stoned
going to school

Baptist

widower

married in hotel

had daughter

went to U.S.

long ocean trip

back to Scotland,
England in 1890s?

back to U.S. 1909?

Grandmother

37

I thought my African relatives looked like that. How disappointing when they turned out to be just pale ordinary Scots.

I can wander back and forth over this map and begin to catch the texture of my childhood. There was the fear my mother had that I would sit on stones; somehow that would give me bone aches when I drew up. I sat on stones; I don't think there's any connection, but I do have bone aches. I've never dealt with the fact that I had an aunt who died in the flu epidemic years before I was born, and that her mother—my grandmother—felt it was good she died because she had dated a man who had drunk beer. If I'm going to write about my grandmother, I'm going to have to deal with the harshness of her faith.

It would take me pages, or perhaps books, to deal with all that is called up by that ten-minute mapping session. If I don't think I have anything to write, I can brainstorm or map, or just sit down and use the third most successful technique I have to discover what I have to say.

Free Writing _____

Another technique I have found productive is *free writing*. When you free write, you sit down and let the writing flow, seeing if language will carry you toward meaning. Sometimes this is called automatic writing. It is writing that seems to be writing without thinking. You have to suspend critical judgment, as you do when brainstorming or mapping, and hope that something will happen.

I'm never sure that anything will happen. In fact, right now I feel the fear in my stomach that nothing will come. It really doesn't matter. Some days the writing comes, and some days it doesn't. If free writing doesn't work, I'll try brainstorming or mapping, or staring out the window, or turn to another project, or get a cup of tea, or take a walk, or otherwise create an interruption. But in a few minutes I'll be back, and something will work, most of the time.

Now I will free write:

> I'm a bit afraid to write about Grandmother. Interesting I don't put in "my." Just Grandmother. Grandma. She was a frightening woman. I felt the fear in all the grownups around me. My mother was a big woman, even bigger than my grandmother, but she was afraid of Grandma. She wore her hair up in a knot on the top of her head like the queen of England. I'm interested in the fear. Yes, I guess it was physical. I said "darn" once and "bugger," and I was hauled down those wooden stairs in the Vassell Street house and she scrubbed my mouth out with Fels Naptha soap. When I came home with a tan from summer camp she tried to scrub it off with a big brush, the kind you use on the floor when you're on your hands and knees. When she fell in the dining room, I must have been in about the first grade, and broke her arm, she had a great big round welt, a big purple lump just rose right up. We were alone; I had to call Dr. Bartlett probably, I had to call someone. Dr. Bartlett always moved slowly and smelled like his pipe. Grandmother didn't let the pain bother her. What a strong woman she was. Some of the best times were when we sat in the gloaming. Harry Lauder had a song "In the

Gloaming" she liked to sing. Sometimes we played it on the huge tall phono-graph—the Victrola. You had to crank it up, and there were cactus needles you had to sharpen by hand. The gloaming was the time before you spent money to turn the lights on, but when it was too dark to do any housework. She sat in the shadows looking out the window. We spent a lot of time just sitting in those days, on porches, in the living room, during those awful Sundays or holidays when there were family dinners and I always felt like the poor relative. Maybe that was good, maybe I worked hard to show them. God, I hated those dark houses, dark woodwork, dark wallpaper, old lamps with yellow bulbs and heavy shades, and all the things that were not said. We never talked, I mean really talked. Silence was heavy. Loud? There was so much silence, so much not saying.

Again, that was ten minutes of following language. Note the threads that are woven through the piece of writing, and how the writing starts to develop its own form, working toward the silences. If I'm going to write about my grandmother, I now know I've got to deal with the cruelty and with the silences.

You see, free writing isn't free. It starts to take you somewhere, to tell you what to say and how to say it. After you free write, you have to look back and see whether you want to follow any of those paths, to fill them so the writing stops being private and can go public. You have to decide whether you want to share what you are discovering with others. If you do, you'll find that the more personal the writing, the more specific and private, the more it will spark memories and ideas in your readers.

Free writing is just as valuable a technique to use as a starting point for a term paper, a historical essay, or a review of scientific literature. It's a way of thinking in which you can preserve the flow of thought.

You should try brainstorming, mapping, and free writing. Good writing often begins when you find out what you know and what you need to learn. These techniques can also be effective when your head feels empty. Free write or map or brainstorm with no topic in mind, and things will start to happen on the page.

Do you have to do mapping or brainstorming or free writing every time? Of course not. Nothing in this book is absolute. There is no way to write. These techniques, and all the other techniques in this book, are thinking and writing tools that should be in your intellectual toolbox. You don't have to use a Phillips screwdriver unless you have a screw with a Phillips head; you don't have to use these techniques unless you have the need to collect and recollect your thoughts, memories, observations, and information.

Making a Tree _____

Another helpful technique to discover what you know and need to know is to draw a *tree* that reveals all the branches that can grow from a single idea.

This is a way of breaking down the subject or a way of letting the subject expand. Some teachers who use trees successfully place the central idea at the

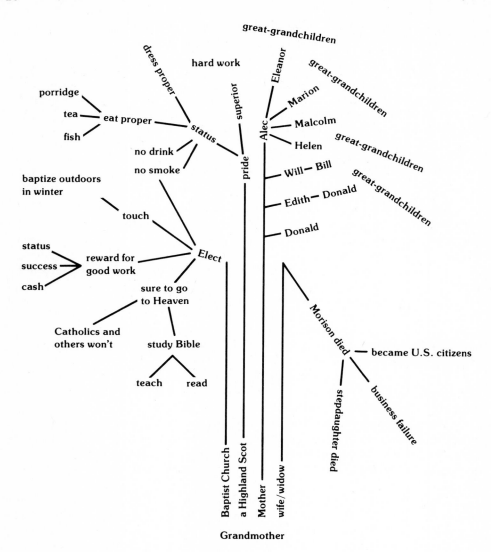

top of the page and let the tree grow down; others place the central idea at the left of the page and let the tree grow to the right. They both produce excellent results. But I am too literal; my trees grow up.

This tree took nine minutes, and, as you can see, it also produced some new insights. I see the tangle of Baptist and Highland beliefs in reward for hard work, and the certainty of being the elect, by God and by birth. But none of the techniques in this book will work the same way all of the time, and some may not work for you at all. They are tools that may help you solve a writing problem.

Checklist for Finding a Subject _____

Develop your own itch list to help you find a subject. Here are some of the questions I ask myself to discover what I want to scratch next:

▶ What has surprised me recently?
▶ What do I need to know?
▶ What would I like to know?
▶ How are things different from how they used to be?
▶ How will things be different in the future?
▶ What have we lost?
▶ What have we gained?
▶ What do I know that others need to know?
▶ Whom would I like to get to know?
▶ What's not happening that should?
▶ What's happening that shouldn't?
▶ Whom would I like to see at work?
▶ What process do I need to know?
▶ What process would it be fun to observe?
▶ How can I switch my position so I will see my world differently?
▶ What have I read, heard, thought that confuses me?
▶ What connections are being made that surprise me?
▶ How are peoples' behavior changing?
▶ How are beliefs changing?
▶ What makes you mad?
▶ Sad?
▶ Happy?
▶ Worried?
▶ Frightened?
▶ Content?
▶ What do I expect to see, hear? What do I see, hear?
▶ Why?

Other Ways of Finding a Subject _____

The photographer using a zoom lens first selects a territory to be explored, then zooms in close. The photographer sees a meadow of wild flowers, a gang hanging around on a city corner, a series of waves exploding against a rocky coast, and then selects the three wild flowers, the hood leaning so carefully and casually against the telephone pole, the seventh wave to catch, print, and develop.

The writer works much the same way, and the following techniques are designed to help you find a territory that you may want to explore with language. Later in the chapter there are other techniques that will help you move in close and concentrate your vision.

Listen to John McPhee, my candidate for the best nonfiction writer working today, as he tells how he got the idea that led to his *New Yorker* magazine piece that ended up as a book called, simply, *Oranges*. "What started me on the 'Oranges' piece was a daily glass of orange juice I would have at a stand in Pennsylvania Station when I worked in New York. I noticed over the course of the year that the juice's color would change depending on the season. I wondered about that. Then I saw an ad for the Florida Citrus Commission that had a picture of six oranges. They looked almost exactly the same, but had six different names. I decided it might be interesting to understand the differences, so I went to Florida, intending to do a short piece."

You can work to develop an insatiable nosiness, such as John McPhee's. Everything that you see, hear, feel, touch, overhear, read, dream, imagine, remember is a potential subject.

Be Nosy

The way that a subject comes clear is by collecting concrete specifics about it, and you can collect the specifics by observing and by asking, why, who, what, when, where, how. The most ordinary things—oranges—can be a subject.

You go to a football game and see the player with the ball tackled again and again. Nothing extraordinary in that—or is there? Talk to the best tackler on the team and you'll find out that tackling can be a complex craft.

How do you tackle a runner moving outside the end of the line of scrimmage? How do you tackle a player coming through the line? When do you tackle low? When do you tackle high? How do you tackle a player who may pass? How do you catch up with a player and tackle from behind? How do you get an angle on a player and use the sidelines to help you tackle? What's a legal tackle? Is there such a thing as an illegal tackle that's okay to do, that's a cheap shot? Have you seriously hurt anybody tackling them? Did you mean to do it? How do you feel about doing it? How did you feel when you did it? What are you afraid of in tackling? Have you been hurt seriously? How did you feel about that? How do you tackle to keep a runner from making a few inches for a first down? How do you tackle to cause a fumble? Where do you place your weight to be most effective? How do you use your arms when tackling? How do you tackle without using your arms? What different steps do you take before tackling?

That's just the beginning. Each answer will bring new questions, and you can ask other players and coaches and read books and articles. You could write a book on tackling. A writer has a license to explore both the familiar and unfamiliar.

There are good pieces of writing in bread, diesel motors, word processors, tea, trees, highway pavement, grass, snow removal, desert reclamation, dormitory design, wood stoves, deer hunting, vegetarianism, sewing, taking photographs, gardening, driving a truck, work habits, passing laws, water, weather—anything that is part of your world.

My Daily Experience

Make use of your personal experiences. You have to go to the dentist to have a cavity filled. What new equipment are dentists using to drill teeth? Are people having fewer cavities? Do most people lose their teeth because of cavities? (No, gum disease. I had a problem with my gums: I wrote an article on that.) What materials are they using to fill teeth? Why do they use different materials? Are people allergic to certain materials? How does the price of gold affect dental care? Can different kinds of metal used as fillings react badly to one another? Do dentists do unnecessary fillings? How do dentists describe a good filling? How do you find a good dentist?

Look Backward

We get good subjects by digging out the history of an event—a law, an institution, or a place. Why did your hometown become a town? How has it changed and moved in response to changes in economics or geography or population? What's the history of your street or your house or the field or alley in which you used to play? How does that history affect the way you think and behave? How are your parents the product of their history? Your grandparents? What are you doing and thinking and seeing today that will become history? What will today look like through the telescope of history?

Look Forward

Speculate about the future. Where will you be in five years, ten years, twenty-five years, fifty years? What will your world be like? How is your hometown going to change? How is your school going to change? How does the past predict the future of your neighborhood? How will changes in transportation or the economy or a new discovery, such as plastics, affect your hometown? What change do you fear the most? What would you like to have remain the same? How will people think differently twenty-five years from now? How will they think the same at that time?

Watch People

People are one of the primary sources for good pieces of writing. Watch how people behave, how they speak with their bodies, how they say what they say, what they don't say, what uniforms they wear, what masks. How do they look when they don't think anyone is watching? Role-play the person you're observing. What is it like to be a policeman or a nurse, a factory worker or an executive, a salesman or a politician, a soldier or a professor? What do they fear? What do they like doing? What are they good at? What qualities do they try to develop in themselves? What is the reason they act the way they do? What rewards do they hope for? What are the limits of their world? Talk to the people who interest you. Listen, and they will reveal themselves to you.

Observe Process

Readers are forever interested in process. How do you arrest a drunk in a college bar? Decide what injury is most important in a hospital emergency room? Tip a slapshot into the net? Sell a used car? Write a news story on deadline? Decide who deserves a bank loan? Keep an assembly line going? Place groceries on the supermarket shelves so people will buy high-profit items? Laws are passed by a process; children are adopted by a process; planes take off and land by a process; plays are rehearsed by a process; and games are won by a process. Readers like to get inside a story—backstage, into the emergency room, behind the banker's desk—to see the process that makes each part of our world go.

Find the Problem

Problems make good subjects. Define a problem so the reader can understand its importance and then see the alternatives. Problem: how to make an icy New England road safe for driving. One solution is to dump salt on the road, but salt gets into the plants and tree roots and water supply along the road. New problem: how much salt to use. When is it important to use it and when not? One of my students wrote a fine piece on this subject. He came from Idaho, where the problems of snow removal are different from those in New Hampshire, and he saw a good story in what was obvious to us. He taught me that I didn't know as much as I thought I knew about my world.

You can reverse this one; if you see a solution—an attractive nursing home, a successful business, a tax, a popular resort, almost anything that works in our society—you may be able to find a good subject by discovering the problem that sparked the solution.

Read to Write

A text—or a movie, television show, or play—can provide a subject for writing. We can examine the text internally. How do the parts of the text work with and against each other? What does it mean? How is the meaning supported? Is it supported well? How could it be improved? We can look at the text externally. How does it compare with other texts? What tradition does it belong to? How does it fit into the tradition? How is it in conflict with the tradition? We can compare the text with our own personal experience. How does the text fit with our reality? How does it disagree with our reality? We can look at a text from the point of view of a writer. What was the writer trying to do? How did the writer try to do it? What did the writer do that made it work? Or not work? What could be changed, and why?

The text can supply us with information that we can use in any form of writing. Or it can simply spark an idea. We read, for example, George Orwell's *Down and Out in Paris and London* and realize there is a story in the kitchen at the resort we worked in last summer. Or we read his "Shooting an Elephant" and it makes us think of a story about a gang fight in our neighborhood.

Use What You Know

Look into yourself to discover what you know that might interest or help other people. What you consider ordinary may be extraordinary to someone else: how to track a deer, bicycle in Europe, tune a car, get a tip from a stingy diner, sail a boat, lasso a calf, repair a roof, develop a picture, service in a subway, light a play, save money by buying used clothes, cook on a hot plate or a camp stove. You are an adult who has had many experiences and performed many jobs that would interest other people. List them, or team up with someone else. Interview the other person and have that person interview you, so each of you will discover what interests the other.

What Do Readers Need to Know?

Imagine what readers outside of the class need to know. If you can answer a reader's need you will have an effective piece of writing. Readers off the campus may need to know how many students have work to pay their way through school, that some parents don't want their children to go to college, that all jocks aren't dumb, that undergraduates often work on important research projects, that some students have to drop out of college because of increasing costs, that alcohol—the drug adults approve of—is the biggest problem on campus. A good way of looking for a subject is to look first for a reader.

What Would You Like to Know?

Writing is a marvelous way to satisfy your curiosity. When I was a freshman, I wondered what college was like from the point of view of a night watchman, so I got permission to go around with him, and ended up with a fine feature for the school paper. Think what you're nosy about: What's it like to watch a football game from the sidelines, or with the coaches watching the film on Sunday? Who cooks the rolls for breakfast and when do they come in? How do they audition for the play? How do they set up the equipment for a rock concert? How can a student rule be appealed or changed? What are the best paying or most unusual summer jobs? How do foreign students see the school? What happens to shop-lifters when they are caught downtown? Look at the world around you and question it.

Use Your Emotions

The way you feel can lead you to a good piece of writing. A while back, someone grilled me about my combat time in World War II. I became very agitated; I didn't want to talk about the killing. But afterward I wondered why I was so agitated, why I had hidden my feelings for so long and hidden them so deeply, why I was afraid to face the complicated feelings of war. My feelings have led me to write paragraphs that are leading me to a book. Your fears, your anger, your sadness, your happiness, your discomfort, your comfort, your reactions to people and situations may produce powerful pieces of writing. The more you face your emotions honestly, the more you will touch the emotions of readers.

Use Your Mind

Writing is, of course, an intellectual activity. Use writing to think about your world. Observe what you see, and ask why, what if, how come, what's the alternative, what's going to happen, what should be changed, how can it be changed? Ask all the questions that do just that: question. Doubt, be critical, speculate, connect, create, make up answers and look for their questions. Create theories and examine their consequences. Look for the roots and the branches of what you see in the world around you.

Subjects Lead to Subjects

The more you become aware of potential subjects, the more pieces of writing you will begin to see. Awareness multiplies awareness. Paint all the colors you find studying the bark of a single tree and you will see all the colors in the grass, on the hill, in the stream, on the rocks.

Your increased awareness will make the world a more interesting place. An experienced basketball fan watches how the good players move without the ball. As you record and explore your world through writing you'll begin to hear what isn't said, notice problems that are not solved, find the ordinary people around you interesting, discover meaning where you saw no meaning before. The writer is never bored, for where others see dull monotony the writer sees potential subjects.

Fine subjects are often found by what isn't as much as what is. What is not being done, said, felt. Be aware of omissions, the space around and within a potential subject.

A couple of questions may help the writer to estimate the reader's response to a particular subject:

▶ Why should anyone read this article?
▶ What do you expect the reader to do—or feel or think—after reading it?

Most of all, pay attention to those subjects you must explore. Write, first of all, for yourself and from yourself. Writing is an act of thinking. Its primary purpose is to find meaning, a meaning so powerful that it should be shared through writing.

The Inventory of Information

Write with information, not words.

Effective writing is built from specific, accurate pieces of information. The reader wants, above all, to be informed. Whatever you are writing, you should try to make the reader an authority on your subject. The writer's greatest compliment may be when a reader turns from the page and says to someone else, "Did you know that . . . ?"

Many students have the misconception that writers write with words, language detached from information. They think that words are pretty balloons filled with air. But writing that is read has words that are firmly anchored to meaning. If you write a science report, a poem, a term paper, a business letter, a short story, an essay exam, a film script, an argument, a newspaper story, a personal letter, you will capture the reader if you give the reader writing that is filled with concrete details.

Words are the symbols for specific information. We use words so that we can arrange information into meaningful patterns. Words are a sort of shorthand by which we can capture, comprehend, and communicate experience. Man is the animal that uses words to think and share.

James Baldwin says, "The importance of a writer . . . is that he is here to describe things which other people are too busy to describe." Maxine Kumin adds, "What makes good poetry for me is a terrible specificity of detail, whether of object or of feeling. The poet names and particularizes and thus holds for a moment in time (and thus for all time, as long as time lasts for humanity) whatever elusive event he/she is drawn to. By terrible I mean unflinching. Honest and sometimes compassionate."

The person who has a full inventory of detailed, significant information has the advantage over every other writer. It is more than an advantage, it is a necessity to have mental shelves stacked with information when you are writing. You must be able to select the statistic, the quotation, the descriptive detail, the anecdote at the moment of writing that will help you understand the subject you are exploring through writing, and will eventually help your reader understand it. You can't write nothing.

Beginning writers often misunderstand this. Young writers often become word drunk on their way to becoming good writers. They dance to the sound of their own voice. They try to substitute style for subject matter, tricks for content, ruffles and flourishes for information. It doesn't work.

Receiving Information

Writers learn to spend a large part of their writing time collecting information from which to build writing. Writers practice a wide-ranging receptivity to information, behaving like great dish antennas collecting signals to which they may decide to tune from satellites and from space. That collecting may be done in response to living or in response to an assignment, but collecting information is the beginning of the writing process.

This process seems random, and it may even feel random, but it is not. Most of the specifics are caught for a potential purpose. I almost always have my daybook or log with me, but if that notebook isn't handy 2½-by-3-inch cards in my wallet are.

I'm always receiving, as every writer is, specific information that can be connected with other information. Sometimes I have an assignment from an editor or from myself and I'm consciously looking for details that will fit that topic. But other times I'm just receiving the gift of details that will produce their own abundance, their own need to be related and understood.

The Process of Collection

We are all writers whether we know it or not. We collect information so that we can survive: What is that noise? What is that smell? Did that shadow move? We learn what brings punishment and what brings reward, what streets are dangerous, what behavior makes you popular. We learn how to dress and walk and talk and laugh. We learn how to make a dress, pass a basketball, make money, get through school. Our brain stores everything we see, feel, hear, taste, touch; and it also stores how we feel and think. Your brain has already collected enough information for thousands of books.

In addition to this spontaneous, unconscious collection process, we also collect information when we are given an assignment to learn something or to write about it. This is usually a more formal, structured activity, but it shouldn't be too formal if it is to work. Even formal research depends on happy accidents, unexpected connections and insights. When we are collecting information, the most significant specific is often caught in the corner of our eye.

Recollecting

We usually start the process of collection with ourselves. We begin not so much by collecting but recollecting, using techniques to remember what we know and what we don't know we know.

The term *research* itself means just what it says—RE-search. We start by searching through our memory bank to see what is there that we can make use of as we write. Don't worry if you think you have a poor memory. Most of us measure ourselves against those freaks on game shows who can remember every irrelevant detail about opera, football, politics, antique autos, or movies. That sort of memory is meaningless when you are writing. The writer needs to know relevant information, information that connects with other pieces of information, information that is available when the writer—and the reader—need it.

That is one of the most exciting things about writing: It makes it possible for us to remember what we didn't know we knew. We all know far more than we think we know. Our brain has recorded, through all of our senses, much more than we were aware of at any moment. Sometimes when we are in a terrifying situation—in a car that skids out of control, in a house that catches on fire—we become aware of how many things our brain is recording. Once, in paratroop training, my main chute didn't open. I seemed to have all the time in the world to consider and reconsider the problem. I had to make sure my parachute was not a streamer, a long tail of an open chute hopelessly wrapped around itself; then I had to open my reserve chute and feed it out. It wound around the legs of another paratrooper, and I became a pendulum dragging us both down dangerously fast. Then my main chute partially opened. I reached for the knife strapped to my right leg, cut free from the reserve chute, and managed to get into position to land.

Writing this, I am back in the skies over Tennessee in 1943. I can feel the glasses strapped to my face with adhesive tape, the wind on my cheeks, see the blue southern sky, hear the planes and the silence as they disappear over the ridge, see the red clay earth rising fast, so fast. But somehow time slows down so I can prepare to absorb the jolt of the earth slamming up at me. I tumble over and over, and roll up on my feet. I could fill a book with the sensations of that one jump. I looked at my watch. It was only forty-seven seconds since I had stepped from the plane.

The material for writing is in your head. It will be recovered, relived, understood, and shared through writing. One of the principal reasons that writers write is to relive life.

Writing is also rethinking. When we write a personal experience, we reexperience it and have the opportunity to give it shape and meaning that may not have been apparent the first time around. This is just as true when we write an academic paper. We combine our living with what we heard in the lecture, what stuck in our notebook during the discussion, what we remember from the reading. All that we are learning is processed by our brain, so that when we write we often find out that we know more than we thought we knew. We can connect theory with practice, history with the present, our ideas with the ideas of others, facts from another course with facts from this course.

But to do all this, we must collect the information—specific, accurate information—from which vigorous writing is constructed.

Increase Your Awareness _____

As writers, it is important that we move out from that which is within us to what we see, feel, hear, smell, taste of the world around us. A writer is always making use of experience and extending experience. This is one of the most exciting things about writing; it increases your awareness of the world around you. To put it a different way, writers are receptive to the life they are living, prepared to receive what life brings, so that material may lead to writing or be stored away in inventory, ready to be used when a writing project needs it.

I watch an old lady moving upstream against the students coming downtown for lunch. She has a stainless-steel walker, a U-shaped contraption that she lifts and pushes eight inches ahead, then shuffles toward. What my grandmother could have done with such a gadget! She spent the last twelve years of her life in bed. Perhaps. . . . The old lady has my grandmother's hair, a wispy halo of white, like the fine, white angel-hair that is sometimes used on Christmas trees. She also has my grandmother's jaw, tough, mean, determined. A friend stops and says, "You're looking good today." The old lady says, "I'd rather be seventy."

I don't know if I'll make use of that, but I received it and stored it away, the same way I clipped and read and stored away an article by William Stafford in which he talks of writer's block. I may use it in an editorial-page essay on the delights of procrastination for a newspaper, in an article for a writers' magazine, or in an academic piece for teachers or researchers into the writing process. The scholar, the scientist, the lawyer, the writer—every thinking person keeps picking up bits of information that may fit into an evolving meaning now or later.

You do this every day without even knowing it. You pick up the latest slang, hear a joke and store it away to repeat it later, notice a jacket someone's wearing and decide you ought to have one, hear a song and think about buying a record. We all use our powers of observation so that we can survive. We receive messages that tell us how to live our lives.

A big difference between the writer and the nonwriter is in the number of messages that are received. Each day we receive conscious and subconscious messages. I see the squirrels this winter madly searching for food in the snowy woods outside my window. I'm conscious of that. It's been a hard winter for squirrels, and this year I've heard neighborhood stories of squirrels trying to get into houses. I can't tell you what I'm not conscious of, but I know those woods are stored away in my memory, and that this summer, or next, if I write about a snowy woods, I will then see again, in my mind, the way snow has clung to the north side of a certain tree.

We can't write without seeing, and by writing we see better. A writer's life is at least twice lived, at the time of living and at the time of reliving.

Becoming a Camera

There are some specific things you can do to increase your awareness. The best is to go to one spot and sit for an hour and just write down the specific details you see. As Christopher Isherwood said, "I am a camera with its shutter open, quite passive, recording, not thinking. Recording the man shaving at the window opposite and the woman in the kimono washing her hair. Some day, all this will have to be developed, carefully fixed, printed." Make yourself a camera that is recording what it sees. Later you can edit the film to find out what it means. If you do this, don't worry about sentences or spelling or neatness. Just record what you see.

It's amazing what happens when you go to a familiar place—the dormitory lounge, the dining hall, the basketball court an hour before the game, the student beer hall, a church, a hospital waiting room, a supermarket—and just write down what you see. It's easy to collect a hundred, two hundred, sometimes many more specifics than that in an hour. You will see things that you haven't seen before and make connections that you haven't made before.

But is this writing? It certainly is, because writing starts long before the first line of a finished draft. If you're going to write a book review, you have to read the book, and possibly other articles and books about that particular book, that sort of book, or the author. You have to do the experiment before you write it up. You have to observe the game before you write the news story that tells who won, how, and why.

I can't go back and observe my grandmother, for she died many years ago. I'd like to go to the island off the coast of Scotland where she was born, but I can't afford that. I can't even take the time to go to the hospital and see stroke victims and how they are treated today, or go to a nursing home. But I can, on my way to school, stop in the supermarket, sit down or walk around with a notepad, and put down some of the things I see old people do.

This took me a few minutes. I had to wander through the supermarket until I found an old lady shopping. I stood at the end of the aisle where she couldn't see me, and then went and sat on a bench on the other side of the cash registers where I could see her shop and then check out. She wasn't at all like my grandmother. My grandmother was large, imposing; the woman I watched was birdlike. But just being a camera, watching her and her ostentatious manners,

Dressed up—camel's hair coat
rubbers make feet big—spindly legs
Hairdo—been to hairdressers
Dressed like lady
Moves slowly—makes shopping last
Superior look on face
     Knowing
     Examines delicacies
No one to cook for but self
Acts as if someone were watching, judging her
Middle class
     (See middle-aged man. I played
     football with him. I see the boy
     in the man. Same grin. Spraddle-
     legged walk.)
Others harried, hurried
Old lady wants to make time last
     (But you have a sense of time
     racing ahead as you get old)
     Lifts up each foot separately and
     plants each one separately—
     scared of falling
Her awareness of others
Alone in aisle, I'm hidden behind display, she acts as if someone is watching (someone is)
Middle class—what will neighbors say
My grandmother's sense of propriety
     Keeps curtains half drawn
     Wears a hat when shopping
     Lace curtains
Does old lady buy "the right brands"?
     If anyone was in kitchen they'd
     see "right" brands. No one in
     her kitchen until she dies.
Wears clean underwear in case of an accident

Go back to what she was examining:
     Spanish olives
     Olive butter
     Sweet pickles
     piccalilli
———
handbag hung on left arm
pushing cart as she pushed baby carriage?
———
tiny, round-shouldered
———
tips head up to read labels—bifocals
———
large cart, few items
———
pursed lips, raised eyebrows
critical lady
———
small-boned, looks like a bird
———
Manners—she makes sure she has manners
Impatient in line but she has nowhere to go?
wrinkled stocking below neat coat
varicose veins
walks flat-footed
———
money from purse, carefully private

her obvious concern with what the neighbors thought, reminded me of the concern with propriety felt by my grandmother, who had been a farm girl from an island off the coast of Scotland sent when she was a teenager to live in a great house in London where she had to work and learn manners. She married an older man who was coming to this country to run a mill. The farm girl had to be a lady. It was terribly important to her to do the right thing, I was both amused by and very sympathetic to the efforts of the little old woman in the supermarket to be a lady.

As you look back through my notes you may see that I have the beginning of a piece about my grandmother, but I also have a character sketch, perhaps even a short story, about the lady I saw, or an essay or newspaper column about the little old ladies who live alone and dress up to go shopping; they make the trip last as long as possible, and the few lines of dialogue at the checkout counter may be their only conversation of the week.

I am never bored, for when I'm waiting in an airport or in a parking lot for a meeting to begin or a movie to start, I am always receiving observations. I see how people dress, move close to or away from one another, walk, act when they don't think they are being seen. I'm a spy, or a sneak, enjoying human comedy, and all that I observe is stored away ready to be called up when I'm writing.

The writer is always receiving revealing details—the way one teacher carries a pile of books to class and builds a little wall of books between himself and his students, the way another teacher uses the latest campus slang in precisely the wrong way.

Use Your Senses

All the writer's senses help the writer become aware of information that may become raw material for a piece of writing. The writer hears and overhears. The writer touches, tastes, and smells the world so the details can be used in writing that makes the reader experience the world through all of the reader's senses.

Practice Empathy

Another way to make yourself receive information that may be helpful to you as a writer is to practice empathy, the ability to put yourself in the other people's skins. We can imagine what it might be like to be rich if we are poor or poor if we are rich, to be a policeman or to be arrested by a policeman, to be selling or buying.

These imaginings are not facts, but they can help us understand the factual elements in the world we observe, and they can let us know what questions we should ask when we investigate a topic. We may be shocked when we see an emergency ambulance attendant respond to an accident without apparent emotion, but if we imagine what it is like to respond to accident after accident, night after night, month after month, we may develop some perceptive questions to ask him or her about the emotional price paid.

Make an Assignment Your Own _____

When most students are given a writing assignment, the first thing they ask is, "What does the teacher want?" Often that question will make the teacher angry. Many teachers do not like to admit they have personal requirements and they do not want to tell students what to think. Yet, too often, students have discovered that teachers—even those who say they don't—*do* have specific requirements that students must take into account. Teachers are so different that no one can give blanket advice on this issue. Students have to decide if they trust the teacher who says, as I do, "Surprise me."

The trick of dealing with any assignment effectively is to make it your own. The skillful writer learns how to shift the ownership of the assigned piece of writing for the teacher—or editor—to the writer. There are guidelines for doing this.

Read the Assignment Carefully

Go over the assignment several times to make sure you know what is expected of you. If the assignment has been given orally, write it out and read it over. Make sure you understand the purpose of the assignment, not just *what* you are expected to do, but *why* you are expected to do it. The reason for the assignment will often help make the assignment clear. If you don't understand it, read what you have written back to the instructor. Writing directions may be the most difficult form of writing. I certainly know I do it badly. I know what I mean and it is hard for me to put myself in the shoes of a person who does not know what I mean.

Ask Questions

If you have studied the assignment carefully and do not understand it, ask the teacher to clarify it. It may be appropriate to ask to see good papers students have done in the past or examples of published writing that practice the lessons being taught by the assignment.

Stand Back

Once the assignment is clear, walk away from it. Circle it at a distance to see what comes to mind. The assignment should be given to your subconscious that will play with it, making connections with what you know, have seen, experienced, thought about. An assignment always increases my awareness. I'm told to do a story on street people and I'm suddenly aware of the bag ladies, the young man mining the dumpsters in the alley, the woman talking to herself on the street corner, the late-afternoon line at the mission or soup kitchen, the early-morning turnout of winos and drifters at the Church dormitory. I see how they dress, I record the sly looks they give people, the way they make themselves invisible, the layers of clothing they wear, the bottles ineffectively hidden in small paper bags, the shaking hand, the shuffling step. Little of this is conscious, I've just been made aware and I see connections with experiences in my past—the refugees who clogged the roads leading to the battlefields they were fleeing and to which we were advancing—and with what I'm reading—perhaps Steinbeck's account of those fleeing the dustbowl in the Depression for California or John Berger's report on the guest workers imported to north European countries from southern Europe.

It is often helpful to stimulate this essential circling of the subject by using the techniques in this chapter such as brainstorming or free writing. You should not just attack the subject the way you've attacked similar subjects but collect and recollect information from which you can discover the most effective way to deal with this particular assignment.

Be Self-Centered

Look at the assignment from your own point of view. Too often we look at assignments from a point of weakness, saying to ourselves that we know nothing about the topic. That is rarely true. Of course, you should do the academic work required by the assignment—read the book, survey the voters, perform the experiment, observe the patient—but you should go beyond that. Look at the assignment from a point of strength. Think what you know that may connect with the subject. You may have had jobs, for example, that will allow you to make a special connection with a character in a book who has moved to a new and alien place, discovered he or she is adopted, or is sent to a nursing home the way your grandmother was. A history assignment may connect with a literature course, a paper in business administration may make use of what you studied in a computer course. Look at the subject from your own point of view so that you shift the position of authority from the teacher to yourself.

This does not mean that you have a license to be prejudiced, to present unsubstantiated opinions, to be unfair. It does mean that in the process of thinking about the topic and writing about it, you take advantage of what you know. If you are writing about the care of the elderly, you may use your experience in working as an aide in a nursing home, your family's guilt in sending a relative to such a home, your neighbor's reasons to stop working as a nurse for the elderly. Such information may give you a way to approach the subject or to document a point in your final draft.

Limit the Subject

The inexperienced writer usually tries to do too much, skimming over the surface of an assignment, trying to cover the history of medical care for the elderly in Western Civilization since 1600 in five pages. The experienced writer severely limits the subject—perhaps concentrating on one nursing home, one disease such as Alzheimers, one day, or even one patient. Limiting the subject allows it to be developed properly, so that one single point can be developed and documented in a way that satisfies the reader's hunger for meaning and information.

Remember the significant relationship between the words author and authority. Whenever possible, try to become an authority on the subject on which you are writing. You can do this by taking advantage of what you know, by researching the subject, by exercising the muscle between your ears and thinking about it before you write, and by thinking through writing, for each draft should be a way of discovering meaning.

Questions about Finding a Subject

- *I'm, well, boring. My parents are boring, their parents are boring. My sister yawned at her own wedding. So did my brother-in-law. We work at being boring. We think it is nice to be nice. We live in a boring house, in a boring neighborhood full of boring people. Mr. Frakus left home in September and his family didn't miss him until October.*

But your writing isn't boring. You've got a great piece there. Tell more about Mr. Frakus, Mrs. Frakus, and all the boring little Frakuses. Tell me about how boring your parents are. Be specific. Describe the neighborhood in concrete detail. You'll have a lively piece of writing.

I've had thousands of students who thought they were boring but only a handful who succeeded in convincing me they were. If students are willing to write in honest, specific language about what they know, see, and feel, they'll start to see their world in a different way. I'm lucky. As a writer, I'm never bored. Waiting in line, stuck in a traffic jam, waiting for the company to come, I turn on my internal recording apparatus and begin watching the world and thinking about what I see.

- *Is good writing always critical? I like my parents and I'm engaged to a wonderful guy who sells insurance. Would I get an "A" if I hated my parents, served them at a barbecue, and gave birth to a gorilla out of wedlock?*

Sure sounds interesting to me. That's a problem that worries every writer and every journalist. Bad news is usually good news to the writer. It's easier to write about a family murder than a family who went to bed happy and woke up happy.

Most of our best writers are people who have had to stand back, detach themselves from the people around them and try to figure out what is going on. That's the intellectual stance and it may alienate you from those about you but most writers are able to be a part of life while examining life. Don't forget that the human animal is inherently critical, part of us is always standing back, listening to how others talk so we can speak the current slang, observing how others dress so we can dress in style, thinking of the marriage manual at the most intimate moments of our lives. It may be ridiculous or not even very nice but that's the way we are. Writing doesn't create the detachment, it allows the human being to make constructive use of it.

- *Before I began this essay, I didn't think I had anything to write about, now I've got too much. Help!*

That's a good problem, like having too much money in the bank or too much power under the hood. Select one topic and explore it. Which one? The one you remember when you walk away from the list, the one you catch yourself thinking about when you didn't think you were thinking.

- *Do I always have to do all these things—brainstorm, map, grow a tree every time before I write?*

Nope. You don't have to do any of them. If you have a subject, write it. If you don't, try these techniques or anything else that will help you find a subject.

- *My teacher won't let me write about what I want to write about or think what I want to think.*

Make sure you are right by talking with your teacher. If you still feel that way, do what you have to do to pass the course but also become a secret writer. Most writers have had to do that. I did. And the writing I did for myself increased my fluency in my other writing, was good therapy, and even gave me a career. The writer has to find the audience for the writer's work. Most writers trim their sails to the demands of the audience. The most courageous ones create their own. That's a dangerous and painful course, but most great artists, composers, and writers were booed when they faced a public that expected what they were used to seeing and hearing.

- *I keep writing about the same subject. Should I have many subjects that I write about?*

You have to learn in school to write about many different subjects in many different forms. When removed from formal requirements, most writers find they return to a few traumatic experiences, the ones that have marked their lives. Usually those are the mysteries of their teenage years. I write about death and disease, marked by the paralysis of my grandmother that you are reading about, and the death of my daughter decades later taps into that deep well of feeling and fear I experienced when I was young. I started publishing in a fourth-grade classroom and began collecting quotations about writing when I was in high school. I went overseas when I was nineteen and I'm still trying to under-stand what I saw and what I was able to do. We each have one or two or three subjects that are so important to us that we keep exploring them all our lives. My mother-in-law in a nursing home, ninety-six years old, muttered about the fact that her mother had sent her to live with relatives when she was only eight years old. She was still trying to figure out if her mother loved her more or less than her sisters 88 years before.

- *You're being awfully personal. Do I have to write about that kind of stuff, take off my clothes and dance around in public the way you do?*

I hope not. It embarrasses me sometimes, I don't always feel comfortable running around in my birthday suit. And I don't always do it. I do it when it's the best way to help others or to say what I have to say. I never finished my master's degree and I don't have a doctorate. My knowledge about writing comes primarily from personal experience. I'm also a pretty open person. I need to share my life with others and have them share their lives with me. It's my way to live but it doesn't need to be yours. Most writers I know are much more private than I am. You don't have to be an intellectual nudist to be a writer.

Not really, but on second thought, all writing is revealing and your distance and detachment may reveal more than you think. If you write about rape only in terms of statistics, that may expose you as much as if you write about it only in terms of feelings.

Subject-Finding Activities _____

1. Brainstorm by thinking of an important event in your life, when you were scared or happy or unhappy or angry, or brainstorm by thinking of an issue, argument, or opinion you want to develop, and put down every detail you can think of as fast as possible.
2. Map by using the same event or topic to see what different things are recalled. But don't worry if the same things come up at first. Just go as fast as you can. Some things will be the same, and some may be different.
3. Free write. Write as hard and fast as you can without worrying about grammar, spelling, mechanics, penmanship, or typemanship. The important thing is to get a flow. You may even want to tape-record to hear what you have written. The important thing is to let language lead you to discover what you know and what you need to know.
4. Work to make yourself more aware. Go to a familiar place and list as fast as possible fifty specific details, or a hundred, or two hundred. The more you list, the more things you'll see you haven't seen before. It may be fun to take a frame or cardboard tube and see what you can see in a small framed area. It may be profitable to take one sense at a time and record what you can smell, hear, taste, and touch as well as see.
5. Make an authority inventory, listing all the things you're an expert on—the jobs you can do, the things you can repair, the places you've lived or visited, the problems you can solve, the hobbies you enjoy, the people you know, the family background you have. Each of us is an authority on many things, and our best writing usually comes from what we know and care about. There is a significant relationship between the word *author* and the word *authority*.
6. Role-play. Watch a situation—a crowd growing unruly, a person making a speech, an ambulance responding to an accident, a person being hired or fired—and imagine yourself in that situation. Figure out how you would act

and react, think and feel. This will give you some interesting questions to ask. Go to a person who is involved in the situation and ask them.

7. Take an assignment you have been given by a teacher and list five ways you could make it yours by responding in terms of an area in which you are an authority.

8. Make a movie in your mind of an important experience. Then turn it into a novel, a poem, a government report, a TV series, a short story, a talk to the Rotary Club luncheon to discover how each genre helps you see the same subject in a different way.

9. Interview other writers in the classroom and outside to find out how they get ideas. Look up books and articles on creativity in the library to discover what others have said about the creative process that could help a writer find ideas or topics to explore. Interview artists, successful businessmen, doctors, lawyers, policemen, nurses to see what sparks their good ideas.

10. Become a stranger to your familiar world. Visit from outer space, become your great-great grandmother, a Russian or Chinese student; look at the familiar as if it were not familiar to see subjects you need to think about and explore, perhaps in writing.

Chapter 3

ᛗ Explore Your Subject: COLLECT

I could keep myself busy for months without moving from one spot, just by leaning now to the right, now to the left.

PAUL CÉZANNE

I would want to tell my students of a point strongly pressed, if my memory serves, by Shaw. He once said that as he grew older, he became less and less interested in theory, more and more interested in information. The temptation in writing is just reversed. Nothing is so hard to come by as a new and interesting fact. Nothing so easy on the feet as a generalization.

JOHN KENNETH GALBRAITH

The more particular, the more specific you are, the more universal you are.

NANCY HALE

Writers write with information—specific, accurate information that the reader needs.

Readers read to satisfy their hunger for information—specific, accurate information that they can use.

Yet students—and some of their instructors—think that writers write with vocabulary, spelling, rhetoric, grammar, mechanics, rules, forms, and traditions. And that readers are drawn to the page by their compulsion to make sure the writer is correct—as if what is said is not important, how it is said is.

Write with Information _____

The writing act begins with the collection of the raw material of writing, information that will be arranged into meaning by that act itself. Writing is thinking.

To think, we have to have information that we can arrange and rearrange until it makes sense; to cause the thinking of others, we have to have a vehicle that will deliver our information and its arrangement.

Words are symbols that capture information, allow it to be manipulated and communicated. I imagine the system of grunts that said that is a BIG dinosaur, get the kids back in the cave. That was information that was needed right now, and it evolved into scratches in rocks that said the BIG dinosaurs are over the ride, watch out.

No dinosaurs, no grunts, no scratches on the rock. As writers, we have to find our own dinosaurs, then use language to understand their meaning and communicate it.

Since we are used to thinking of the superficial aspects of language before we have collected the material of writing, it may be helpful to become aware of some of the forms of information writers collect.

- *Facts.* Specific, concrete, accurate details that reveal meaning, convey authority or believability, provide liveliness, spark insight, add texture.
- *Statistics.* Numbers. In context. Used with care, they convince the reader and may even reveal significance. It may be helpful to communicate them in special ways—lists, charts, diagrams.
- *Observations.* Put the reader in the piece. Allow the reader to stand behind the camera—a camera that records sights, sounds, smells, tastes, and touch.
- *Quotations.* Statements by other people about my subject that give me essential information or will provide, in my writing, a special authority or a different voice from mine.
- *Reports.* Excerpts from reports that record the results of detailed studies of the writer's subject.
- *Anecdotes.* Little stories that show more than tell. They are mininarratives—

60

shorter than Uncle Harry's fishing stories—that include character, dramatic action, setting, dialogue, and theme.
- *Theories.* The thoughts of others that explain what you are writing about.
- *Images.* Pictures in the mind that reveal meaning—and often emotion—to writer and reader.
- *Principles.* The accepted lessons or laws that may be wrong but are accepted as truthful. They may be used or attacked—with significant documentation.
- *Faces.* Individuals who are responsible for the subject, participate in it, are affected by it.
- *Evidence.* Material that will educate and persuade the writer and the reader.
- *Questions.* That the reader will ask. Count on it. You can play reader and anticipate them. And you'd better.
- *Answers.* To the questions the readers will ask.
- *Patterns.* That emerge from the material. Writing may be built from a preconceived concept with the writer seeking documentation to fill in the blanks, but the best writing arises from the material with the specifics making connections and those connections growing into patterns that reveal meaning.
- *Problems* That reveal the importance of the subject.
- *Solutions.* That the reader can see being solved and that show the significance of the topic.
- *Ideas.* Guesses. Estimates, Hunches. Thoughts stray and not so stray. Clues. Hints. Things to think about and things thought.
- *Processes.* That show the subject at work or that the reader needs to know and understand.
- *History.* What's past of the subject? What meaning comes from its history?
- *Implications.* What's the subject's future?

Collect the material to fill out such a list and you'll stop feeling empty. In fact, you'll feel so full, that you'll be eager to write to relieve yourself of the information.

Make your own list so that you realize all of the forms of information you need to have on hand when you start to write, the way you have pots and vegetables and butter and knives and fish and seasonings and milk and eggs and cheese and dozens of other supplies on hand when you start to cook. Some of them are already on the shelf, the way you may use your memory to collect some of the information you need to begin writing, but you may have to go out shopping for other ingredients, the way you need to do research before you begin to write.

Primary Technique for Collecting Information: Find Revealing Specifics _____

What Is a "Revealing" Specific?

A revealing specific is a fragment of information that gives you a hint of significance. It causes an itch, a curiosity, a wonder, a "what if," an invitation for further exploration.

The revealing specific may take many forms. As the column published later in this chapter was conceived—long before there were words on paper—specifics would pass through my head:

• *A Scene.* The dining room of our apartment, brown woodwork, brown wall paper, brown shades half drawn, brown rug, brown furniture, brown people all dull, and my father yelling at me for the noise I had put on the phonograph. Evil dance music, swing—sounds that were just noise to him and were the work of the Devil to deacon Murray.

• *RKO.* The theatre in Boston where John Divine and I went to hear Count Basie, Dorsey, Goodman, the big bands when we cut high school on Thursdays.

• *Columbus Avenue.* The colored neighborhood in Boston. It was decades before the term black became popular. Record stores where I could buy 78s of the real Louis Armstrong, King Oliver, examples of New Orleans jazz, KC jazz, Chicago jazz not available in the record stores of my neighborhood.

Each of those specifics are surrounded by a galaxy of memories, tastes, sounds, odors, moods, feelings, images, details, stories. I could write pages on each of them. This tells me I will have the material I need when I write—and it tells me I'm on to something I had better explore by writing.

These revealing specifics are, at this stage, private. I do not have to explain them to myself as I have to you. They are a private code. Later, if I use any of them in writing a piece for you to read, I will have to put them in a context so that they will communicate.

How Do You Recognize a Revealing Specific?

By that galaxy of thoughts, feelings, and memories that surrounds it. Each of us has songs that will always spark memories in you. Hum the beginning of "Stardust" to me and I am back at a dance a lifetime or more ago. It was played as the last dance—slow, and the lights were turned down and often we were in our overcoats and dancing with the person we came with, close, slow, very close, the overcoats open and wrapped around us, very slow. Memories, emotions, details—more details, more revealing specifics.

How Do You Hunt for a Specific That Reveals?

The same way you hunt for an enormous grizzly. Tracking. waiting. Using every sense. Keeping alert for significant sound, smell, shadow, move, feeling.

Your hunting technique may change according to what you are hunting. If you are hunting for information about a corporation that has been selling stock illegally, you will hunt through financial records. If you are looking for the causes of the French Revolution, you will search primary and secondary sources. If you are writing a nostalgic piece about your childhood, you may enter into a mood of reverie.

In every case, however, you will be searching for those accurate, concrete specifics that carry a galaxy of information around them and that, when they are connected with other specifics, will create a meaning that will interest you and, later, readers.

A Necessary Abundance

To write well, the writer must have much more information on hand than the writer can ever use. When I wrote *Reader's Digest* articles—seven to nine pages triple spaced—I would have collected three or more milk crates of material.

All the material you do not use is somehow in the text. The reader knows if what you write is backed up with additional documentation.

And when you write, you need to choose from an abundance of evidence, pick the most effective anecdote, fact, revealing detail, statistic, image, description from the many you have on hand, the one that is just right in this particular place in the evolving draft, the one that will serve the reader well.

Additional Techniques for Collecting Information: Remember ⸻

The first place to collect is from memory. We have recorded far more than we realize on most subjects or we put a new subject in a context of memory. When I visit a new high school I always remember North Quincy High School and failing and dropping out and, finally, flunking out. I collect information about the new school, first of all, in the context of my own autobiography.

Start your collecting process by listing in your daybook, journal, on a piece of paper, code words and revealing specifics that remind you what you know about the topic. For the column at the end of this chapter I would have put down:

▶ Rock
▶ Beatles
▶ Loud [I went out and bought wax ear plugs for my wife and myself].
▶ Going to field house and getting Hannah who had stayed past her deadline at her first rock concert and seeing a girl who had OD'd being carried to ambulance.
▶ REM. The name of the group I was going to hear. The name of a cough syrup I hated in my sickly childhood.

I knew I knew little about the world of rock music that had pounded away just over the horizons of my life. I was surprised at the extent of my ignorance and that was important for me to know before I started reporting and writing. It is not so much the people who don't know as the people who don't know they don't know who get in trouble.

Read _____

There are as many ways to read as there are to write, yet people usually read in the same way, at the same pace, no matter what the reading task. In this text, you will be introduced to a number of reading styles, each tied into a stage in the writing process. Try them out, develop your own, and use them at every stage in the writing process—and away from the writing process—when they help you with an intellectual task. And never let school give you the impression that reading always has to be work, a purposeful job of collecting information. Reading should often be play because it is one of the best ways we can leave our world and escape to others.

This may be the time to mention reading fast. Many people say that they read slowly but they remember what they read. The research I have read—and my own experience—denies that. Of course there are times when you have to—or want to—read slowly to savor or decode a text, but speed itself can be a benefit to reading. When you read fast, it is an effort and that effort concentrates the mind. You pay attention, your mind doesn't wander, you enter into the text and are carried along by the logic, the emotion, the music of language. Many times you have to read fast to allow the threads of the text to weave themselves into meaning. Read too slowly and you see only an individual thread or two, not the pattern evolving. Try it. There are many schools that teach speed reading, but you can do it yourself by forcing yourself to read at the point of discomfort. Read in groups of words or lines, not single words. And, naturally, if you have to stop or go back to understand, do it. In some cases, you'll want an entire second reading, but you'll make that commitment only when fast reading has shown you it is worth the investment.

Skimming

To collect information efficiently, the reader has to get through many books, articles, and reports to discover what needs close attention. Some of the techniques of skimming seem obvious, but I have found not only students but professional journalists who waste a great deal of time in a disorganized sample rather than an organized skimming of material that *may* include information worth mining. Here's a checklist that may help.

► Title
► Author's name *and brief biography* to discover the relationship of the writer to your topic.
► Table of Contents to see if there is a chapter or section to scan.
► Index to discover specific references.
► Bibliography to find out if there are other sources you should explore.
► The areas in the text itself that may reveal information you need, moving very quickly through the pages and paying attention to:

abstracts
summaries

introductions
conclusions
cross or section headings
key words your eye will catch at high speed if that is all the eye is trying to do at that moment

Interpreting

Once your eye has caught a key word or specific, you should interpret its meaning by putting it in the context of the piece you are reading or writing or both. A college may, for example, brag that 60 percent of its student athletes graduate and one writer may say that is responsible and another may be appalled at the 40 percent who are exploited and do not earn a degree.

Meaning never lies in isolated facts, but in a context. It is the job of the reader to understand the information in the other writer's context and to use that information in a context that is appropriate and accurate.

Immersing

Some writing deserves a fast reading where you do not just skim for facts that jump off the page but demand a quick immersion. You read fast, but you read to catch the mood, the poetry, the sweep of the account that puts you on a street in a strange city, in the hospital waiting room, in combat. By reading fast, you get the feel of a subject.

Connecting

Fast reading will reveal information that connects with other information in the text, in other texts, in your notes and drafts, in your mind. Remember that you are writing to discover meaning; to allow specific pieces of information—represented by words—to arrange themselves in many patterns until there is one that reveals significance.

Interview

The interview in which you ask an authority questions is one of the basic tools of getting information. Most of us are shy about interviewing someone else, but we have to remember that the person who is being interviewed is being put in the position of being an authority, and most of us like to be an authority, to tell someone what we know. It is an ego trip for the interviewee.

Interviews can be informal—just a casual conversation—or formal—when we make an appointment, prepare carefully, and probe deeply into the subject.

You should prepare yourself for interviews by knowing as much as you can about the people you are going to interview—who they are and what they do— and by preparing at least four or five principal questions you have to ask if you are going to get the information you need. Those are usually the questions the reader would like to ask if he or she were there. Think of the reader; ask the reader's questions.

It's important to listen to what the person is saying so that you don't go on asking the potter about how he prepares the clay when he is telling you why he put his wife in the kiln. Many times the interviewee surprises us by what he or she says, and we have to decide on the spot which lead to follow.

Most interviewers take notes by hand, but it is more and more common to use a tape recorder. You should, however, practice taking notes by hand, capturing the essence of what people say, even if you use a tape recorder. Sometimes the tape doesn't work, and if you're not taking notes yourself you may become lazy and miss what's being said—that the wife was popped into the kiln.

It's always best to interview a subject in person so that you can see the expression on the face, the body language that emphasizes or contradicts what is being said, the environment in which the person lives or works, the way the person interacts with others. If you can't interview someone in person, you may have to do it on the telephone, or even by mail. But you lose a lot by doing it without seeing the person face to face.

How the Interview Can Lead to Writing

When you are doing research on any topic, from criminal justice to World War II to urban blight to environmental hazard, don't forget to use live sources, and talk to the people who are involved. They will not tell you the truth, they will tell you their own truths, and you will have the challenge of weaving all the contradictions together into a meaning.

Use the Telephone and the Mail

Sources of information other than individuals are organizations. The library has directories of organizations that will help you find groups that have come together, and one of those organizations' main functions is to educate the public or to serve the public. They will often send you pamphlets or brochures or reports and answer questions you have.

Governments—local, county, state, federal, and even such international organizations as NATO and the United Nations have many groups that will provide you with reports, speeches, laws, regulations, proposals. Your local Congressmen—and women—can help you find the right agency and the office in the agency to contact.

Use the Library

One of the greatest sources of material, of course, is those attics that exist in almost every town, city, and state in the country, as well as in schools, universities, and the nation's capital itself. These attics collect books, magazines, newspapers, pamphlets, phonograph records, films, TV tapes and audio tapes, photographs, maps, letter, journals—all the kinds of documents that record our past—and we call them libraries.

Every library has a card catalog—or computer file—that shows what is in the library and gives the location where you or the librarian can find it. The wise writer always makes sure to have a good working relationship with the library and its librarian. When I was free-lancing in New Jersey I found it a good investment to pay to have cards in four library systems. Libraries are an elemental source for a writer, as important as wind is to a sailor.

If you are going to write, it is vital that you become familiar with your library. Most college libraries have tours that will show you how the library works. Take the tour. Most libraries also have mimeographed sheets or pamphlets that will help you find what you need to know. Study such materials. And most of all, use the library. Browse. Wander. Let the library reveal its resources to you. And if you need help, ask for it. Librarians are trained to be of service, and all of us who write are indebted to their patience and skills in finding information for us.

It's important when you find a reference in the library to make a note of all the essential information about the book so that you can use the library easily the next time, and so that you can use the book in footnotes or bibliographies. Even if you write something that doesn't have footnotes or a bibliography, you should know exactly where you got the material so that you can respond to questions from editors or readers.

Usually you record the author's last name first, then first name, then the middle initial, the title of the work, underlined if it is a book, put within quotation marks if it is an article, the publisher, the place published, the date, the number of pages, and, for your own use, the library reference number together with the name of the library.

The purpose of such notes is to tell you where the information is and isn't. It's important to keep a record of the books you found worthless, so you won't go over them again, as well as the ones that are particularly valuable. Most research doesn't result in big breakthroughs, but a slowly growing understanding of the subject.

Observe _____

Schools often overlook one of the writer's primary sources of information: observation. In the column at the end of the chapter that was my primary source. I went to a rock concert and observed with my *ears*, my eyes, my feet, my nose, but not my taste buds. Try to see how many of your five senses you can use to capture information—and to communicate that information to your reader.

Go to a place that is important to your story. It may not be the place where your writing takes place—you may be writing about the continental congress in which our nation was born—but you will understand that process better if you visit a legislature, a city council session, a town meeting.

Experiment with Form: Description _____

Description is the basic form of writing, but when I first taught Freshman English, it was outlawed in our program as being too simple for academic discourse. Simple? That was the opinion of those who did not write. Description is not simple, but it is fundamental and the best way, I believe, to lay the foundation of the writer's craft.

At first we use description to capture a place or a person, then places with persons, then persons interacting with other persons, and we end up describing ideas, theories, concepts, thoughts and feelings, propositions and conclusions, speculations and facts. All forms of writing contain descriptive elements that make the reader see, think, feel, react.

Writing description can introduce you to the discipline of recording information, ordering it into meaning and communicating that meaning to readers. All the elements of effective writing—accuracy, concreteness, meaningfulness, context, development, form and order within it, emphasis, documentation, flow, grace, style, reader awareness, proportion, pace, voice—may be called on when you write description.

Tips on Writing Effective Description

• *Be Accurate.* The writer has to earn the reader's trust. A single error in fact or an accurate fact in the wrong context and the writer loses the reader's trust. Unfair or not, the reader will suspect everything the writer says.

• *Be Specific.* Readers hunger for concrete details. The specific carries authority with it. Inexperienced writers use words such as beautiful and ugly that carry no meaning out of context. What is beautiful or ugly to one person is the opposite to someone else. Give the reader specifics and the reader will feel or think the reaction to it. Don't tell the reader what to think or how to feel; make the reader think and feel. You do that with specifics.

• *Create a Dominant Impression.* Don't catalogue your details from left to right or top to bottom. Establish a focal point and have everything relate to that point, developing and supporting it. We walk into a trauma center and our eyes go to a stretcher or to a team of people working on someone or parents sitting waiting. Everything in our description must flesh out the dominant impression.

• *Establish an Angle of Vision.* The reader should see the trauma center from a particular angle: the waiting room, the swinging doors of the ambulance bay, from the patient looking up, from a nurse or doctor looking down. This position can move, but slowly. Think of how a professional moves the movie camera and how the amateur blurs the screen by panning the video camera too quickly.

• *Distance.* Stand at an appropriate distance to reveal what you want to say. Zoom in close for intimacy and immediacy, draw back to put the subject in context, move back and forth so that the topic is revealed effectively.

All of these issues exist in other forms of writing, but they are especially clear in the writing of description. Read descriptions that help you understand a subject, make notes on the techniques the writer uses. Try them yourself.

Case History of a Professional Writer ────────────

I write a column for *The Boston Globe* called "Over Sixty" that allows me to look at the world from the point of view of one who is over sixty years old. I write, in other words, the kind of personal experience essay that is central to so many Freshman English courses—and get paid for what I did years ago for a grade. My case histories in this chapter and the four following have all been published in the *Globe*. They were not written for this book, but for publication in the newspaper. When writing this edition, I thought they might show one writer at work, demonstrating many of the techniques presented in the book.

This column came from a class experience. I had assigned my class to go to a classical music concert with my favorite group, the Beaux Arts Trio. The class fought back, asked me if I had ever gone to a rock concert—"well, no"—charged me with cultural illiteracy, and challenged me to hear R.E.M. I did, and they responded to my draft as I had been responding to their drafts.

Description was a major part of this "essay." I wanted to take readers of my generation to a rock concert. I wanted to be light but fair, accurate but not patronizing. I had to make the readers see and hear before they could join me in discovering the meaning I found in writing the piece.

And I did discover the meaning in writing it. It was in the act of writing more than in attending the concert that I found out what it meant to me. Second-guess my description—and everything else in the article. Mark it up, attack it, find out what works for you—and what doesn't work. Put yourself in my place with this assignment. Decide how you'd do it; learn along with me.

Here is the column as it was published:

═══════ ♫ ═══════
Making Peace with the Rock

1   I told my Freshman English class to attend a performance of the Beaux Arts Trio and write a paper about this cultural experience. From the expressions on their faces, I knew they felt they had been assigned to parachute into a Siberian prison camp. Apprehension, disbelief, fear.

2   That made me warm to the task. Of course it would be different but it would be good for them. The Beaux Arts were my favorite "group." They ought to know Mozart, Haydn, Beethoven firsthand if they were going to be educated.

3   Professors tend to go on a bit too long—like parents—and I did. The more you feared music, painting, a book, the more you should confront it. You owed it to yourself as an educated person to put aside prejudice; college was the time to experience the unfamiliar, to turn to primary sources, to begin to think as....

4   "Professor. Have you ever been to a rock concert?"

5   "Well, no."

6   "If we have to go to Beaux Arts; you ought to go to R.E.M."

7   "That's a cough syrup."

8   "No. It's the top college group. You ought to know our music. The more you fear something, the more you...."

9   I held up my hands in surrender. I would dare an expedition to the cultural frontier of rock, lose what hearing I have left, suffer a "location high" from the exhaust fumes of strange drugs, be trampled to death by swaying natives or speared on a purple crescent hairdo.

10   Six weeks later my wife and I were in the bleachers at the Field House molding plastic ear plugs in our hands and trying to appear natural. They were dressed in untied boots, rags that were rags, hair cut by apprentice barbers. Some had interrupted pink or purple hair dye jobs to come to the concert; others were wrapped in leather and hung with chains; all of them were dressed so casually that it must have taken hours to achieve such careful and haphazard inappropriateness.

11   And they were all trying not to stare at us aliens in a building only a mile and a half from our home. They were courteous but curious. White was not the color anyone had dyed their hair. There were a half-dozen or so middle-aged rock scholars—29 to 34 years old—but we were generations older than anyone there, Rip van Winkles who had slept though decades of rock 'n' roll.

12   This was their world and they knew it. It must have been satisfying to them to see more police than at a cop's funeral. They must have felt wonderfully rebellious, dangerous, a marvelous self-selected community of outcasts, superior to those who did not understand and appreciate and belong. I was critical of how they strolled back and forth obviously declaring their belonging, until my writer's eye revealed my casual parade among the faculty at the Beaux Arts intermission.

13   Enough. I wasn't here to reflect on the cultural behavior of academic pseudo-intellectuals but to observe *them,* to appreciate *their* music. B-O-O-M. I felt the first beat in my chest before I heard it. Two rows of speakers, each at least ten feet high—24 speakers in all—were pointed right at us. My ears might be stuffed with plastic but we were inside the music, the beat pressed against the breastbone, stone deaf I would have "heard" the beat.

14   And I liked it. The beat was insistent, fascinatingly predictable and unpredictable. It came in through the feet, the stomach, the spine, and the ears. I wasn't standing back watching a performance, I was somehow *in* the performance.

15   Soon everyone was standing, even my wife stood up and I stood too. The audience was dancing and I felt my own knees bend, even a hip creak in rhythm once in awhile. I was struck by the powerful sense of community, of belonging, of being in, of sharing a, yes, cultural experience. And I was astonished at the self-absorbed loneliness at the same time.

16   Only a few couples danced together in the aisles, facing each other while practicing the mating dance of the fuzzy-tailed Ibis before turning

back to themselves. Everyone else danced alone on chairs, on the floor, in the bleachers, off to the rest rooms and back.

17   It might have been the chewing gum whose smell was stronger to me than that of more natural substances, but these natives were listening to their own music. Each to their own music.

18   Since they paid no attention to each other as they twitched, bent, bumped, ground, hopped, tangled and untangled, no one was critical of how the others danced. Men and women performed as if each were in a room alone.

19   And a good thing that was, because I must report, that most of the scholars around me couldn't keep to a beat that probably cracked the paint on my house across town. One young man with a triple-jointed spine two rows down was wonderful. He must be an osteopath's delight, but the rest of those around me were transported, but not gracefully. Maybe it was New Hampshire, but they lifted their feet as if they were avoiding barnyard obstacles, bent and buckled as if they were trying to load pigs on a truck. Yet it made no difference. They all enjoyed the music in their own private way.

20   Music? Yes. the sounds and the beats were different from group to group, song to song. There was real singing at times, often something as close to a melody as the modern composer Rochberg had allowed at the Beaux Arts performance. The musicians performed with extraordinary skill and teamwork, but this was music for and of our times: the musicians fought the technology but I think the machines won.

21   The flashing, computer-coordinated lights; the electronic sounds, amplified, torted and distorted; the jungle of wires; the dozens of mikes; the island of soundboards, cameras, and slide projectors in the middle of the audience; the backstage crews; the huge trailer trucks to carry the equipment; the three-story towers of lights and screens and speakers all dwarfed the performers. It forced them to yell and scream and jump and struggle, but they lost. No wonder the four performers struggled so hard. The drummer was imprisoned behind his drums, the performers tiny beside their speakers.

22   It did, however, make the music I like best seem out of date in an age of missiles, reactors, computers, even if I play their melodies on my own "sound systems." My music seems more appropriate to a time that appears safer, more ordered, nicer from a distance than it ever was. Perhaps that is why I like it, need its quiet, depend on its order.

23   But standing, twitching sedately to the beat, I couldn't help thinking what Mozart, Beethoven, even Brahms might have done with such electronic toys. Each of them seems safe now they are long dead, but they frightened governments and critics in their day, scared the living daylights out of the old, the established, the whitebeards like me.

24   Walking home, we were glad we had gone. What I had preached in class was true. You should, perhaps especially on the eve of retirement, reach out to what is new, different, even frightening. What does it matter if you dance well, as long as you hear your own music and dance.

Now read the essay with me as I talk you through it, writer to writer, telling you the things I see that were problems and solutions, but remember that I wrote it instinctively. My reading afterward is more detached and intellectual than the way I "read" it during the writing. Then I was hearing a text, reading what was being written, reading what wasn't yet written. Now I have a text to read.

============== ℳ ==============

Making Peace with the Rock

1 I told my Freshman English class to attend a performance of the Beaux Arts Trio and write a paper about this cultural experience. From the expressions on their faces, I knew they felt they had been assigned to parachute into a Siberian prison camp. Apprehension, disbelief, fear.

I have a serious subject, the differences between cultures and the difficulty we all have in crossing such boundaries. But, although the subject is serious, I wanted the tone to be light. Why? Because there is something ridiculous about our fear of other cultures and because the readers I want to reach with this column will not read a solemn essay or sermon on the subject.

2 That made me warm to the task. Of course it would be different but it would be good for them. The Beaux Arts were my favorite "group." They ought to know Mozart, Haydn, Beethoven firsthand if they were going to be educated.

In the first paragraphs I say what I want to say about my position but poke fun at myself and then show the lecture turned on me. The structure is narrative, a form that allows me to invite the reader to experience the story with me.

3 Professors tend to go on a bit too long—like parents—and I did. The more you feared music, painting, a book, the more you should confront it. You owed it to yourself as an educated person to put aside prejudice; college was the time to experience the unfamiliar, to turn to primary sources, to begin to think as....

4 "Professor. Have you ever been to a rock concert?"

5 "Well, no."

6 "If we have to go to Beaux Arts; you ought to go to R.E.M."

7 "That's a cough syrup."

8 "No. It's the top college group. You ought to know our music. The more you fear something, the more you...."

9 I held up my hands in surrender. I would dare an expedition to the cultural frontier of rock, lose what hearing I have left, suffer a "location high" from the exhaust fumes of strange drugs, be trampled to death by swaying natives or speared on a purple crescent hairdo.

I want to look at my students through the eyes of a prejudiced elderly. Here I use stereotypes and clichés but when you do that, you have to let the reader know you are using them on purpose. I hope I did.

10 Six weeks later my wife and I were in the bleachers at the Field House molding plastic ear plugs in our hands and trying to appear natural. They were dressed in untied boots, rags that were rags, hair cut by apprentice barbers. Some had interrupted pink or purple hair dye jobs to come to the concert; others were wrapped in leather and hung with chains; all of them were dressed so casually that it must have taken hours to achieve such careful and haphazard inappropriateness.

A transition—"six weeks later"—and now I describe the students at the concert. We have talked about description in this chapter and you should look critically at the description I use in this piece describing the world you know better than I do. I checked this draft with my students because I wanted to be accurate—from my perspective—and have some fun, but I wanted to be fair and certainly not patronizing.

11 And they were all trying not to stare at us aliens in a building only a mile and a half from our home. They were courteous but curious. White was not the color anyone had dyed their hair. There were a half-dozen or so middle-aged rock scholars—29 to 34 years old—but we were generations older than anyone there, Rip van Winkles who had slept though decades of rock 'n' roll.

My audience for the column was over sixties. I wanted them to identify with how my wife and I felt visiting this alien world a mile from our home.

12 This was their world and they knew it. It must have been satisfying to them to see more police than at a cop's funeral. They must have felt wonderfully rebellious, dangerous, a

I try to get inside the student's emotions through

marvelous self-selected community of outcasts, superior to those who did not understand and appreciate and belong. I was critical of how they strolled back and forth obviously declaring their belonging, until my writer's eye revealed my casual parade among the faculty at the Beaux Arts intermission.

empathy—putting myself in their skin—and by memory—how I felt when I went to big-band swing concerts when I was their age. At the end of the paragraph, I reveal the writer's double vision, standing apart and seeing myself at a classical-music concert as I see them at a rock concert.

13 Enough. I wasn't here to reflect on the cultural behavior of academic pseudo-intellectuals but to observe *them*, to appreciate *their* music. *B-O-O-M.* I felt the first beat in my chest before I heard it. Two rows of speakers, each at least ten-feet high—24 speakers in all—were pointed right at us. My ears might be stuffed with plastic but we were inside the music, the beat pressed against the breastbone, stone deaf I would have "heard" the beat.

I want the reader, through description, to hear and feel the music. Of course, I fail, but I want to give it a good shot by focusing on the dominant impression I had of the music.

14 And I liked it. The beat was insistent, fascinatingly predictable and unpredictable. It came in through the feet, the stomach, the spine, and the ears. I wasn't standing back watching a performance, I was somehow *in* the performance.

Surprise: I liked it. It is surprise that brings me to my writing desk each day. I write to learn and am surprised by what I learn. And I want my text to share that surprise with my reader. But remember, the surprise has to be honest. If I hadn't liked it, I wouldn't have said I did. Even if I wanted to lie, I know I couldn't. I feel the page would expose me.

15 Soon everyone was standing, even my wife stood up and I stood too. The audience was dancing and I felt my own knees bend, even a hip creak in rhythm once in awhile. I was struck by the powerful sense of community, of belonging, of being in, of sharing a, yes, cultural experience. And I was astonished at the self-absorbed loneliness at the same time.

If your description is strong enough, then you can weave in commentary: my discovery of loneliness within community.

16 Only a few couples danced together in the aisles, facing each other while practicing the mating dance of the fuzzy-tailed

Ibis before turning back to themselves. Everyone else danced
alone on chairs, on the floor, in the bleachers, off to the rest
rooms and back.

17 It might have been the chewing gum whose smell was
stronger to me than that of more natural substances, but
these natives were listening to their own music. Each to their
own music.

I like to use as
many senses as
possible and the
smell of chewing
gum was loud. In
this description, I
am going back to
the old timers'
fears. It is safe to
be among your
young and I also
make a transition:
"Each to their own
music." This sets up
the ending for the
reader but, before
that, it led me to
the ending as I
wrote the first
draft.

18 Since they paid no attention to each other as they twitched,
bent, bumped, ground, hopped, tangled and untangled, no one
was critical of how the others danced. Men and women
performed as if each were in a room alone.

I show and tell what
it means to me; an
insight that tells my
readers that the
dancing I observed
bears little relation
to the dancing we
did to Benny
Goodman and
Glenn Miller.

19 And a good thing that was, because I must report, that most of
the scholars around me couldn't keep to a beat that probably
cracked the paint on my house across town. One young man
with a triple-jointed spine two rows down was wonderful. He
must be an osteopath's delight, but the rest of those around
me were transported, but not gracefully. Maybe it was New
Hampshire, but they lifted their feet as if they were avoiding
barnyard obstacles, bent and buckled as if they were trying to
load pigs on a truck. Yet it made no difference. They all
enjoyed the music in their own private way.

I hope I've earned
the right to have
some fun. My
description is
accurate—in my
eyes—but it is not,
I hope, unkind.
Remember, I have
made fun of myself
in all this and
showed my
willingness to learn
and pass beyond the
stereotypes and
clichés about rock
concerts. I hope I
have earned this
paragraph and I did
check it—and the
whole piece—with
my class.

20 Music? Yes. The sounds and the beats were different from
group to group, song to song. There was real singing at times,

I compare rock
music to

often something as close to a melody as the modern composer Rochberg had allowed at the Beaux Arts performance. The musicians performed with extraordinary skill and teamwork, but this was music for and of our times: the musicians fought the technology but I think the machines won.

contemporary classical music and work my way to the effect of modern technology on music.

21 The flashing, computer-coordinated lights; the electronic sounds, amplified, torted and distorted; the jungle of wires; the dozens of mikes; the island of soundboards, cameras, and slide projectors in the middle of the audience; the backstage crews; the huge trailer trucks to carry the equipment; the three story towers of lights and screens and speakers all dwarfed the performers. It forced them to yell and scream and jump and struggle, but they lost. No wonder the four performers struggled so hard. The drummer was imprisoned behind his drums, the performers tiny beside their speakers.

More specific description, but it makes a point, reveals man against machine and man loses—in my judgment.

22 It did, however, make the music I like best seem out of date in an age of missiles, reactors, computers, even if I play their melodies on my own "sound systems." My music seems more appropriate to a time that appears safer, more ordered, nicer from a distance than it ever was. Perhaps that is why I like it, need its quiet, depend on its order.

I question my own music and suggest why I like it. I'm not especially proud of my reasons.

23 But standing, twitching sedately to the beat, I couldn't help thinking what Mozart, Beethoven, even Brahms might have done with such electronic toys. Each of them seems safe now they are long dead, but they frightened governments and critics in their day, scared the living daylights out of the old, the established, the whitebeards like me.

I make the obvious but necessary point that my "tame" composers were radical in their day and that Brahms might have a rock group if he were alive.

24 Walking home, we were glad we had gone. What I had preached in class was true. You should, perhaps especially on the eve of retirement, reach out to what is new, different, even frightening. What does it matter if you dance well, as long as you hear your own music and dance.

I end by resolving the experience, saying what it meant to me and, therefore, suggesting what it might mean to the reader. I hope I wasn't too preachy at the end, that I allow readers to come to their own conclusions based on their own experience, their reading of my experience and our combined thinking.

A side note that still shocks me: I promised before the class to go to the concert. They had to buy me tickets—with my dollars—because it was a student-sponsored concert and they would not sell to faculty. And yet many students were surprised to see me there. They expected me—and all teachers—to say they would attend and then not do it. That haunts me. What kind of an education are we modeling for our students? Someday that will spark another column.

A Student's Case History: Sarah Hansen _____

This edition of *Write to Learn* includes five case histories of students who used the first edition. The case histories are honest accounts by experienced instructors, who are very different in background, training, and personality. They are all excellent teachers, each in their own way. And the students are different from each other.

Bruce Ballenger does an excellent job of getting his students to see and to communicate what they see to the reader. Here is his account of how he does it, followed by the case history of one of his students, Sarah Hansen.

The Instructor's Account by Bruce Ballenger

1   One of the easiest things for student writers to learn is the importance of detail. "It's not just a car," I tell them, "it's Frank's twenty-year old beige BMW 2002, with the rotting fenders and the engine that coughs like a camel."

2   It isn't hard to see what happens when we move from vague or abstract prose to something more concrete: the writing comes to life. Details are like a rock climber's handholds. They give us as readers something solid to hold on to as we make our way through a piece of writing. In this case, the details help us to see and hear the car, engaging our senses and minds.

3   That details can do this, and therefore make writing more interesting, isn't much of a revelation for most students, and pretty soon they start trying to be more "descriptive." Drafts that once said there were "green forests covering the rolling hills," acquire "verdant oaks and maples thickly carpeting the undulating hills against the azure August sky."

4   Though the second version has more descriptive detail than the first, it doesn't seem better. The details call attention to themselves like loud wallpaper.

5   There was a time when I thought that's what details were for—to pretty up the prose—rather than giving readers purposeful information. Many of my students share that mistaken assumption, and the "descriptive essay" becomes paragraph after paragraph of sensory details and similes that don't seem to add up to anything at all.

6   Fortunately, Sarah Hansen knew that like any other piece of writing, she must discover her purpose in writing this essay. Then she would know which details would further that purpose and which would not. It wasn't easy. Once she found her topic—her recollections of growing up in Birch Grove, Illinois—she began by brainstorming specifics and freewriting about

some of them. Soon a pattern emerged: her sense of her hometown was colored distinctly black and white. She was bitter about its racism and narrow-mindedness, yet now could also see its simple strengths.

7   But this was only the beginning for her. For the next six weeks, she wrote draft after draft, adding new details and taking some out, trying new leads and new ends. But what she struggled with most was trying to figure out what it all added up to: what was she trying to say?

8   Because Sarah is a good writer, she had less difficulty composing effective description. She gives us the bigoted Miss Gooch, who is as superficial as her thin, tight-curl perm. There is Sam Ritchel, former salutatorian of his high school class, now with shaven eyebrows and black lipstick—a burnt husk of his former self. And there are the flat fields ouside of town in summer, where the blinking lights of fireflies hang over the soybeans and the wheat at dusk.

9   What makes such description effective is not simply that it helps us to see, it also *reveals*. We not only see Miss Gooch's perm, we know what it says about her. And effective description sometimes helps us to see something in a way we haven't before. Though Midwestern wheat fields may be a familiar sight to some, few readers will know them at dusk under a constellation of fireflies.

10   Even Sarah's early drafts resonated with such details. Being "descriptive" was not a problem for her. Digging more deeply into the meaning of the essay was.

11   Thinking as much (or even more) about *what* you're trying to say as *how* you say it in a draft is difficult for all writers. But it's the place to start most revisions. The process begins by finding the questions that might help you think more about what you're trying to say, hoping to discover the less obvious ideas or insights that might be buried under the surface of the draft.

12   I asked Sarah lots of questions about what she seemed to be saying: "Why does it take going away from your hometown to see it freshly?" "What did you learn about Birch Grove since you left there?" "Why is it so hard for many of us to forgive our hometown's faults?" "Have you forgiven Birch Grove?" "Is it important to?" "Why?" "What do you mean when you say you hope Birch Grove will be 'safe'?" "From what?"

13   I asked a lot of questions that were the wrong questions, but slowly Sarah found her own way to the heart of her essay, and by the eighth draft had finally figured out what she wanted to say. Sarah tells us that leaving Birch Grove helped her to see its simple strengths—the energy in the fields, the uncomplicated kindness of the hardware store man—but these don't offset the bigotry and the narrow-mindness. Birch Grove, and other places like it, may be a "safe" place to raise children in some ways, but it will never be truly safe until the people there come to terms with its sad, ugly side.

14   Though a descriptive essay has some qualities that set it apart from other kinds of writing, in many more ways it is not unique. Like virtually all writing, it must have a purpose that can be made clear to readers through

skillful, and selective use of detail. There must be a reason the writer shows us the things she wants us to see.

15   And like the best writing, descriptive essays succeed—as Sarah's does— when it goes beyond the obvious, helping us to see freshly something we may have seen before, whether it's places like Birch Grove or the dance of fireflies over a wheat field.

Now we hear from the author, speaking from within the context that her instructor has established.

The Student's Account by Sarah Hansen

1   This descriptive essay is the result of eight drafts, conferencing, work-shopping, journal writing, thinking, and sharing. It was hard to work— sometimes frustrating but mostly rewarding. I have learned to have confidence in my own writing. But I still have not tackled procrastination, and wonder if I ever will.

2   To come up with a topic, I brainstormed places and people that I would like to describe and that I know a lot about. I picked my hometown, Birch Grove, Illinois, because I have a lot to say about it and at that point I was confused about my feelings for Birch Grove. My English teacher, Bruce Ballenger, says confusing topics are the best to write about because my writing about them a discovery might be made that will help to end the confusion.

3   Before I began a first draft, I brainstormed another list of Birch Grove people, places, and events. The list I made ended up in two piles: one bad and one good. This was something I hadn't expected. I circled the most controversial and the weirdest things on the list. Directly after this, I began to freewrite about the circled things.

4   I thought about the paper for a few days and then went to the computer to type what I had written during the freewrite. I added more stuff to it that had been in my head and took the first draft to my conference with Bruce. He liked it. But the point I was trying to make was not clear. It wasn't clear because I didn't really know exactly what the point was. Ideas about a hometown are complex. This was the most difficult part of writing this essay: trying to find the point.

5   Also, my first draft had too much description. I had to find the places where the description didn't fit the purpose of the essay. I actually used scissors and tape on the first draft to cut out unnecessary description. The second draft had less description but was no closer to realizing a point than the first. I was frustrated.

6   Our writing class had group workshops where we shared our pieces with three or four other students. I read the Birch Grove paper to my workshop group because I needed fresh perspectives. I also needed some positive reinforcement. All three students liked my paper—that made me

feel more motivated to work on it. One woman in my workshop agreed with Bruce and me that the point of the essay needed to be clearer. The most valuable thing I learned from the workshop was that the topic of the essay wasn't clear until the middle. They suggested starting the essay with a paragraph or idea from the middle.

7   With this in mind, I changed the first paragraph and fiddled around with various parts of the essay. But I was still frustrated with the meaning. I knew that the essay was slowly progressing with each draft, but from drafts two to six I made little progress finding exactly what it was I wanted to say without sounding boring, clichéd or obvious. I started to share the essay with a lot of different people. Most close friends tend to like just about anything you do and aren't objective enough and don't give much criticism. Older English majors and my parents and their friends, people that read a good amount of writing, turned out to be the most helpful.

8   With each draft from two to six, my English teacher and I became more and more discouraged. I couldn't reach exactly what it was about Birch Grove I wanted to say. Did I want to say how I felt, did I want to say something to the people of Birch Grove, did I want to make a point about all hometowns, did I want to make a statement about the world by talking about one hometown? My biggest mistake was not writing in my journal enough. I procrastinated writing about my feelings for Birch Grove because it was too frustrating.

9   Around draft four or five, I couldn't look at the paper with objectivity anymore. I was too close to my subject and practically had the words memorized, as did my English teacher. Finally, after draft five, Bruce gave the draft back to me with questions written all over it about what it was I was trying to say. In my journal I wrote answers to his questions. It was this way, by talking to myself in my journal, and by answering questions, that I nearly found what I wanted to say.

10   I wrote that the good in Birch Grove I had realized by going away, far outweighed the bad. The energy of the good things is what makes Birch Grove all right. When people realize this, then Birch Grove will be safe. We decided that this would be the final draft. I thought I was done.

11   But when my father read the essay out loud that night I realized what I had wanted to come across did not. In the sixth draft it seemed I had forgotten the racism and the close-mindedness. I intended just the opposite. I wanted to say that I have realized the good in Birch Grove but that the bad needs to be changed.

12   The biggest problem I had writing this essay was attempting to find exactly what the meaning was. I also needed to spend more time talking to myself about the essay in my journal. In hand with this, I needed to spend more time writing than thinking about the essay. A good idea can sometimes surprise me as I write, but that rarely happens when I think about my writing without a pen in my hand.

13   I learned to share my work with as many people as I could who were willing to take the time to read it and give their response. It is motivating

to hear fresh and new ideas. The conferences helped in that Bruce and I would talk about what it was I was trying to say. The discussions helped each draft to come closer and closer. It was also good to hear someone give positive comments about my writing.

14   Writing a descriptive essay can help with any other kind of writing. It is not only a creative type of essay. Description is about saying things so that other people can see, feel, hear and smell what you have. These things are revealed through specific details. It is exactly the same concrete writing that is needed to critique a novel or write a term paper.

Sarah's daybook started out with the following entry:

> I have to write a paper for a book—a descriptive essay—to be published. I have no idea what to write about—just knowing it's for a book makes me nervous. I've even been avoiding thinking about it. Dad—Heather—East H------commune--------expectations—grandma—Birch Grove—Berry Farm—trip to France—2nd semester at UNH.

She starts out with a writer's apprehension and makes a list of possible topics. She did put a mark like a rising sun after Birch Grove, and then she wrote a draft that plunged into the subject: "The round and friendly minister of the Methodist Church of Birch Grove, Illinois was found in Sanderson's three story department store stealing a large pair of light brown corduroys."

In her daybook Sarah writes:

> I showed my first draft of the essay for the book today. Bruce liked it. I was so relieved. He's really helped me to be more confident about my writing. We decided that the point of the paper wasn't too clear. He said that I need to "peel the onion." In class we talked about how the layers of the onion are like layers of ideas and points to an essay or a piece of writing. The deeper into the onion layers you get, the closer you are to your main point. I know a few things that I am pointing out but I don't know exactly how to say them. I think my main point is about how Birch Grove was all bad to me at first, and then, as I went to UNH, I realized the better things about it. But the better things don't excuse the bad things. I'm still confused about it. I don't think this paper is very interesting. I don't think it will keep the reader's interest. We also talked about how there are too many descriptions.

I find this sort of writing to myself important. It helps to put into words what you got from a conference and to identify your feelings about the text and about the process of writing.

Later she writes in her daybook:

> I've decided to show my paper on Birch Grove to my workshop group. I don't know where to go with it. I have been thinking a lot about the focus of this paper and it's getting me nowhere. Hopefully, they'll have some insight to it that will get me motivated for revising this paper. I spend too much time just thinking—I should be writing in this journal more but don't have discipline—I procrastinate too much.

> My workshop group really liked my paper. Lin said it reminded her of her hometown which is cool cause that's sort of a point I'm trying to make— every hometown for every person is both good and bad—end up blaming hometown for everything—have bitterness towards it. A love-hate thing. I don't know that's quite what I want to say though—seems cliche. Brian and ------ both thought that the beginning isn't clear—maybe start with paragraph that starts, "I moved to Birch Grove, where life offers more," when I was four...." They said as it stands now it's a little unclear what I'm talking about. So I'll try to rework that into the beginning and Brian thought that my point was perfectly said—that I shouldn't add more but ---- said I should make my point clearer. I agree more with ----- cause at this point I don't even know what my main point is. I asked them if they thought it was boring and if it caught and kept their attention. They said it was interesting and kept their attention well so that made me feel better. Asked if there was too much description and they said no.

In all her daybook entries, Sarah reveals the way a writer's mind—and emotions—work. I certainly feel the same way about my drafts as Sarah does about hers. To learn to write effectively, we need to be open and realize our feelings and how to deal with them. Later in her daybook Sarah writes:

> I'm annoyed with my paper about Birch Grove. I'm sick of it. I'm too close to it and can't see it correctly any more. It seems so trite and boring and cliche. Bruce seems to not like it much either. That's really discouraging. I don't know what exactly I want my point to be that's creative and fresh.

These excerpts from her account reveal the writer at work, what goes on backstage that is essential to the creation of an effective piece of writing. There is not space here to reproduce her drafts, sometimes marked up with her comments, other times with the comments of her readers, but they document the evolution of her essay. In the third draft, for example, Sarah begins, "When I was four, my mother, my dog, and I moved to Birch Grove, Illinois. I've spent all my time there minus the summers which I've spent with my father. Passing the town border a cheap billboard reads: 'Life offers more in Birch Grove.'"

By the fifth draft her lead reads, "Passing over the town border into Birch Grove, Illinois, a billboard, paint peeling off, reads: 'Life offers more in Birch Grove,' When I was four years old my mother, my dog, and I moved to this Midwestern town. As I grew up, I'd pass the fading billboard and my tolerance for Birch Grove faded along with it." By the eighth draft, the lead was as it appears below. Most of us have to learn by writing and by considering what we have written and how it can be improved. We are fortunate that Sarah Hansen was willing to let us see her learning and to observe what she had to write to produce an excellent essay.

Simple Birch Grove
Sarah Hansen

1   Passing over the town border into Birch Grove, Illinois, a billboard, paint peeling off, reads: "Life Offers More In Birch Grove." When I was four years old my mother, my dog, and I moved to this Midwestern town. As I grew up, I'd pass the fading billboard, and my tolerance for Birch Grove faded along with it.

2   The owner of Sanderson's three-story department store found the round and friendly minister, Donald Morison, of the Methodist Church of Sycamore stealing a pair of brown corduroys. Most of the bank presidents and company founders and Mercedes Benz owners of Birch Grove belonged to the Methodist Church on the corner of Third and Main. They put up a big fuss about having a kleptomaniac as a minister. There was great pressure on Don to leave. These influential people weren't seen at Sunday service anymore to listen to Don with his brown, shining eyes give the sermon. Only a few members forgave Don, told him so, and asked him to stay. One Sunday, a woman slowly stood up and told the churchgoers that the bible says to forgive, and that we should forgive Don, and help him out, because his problem is a disease, just as alcoholism is a disease. Don left the Methodist Church two long months after the incident, and the members are now content to sit in the pews and sing out of the worn, red cloth-covered hymnals.

3   Miss Gooch, the assistant counsellor at Birch Grove High School wears her thin, grey-brown hair in a tight curl perm. I was the student council president my senior year, and we were discussing some upcoming activities. Miss Gooch liked to gossip; she asked me how my friend Peggy was doing. Peggy has fair freckled skin and blonde curled hair—like most other girls at Birch Grove High School. Her boyfriend is thin and has beautiful, chocolate brown skin. What Miss Gooch meant was, "How is she dealing with having a black boyfriend?" Miss Gooch said, "I am not prejudiced, but I don't think the races should intermingle ... and I hate Mexicans." Sixteen black students and forty Mexican students attend Birch Grove High School where Miss Gooch is the counsellor and student council advisor.

4   At age eleven, my sister Traci walked to the Save and Shop, three blocks down Walnut Street from our house, to buy groceries. As she crossed the supermarket parking lot, a little girl, not over seven years old was left alone in a beat up station wagon. The girl rolled down the front seat window. "Nigger," she said to Traci, my adopted sister, now one of the sixteen black students at the high school. Traci is startled as she looks in the mirror to see her own black face. Her eyes are so accustomed to whiteness.

5   Sam Ritchel was salutatorian of my class. Now, when I come home for Christmas or Easter vacation, I see Sam wandering around Birch Grove, or staring off in a booth in the coffee shop. He's taken too much acid, refuses

to get a job, dropped out of the University of Wisconsin, shaves his eyebrows, wears black lipstick, black eyeliner, and black clothing. He listens to Jim Morrison on his tape recorder, and says nothing but "black, melancholy, darkness, despair ..." In the Weston Elementary School, Sam's nickname was Happy.

6   I hated everything about Birch Grove. I hated its conservatism, its hypocrisy, its ignorance, its racism, its close-mindedness, and its ugliness. I hated what it did to bright, open-minded people who could not escape. In Birch Grove, I could only think about itchy, depressing, angering things. Times when snotty Claire Saunders knocked over my newly painted three-speed bike in the fifth grade, when the whole of Birch Grove watched "Top Gun" perpetually for weeks after it came out on video, when high school students egged our house five times in two months because my step-father is the assistant principal of the high school—a fair, kind man who must punish students for skipping a study hall, for smoking in the music wing.

7   But since I've been at college, far away from my hometown, I can remember eating macaroni and cheese on Kiersten's sunny, white porch with her mother and mine, enjoying the lunch hour before returning back to the third grade. I can remember the annual January snow sculpture competition in front of Prince's restaurant across from Birch Grove Park. I remember my very first valentine in seventh grade from my very first boyfriend: shy, curly white-haired Jim Morse, a farm boy. The homemade card was caringly shaped and cut out of red, pink, and white construction paper. Two white rabbits kissed on the front; inside, pencil cursive writing read, "I'm glad that you're my valentine, Sarah."

8   I remember the annual Birch Grove Pumpkin Festival where all of Birch Grove competes in a pumpkin competition, decorating them as a scary monster with orange peels for hair and gourds for arms and legs or a pumpkinphone for goblins and ghosts to use. The Miller family won the grand prize one year and got to go on the Bozo Show. There was a pumpkin princess or prince award to the best essay in the junior high, and the grade schooler with the best scary picture got to ride on the fire engine at the front of the Sunday Pumpkin Parade. I watched the parade from the Abbens' house on Somonauk Street with people from our church, eating warm carameled (sp?) apples, and drinking hot apple cider sitting on fold-out chairs along the street. The huge oak, maple, and sycamore trees lining the street screamed autumn with their yellows, golds, reds, and oranges.

9   I remember Mrs. Munter, my junior and senior year English teacher, my most influential teacher, sneaking chocolate M&M's out of the second drawer down. I remember her strong, clear, enunciated voice demanding and challenging us to accomplish more in her class than we ever had before.

10   I remember driving along the smooth and winding North River Road just after dusk on a hot summer day, windows rolled down and arms out waving, watching the thousands of tiny blinking lights of the fireflies just above the soybeans and wheat fields. Although I used to hate the flatness of the land, now as I return I appreciate the great big sky and lie in the

middle of a cornfield with Steven and Pam, watching the silver white shooting stars stream across the blue black expanse.

11   I see Sean Allen in the store window of Ben Franklin, the five and dime, and wave back knowing he's still the same friendly, simple person he always was and will be. I know that every summer the woman with the wrinkled face will bring out her popcorn stand, and my mother and I'll buy sweet caramelcorn and eat the whole bag as we walk slowly home in the hot night air.

12   Mom says Birch Grove is a good place to bring up children. Maybe it is in some ways. Friendly Sean Allen, the sun on a white porch that makes the skin hum, and Mrs. Munter's deep, resounding voice are as pure and warm as the wealthy churchgoers and close-minded Miss Gooch are tarnished and cold. But even as the sweet smelling fields, the wide Midwest sky, the leaves of screaming colors that crackle under foot seek to balance this out, I know that Birch Grove still is no place to bring up my children.

Collect for the Reader ──────────────

Throughout the collecting process you've certainly been aware of one reader—yourself. You have found information that interested you and other information that didn't. You have seen things that relate to other things and things that had no apparent relation. In all this process, you have been role-playing, consciously or unconsciously, the reader. Writing is not writing until it is read, and so, throughout the writing process, there is a continual attention to audience.

Many times this audience is specific. We are writing something that will be read by a teacher, a classmate, an employer, a friend, someone who needs to know the information, someone we want to persuade or educate or entertain. In some modes of writing the audience is paramount. This is true when we're writing a memo asking for financial support from a college administrator, or when we're writing an examination for a teacher. In other forms of writing, the personal essay or the poem, we may be at first writing for ourselves, and later realize that others would be interested.

The reader should help us write. Being aware of who may read what we write gives us additional eyes with which to see the subject. The reader's eyes help us collect and select, and they will be with us throughout the writing process.

Being aware of the reader does not mean that we change what we see, avoid what we think is important, or in any other way pander to the reader. Our job as writers is, above all, to be truthful, accurate, fair, even if the message we deliver does not please the reader.

When collecting, I generally work from inside myself out. I realize I will remember more as I write, but I have stimulated my memory and each day I am remembering more things. I have reached out from myself to collect those bits of information that I can find around me, and I've worked outward using books and documents from other times and other places.

What I have are fragments: facts, quotes, memories, images, pictures, notes, lines, phrases, and questions—many, many questions. It's a mess, a great big, glorious, confusing mess. This is usually what happens in the collecting stage of the writing process. We don't get all the information we want, and we often get much information that we don't want. There are contradictions, vagueness when there should be concise accuracy, fragments instead of completeness, disorder and chaos.

That's the writers' raw material. Most people think the writer works with neatly organized material. That hardly ever happens, and it wouldn't be any fun to be a writer if that were true. It's not the job of the writer to write what the writer already knows and what the reader probably knows. Writing is thinking. As Joyce Cary says, "The work of art as completely realized is the result of a long and complex process of exploration." The writer's challenge is to think about the material, to select from the chaos what is significant, and to order it in such a way that a meaning is created for the writer, and therefore for the reader. The writer writes to learn first and then to teach by sharing that learning.

Remember that the process of collecting material continues all during the writing, but when there is a wonderful stew of raw and contradictory information it's time for the writer to begin to see how to discover a way to focus it, to catch a glimpse of meaning in that challenging mess.

Questions about Collecting _____

• *When do I know that my research is finished?*

You'll never know. You'll always feel there will be a new and wonderful piece of information in the next book you read or the next interview you do—if only you had the time. Some writers get so involved in research that they never become writers. Most professionals stop when they know the answers they will hear as they ask the questions. In other words, they aren't finding much new. When that happens it's time to write.

And of course, there's the deadline. You have to figure back from when the writing is due and allow time for clarifying, drafting, ordering, and focusing if you're going to have a good piece of work.

• *Who is an authority?*

The best way to find out the authority you should interview is to ask the people in that business who's the best. Ask nurses in the hospital, policemen on the force, teachers in the school, scientists in the lab who you should talk to find out about your subject. They work with all the authorities. The ones you want to interview are those whom the people in the trade turn to when they have a problem.

• *How do I know who's telling the truth? If a fact is a fact?*

By checking. It's a good idea to have three sources for any important fact or piece of information. It's not so much that people lie as that they're uninformed;

they believe what they're telling you, but it may not be true. As a researcher, you have to keep your common sense in good working order. When you are suspicious about a statement or a detail, pay attention to that hunch and check it out.

- *I'm shy; I don't like talking to people.*

Most reporters are shy. I used to hide in the closet when I was a kid and company came to the house, but it got uncomfortable sitting on a pile of shoes. I still get a funny feeling in my stomach when I go out to interview people. I was just reading an article about the most famous reporters in the country and they all shared a common difficulty—making the first phone call.

What you have to realize is that interviewing someone is very flattering for the person being interviewed. If you come in saying, "You're the greatest living authority on cockroaches," you won't be able to shut the delighted authority up.

- *What if people won't give me information?*

You have to give them a reason to give information to you. Flattery, as above, is a good reason. If that doesn't work, you have to find out what is a good reason for them—they want to educate the uneducated (you); they want to persuade; they want to raise money. There are many reasons people will give out information, and you have to find the reason that will unlock the information you need.

- *I've got too much information; I've got more notes than I've got dirty socks. It's a mess.*

Good. Strong pieces of writing come from an abundance of information. Walk away from your notes. Take a pad of paper and sit down somewhere quiet and put down what you've learned from your research, the things that have surprised you the most or that seemed the most significant or that connect. What you remember will usually be what is most important.

And read the next chapter. It tells you what to do with a mess of contradictory, interesting, confusing information.

- *How can I keep track of what I'm learning while I'm doing? I keep getting lost.*

I like to take a few minutes at the end of the day and make a quick note on the outline or trail I've been following. Sometimes I do this in terms of what questions I still have to have answered; other times I keep a short list of key items: "What I Know" and "What I Need to Know." While writing a book I often have a draft table of contents I keep changing as I explore the subject.

- *What are the qualities of a really good piece of information?*

Of course that depends on the story, but here are some elements:

▶ It is true.
▶ It connects with other pieces of information to help create a pattern of meaning.
▶ It reveals significance. When we went overseas, the average age of enlisted men was nineteen, of officers twenty-one. Wars are made by old men and fought by young men.
▶ It surprises. Officers were twenty-one, younger than most readers would expect.

● *What if I don't work like you or the student in your case history?*

You won't. There's no way to write. There's not even a right way and a wrong way. What works for me, may not work for you; what works on one task, may not on the next. But we can pick up tricks of our trade and store them away so they'll be in our memory bank when we need them.

Collecting Activities _____

1. Make an authority inventory, listing all the things you're an expert on—the jobs you do, the things you can repair, the places you've lived or visited, the problems you can solve, the hobbies you enjoy, the people you know, the family background you have. Each of us is an authority on many things, and our best writing usually comes from what we know and care about. There is a significant relationship between the word "author" and the word "authority."

2. Interview someone else to find out what the other person is an authority on. Dig in to find out how the person became an authority on the subject. What makes the person angry, satisfied, happy, interested, sad, laugh when they talk about their subject?

3. Go to the library and find out what sources exist on a subject that interests you. The people who work at reference desks are very helpful in showing you all the places in the library where there might be information on a specific subject.

4. Practice scanning—quick reading—to find out what interests you by taking a book that covers the subject in its broadest terms. For example, if you're interested in one variety of seagull, take out a book about birds and go through it fast to see what you can find out about your seagull.

5. Practice making quick notes by watching television news and taking down the essential details.

6. Collaborate with one or two other classmates to research a limited topic. It's interesting to learn from others how they approach a subject differently from you. Each of us has our own researching style and tricks, as well as a different background that changes our angle of vision on a subject.

7. Look up a piece of writing on a subject you want to research and try to figure out where the writer got the information. Some books have interesting

appendixes in which the authors talk about the problems of research and how they solved them.

8. Try to apply the research techniques in this chapter to a problem in your own field so that you can see how these techniques can be adapted to a problem in social work or hotel administration or physics or history. Ask a professor in your major field to share some of his research techniques with you, and report on these to the class.

9. Role-play. Watch a situation—a crowd growing unruly, a person making a speech, an ambulance responding to an accident, a person being hired or fired—and imagine yourself in that situation. Figure out how you would act and react, think and feel. This will give you some interesting questions to ask. Go to a person who is involved in the situation and ask him or her.

10. Practice looking for the detail that reveals—how the doctor walks calmly when there is a crisis, how the expert teacher uses silence to control a class, how a politician uses first names, how an expert programmer plays with a computer. Try to catch the action in a few words that reveal.

11. Write down as fast as you can a list of all the details you remember from last week's activities. Use all your senses. Doing this, you'll be surprised at what you remember, and you may find things you want to explore more. Doing this kind of collecting will also make you more aware in the week ahead. And the more you see, the more you'll have to learn by writing.

12. Write your own case history to discover how you work and how you may work more effectively in the future.

Chapter 4

ᛟ Explore Your Subject: FOCUS

The writer . . . sees what he did not expect to see. . . . Inattentive learner in the schoolroom of life, he keeps some faculty free to bear and wonder. His is the roving eye. By that roving eye is his subject found. The glance, at first only vaguely caught, goes on to concentrate, deepen; becomes the vision.

ELIZABETH BOWEN

That could almost be cited as the definition of a poet: Someone who notices and is enormously taken by things that somebody else would walk by.

JAMES DICKEY

That's what a writer is: someone who sees problems a little more clearly than others.

EUGENE IONESCO

The most obvious difference between the amateur and professional writer is a matter of focus. The amateur rides off in all directions at once, including this fact, developing that point, tossing in a fascinating but irrelevant anecdote, luring the reader off the track of meaning with unnecessary facts or quotations, repeating what has been said, or making the reader circle back again and again to try to figure out what it all means.

The professional says one thing in the piece of writing. A single meaning dominates the essay, report, poem, argument, memo. Of course, there may be other meanings in the text, but each of those relates to the primary message. Kurt Vonnegut, Jr. says, "Don't put anything in a story that does not reveal character or advance the action." This can—and should—be adapted to any piece of writing. Make sure there is a dominant message to the reader and that everything in the piece of writing—the tone, the documentation, the genre, the structure, the pace, the word choice, every element of writing—supports and advances that message.

Too often, however, focus before the first discovery draft is confused with thesis statement, what is discovered by the writing. The trick for the writer is to start writing—most of the time—with a sense of direction, then refine that sense of direction through the draft—or find a new one—and, finally, to revise and edit so the reader experiences the discovered focus.

How a Potential Focus Helps the Writer _____

We all know as readers that focus is essential. We like to read the result of focus, the feeling of riding a clear flowing river toward a certain destination. We are far less familiar with the process by which the writer senses, then follows a possible focus toward a draft.

Such a focus is our starting point. Before the moment of potential focus all is possible—we can go to the beach, to the city, stay home, fly, walk, run, drive, kayak, balloon—and all is confusion.

The trap is in thinking—or being taught—that we should know what we want to say before we say it. That sounds good but it is rarely the writer's experience.

If we think we should know what we want to say in advance of writing and think others, brighter, more talented than we are actually do, then we will sit paralyzed at the writing desk.

We need a starting point, something that causes us to start putting words on paper. There are many starting points and we will discuss a number of them later in the chapter but the one that works best for me is what I call *The Line*.

Primary Technique for Finding Your Focus: Hear the Line _____

Although I have been hearing the line all my writing life, I didn't realize it until I started doing my newspaper column. I would half think about what I might write, make a few notes in my daybook, daydream the subject while walking, driving, watching a dumb TV show, reading, and then, suddenly, I would know I had a column to write.

I didn't see the column entire, didn't know just what I was going to say, but I knew I had a writing experiment to begin. I had a starting point.

I began to observe myself, to become my own laboratory rat, and found there was a clear starting point that I could describe. It was a fragment of language that might be as short as a single word or, rarely, as long as a complete sentence. That fragment of language contained a tension that could be unleashed by writing and would provide the energy for the writing. Within that tension was something—an idea, a feeling, a mood, a memory, an observation, a thought—that I needed to explore through writing.

Although I recognized this crucial point in my writing process while writing my column, I found that I had been depending on the line while writing articles, difficult letters, talks, poems, and books of fiction and nonfiction. Of course, this is only *my* way of writing and I follow it only when it works. I'm not suggesting that anyone else *should* work this way, but I do suggest that we all pay attention to what works for us and that we share those methods and techniques with each other as I am sharing this one with you.

Let's try to define the line without being too restrictive. It might be described as a question that demands an answer, an experiment that I must perform, an itch I must scratch, a path I must follow, a hint, a clue, a vague shape I cannot yet make out and must.

Elements in a Line

The elements that exist—most of the time—in this linguistic trigger mechanism include:

• *Tension.* A sense of forces headed for a collision [courtship?] or of forces exploding in opposite directions [marriage?].

• *Conflict.* Irony: a tension between what should be and what is. An energy that will be released by the writing of the story.

• *Play.* The possibility of surprise, discovery, contradiction, learning—the writing of the draft will teach me something I do not yet understand. Knocking down the blocks of a previous meaning; stacking up the blocks of a new meaning.

• *Music.* The sound of the *voice of the text*. This is my voice and more, the child of my voice, adapted to the purpose and audience of the to-be-written text. The rhythm or beat of music, the sound of what I will write, leads my writing ear toward meaning.

• *Form.* A hint of the shape of the piece. Its length, pace, proportions. Not a rigid pattern, but a territory to be explored—hill country or river valley, coast or plain—and a sense of the time it will take.

• *Ease.* I never start without the illusion of ease, which may be false, but often is not—when I have found the line and follow it.

All of those elements are usually in the line and they are so important for me that I will not start a draft, even on deadline, until I have found the line, the path of possibility. That is my starting point.

The Form of the Line

The line comes to me in many forms. Often it arrives in my head when I least expect it, but almost immediately it is written down in my daybook, a spiral notebook I keep near me most of the time or on a scrap of paper. Other times it comes as I scribble in my daybook, more consciously thinking about what I may write. In either case, the scribbling is vital: Writing the line usually changes it in small but crucial ways that are constructive—it starts to grow its own meaning. And writing down the line preserves it—last week's line becomes this week's column.

I am going to share some of the lines that have worked for me because of their very ordinariness. The lines I share with you will not impress. This is private language, private notation. I hear the mystery and the music and the potential meaning in what is meaningless to others. If I am successful, I will turn it into public language and during the process, I, the writer, and others, the readers, may experience the magic, the music, and the meaning.

But first I have to be able to hear and see what is not yet there. I have to be able to catch the vague shape of possible meaning, the hesitant, quiet sounds that may grow strong.

The line appears to be in many forms:

• *Word.* The word "playground" keeps appearing in my daybook. That single word contains significant tension for me because my family religion combined with my native cowardice, made the playground a place of terror, testing, and failure. I will explore that word in a piece of writing some day.

The word "ghostwriter" has just ignited a revision of the novel I'm writing. It's a word I've often used for a trade I've practiced, but within the context of my evolving novel draft, it has a special and surprising resonance for me.

• *Fragment.* This is the most common way the line appears to my ear or my eye. I read "I had an ordinary war" on my daybook page and started to pursue a novel. Obviously, the horror of war is what becomes ordinary.

The columns that have received the most reactions started with lines that contain good examples of tension: I heard myself say on the phone, "I'm proud of my wrinkles" and knew I had a line and a column making fun of a new antiwrinkle drug; sitting in a bank parking lot I scribbled, "I didn't know it would be a full-time job to do nothing" and I knew I had another line and column about the time-consuming errands retired people use to fill their days.

• *Image.* One unexpected moment I saw the way my mother kept the three places always set at the kitchen table ("the places at the kitchen table were always set") and as I captured that image in a poem, I recaptured the lonely silence of my home. The imagined image of the surgeons waving good-bye when I almost died between my by-pass operations ("the doctors, happy in green, wave at my leaving") lead to another poem that was, at least, good therapy if not good poetry.

• **List.** The list is a powerful thinking tool. When young children start making lists, we know they have made an enormous stride forward. My line is often a list:

► touch
► old
► NY *Times*
► hands in middle of night
► football
► parents' marriage bed

That led to a column on touching. All the elements on the list were in the column—in a very different order. It was not an outline but a confusion of items that were significant to me and became ordered and meaningful through their writing.

• **Lead.** I do not try to force a marriage between the line and the lead, the first sentences or paragraphs of a draft, but, of course, that relationship often develops. The line is the starting point for my written exploration. "I am not going to write a column about my daughter Hannah's wedding" became, of course, the lead from which the column grew. Many lines are shaped and developed in my head, in my daybook, on my word processor until they become the lead. I am one of those writers who must have the lead before I go on and I have come to realize that it is usually the line that gives me the lead.

Those are the most frequent forms of the line that come to me, but there are many others. One is a quotation. A surgeon told me he was going to sit by the pool and write when he retired. I got him in a column. Often a fact—or the illusion of factualness—in a statistic, or report finding, will contain the acorn of a piece of writing. A revealing detail—the colonel who ordered one of our regiments to attack another was promoted to general and sent back to safety in England—may lead to an article, a story, an essay, a book.

Pursuing the Line

Making use of the line is, for me, a strange form of pursuit that has taken me years to perfect—and to grow comfortable in using. It is not a chase. That's the first lesson.

I may have to force myself to my writing desk, but once there I have to relax, to become receptive to language, to write easily. I do not pursue the line as much as put a tail on it. I am the private dick following a suspect who may saunter through a shopping mall or race along a mountain road. My job is to stay in sight, out of sight. I follow language to see where it will take me, influencing the text as little as possible.

I write my first draft quickly and uncritically, allowing the text to tell me what it will say. I am stenographer more than maker.

Then, once I have a draft, I cut and add, shape, form, polish, clarify. But it all begins with the line. That is where the text begins. I write as I draw, by following the line.

Additional Techniques for Finding Your Focus: Voice of the Text

We often think of voice as style, something we put on after the shower to make us appear something more than we really are. But voice is what we are; voice is the person in the text; voice is what persuades the reader to listen and draws the reader on.

The Personal Voice

Each of us has a personal voice. I can recognize family and friends in the other room and on the telephone. We have our own music made up of genes and hormones, regional and ethnic influences, professional training, and daily exercise in speaking. Our natural tendencies in speech are influenced by those we hear speaking and by what draws the best response from those to whom we speak. How we pace our speech, our pauses and the way we underline phrases, our sense of humor, anger, irony, despair, joy are all communicated by voice. We relate to people by speech: As the father of daughters, I read their relationships by how they spoke on the phone to young men.

The Text's Voice

Just as we have a voice, so does everything we read. The writer's voice is adapted to each text: its subject, purpose, audience, traditions. We hear the texts we like, trust, believe. The texts speak to us in the individual, human voice of the writer tuned to the needs of the text.

The Revealing Voice

As we learn to write, we speak on the page and then listen to that evolving voice to understand the meaning of what we have said. It is the music of the text that tells us its full implications in the way that the background music of a movie supports and advances the meaning of the actions on the screen.

Voice is not after-the-writing decoration but it is voice as much as anything that leads the writer to meaning. I have trained myself to hear the music in the line, that fragment of language I have described above, so that I will catch a hint of what I may write.

As I draft, I write with my ear, hearing the language before it is on the page, following the beat, the melody, the phrasing that will reveal meaning to me—meaning and feeling—and eventually to my reader. If you work on a word processor, turn off the screen. If you write with your ear, you do not need to see the words of a first draft; you hear them and write what you have heard.

And then, in revising and editing, I listen to the text, reading it out loud as the final test, tuning it to its own meaning. The voice of the text gives me focus.

Steinbeck Statement

The great American writer John Steinbeck used to write what a book was about on a 3-by-5 card. He might write 500 pages, but his focus would be on that sentence or two on the card. I have found it a valuable technique to do this when I have trouble with focus. That statement includes and excludes. It keeps my eye on target.

But—and don't forget this but—the statement will have to be revised as you write. You may know what you hope to write about when you start but all writing is a voyage of discovery. Columbus thought he was going to India. You have to make course adjustments, refining and revising that statement as you discover what you have to say.

Begin by Ending

Many writers, including Truman Capote, Raymond Carver, John Gregory Dunne, William Gibson, Joseph Heller, John Irving, Toni Morrison ["I always know the ending; that's where I start"], and Eudora Welty write to a perceived end. They have a destination that may change in the writing in the way that you decide to go to the lake and end up at Ruth's along the way. But that destination gives you purpose and direction: focus.

It may be helpful to write a dozen, two dozen last sentences. Once you choose one and know where you are headed, you may know where—and how— to begin.

Controlling Image

When you started to write as a child, you usually drew a picture, then wrote a caption. Sometimes you reversed the procedure, but you worked back and forth calling both drawing and writing, writing. I think writers still work that way. I see what I write and many times the focus of my writing is in an image—my grandmother ruling the family from her sick bed, my first dead soldier and his look of surprise, the kitchen table that was always set at the end of a meal, ready for our next silent meal.

Pay attention to what you see with your mind's eye—or with your real eye—as you research or think about what you are going to write. The focus may lie in that vision. You may have a controlling image that will give a landmark to guide you through the writing.

Reader's Need

The focus of a piece of writing may come from the reader. In writing memos to a dean when I was English Department Chairperson, I knew what the dean wanted to hear and how he wanted to hear it—in numbers. My job was to focus a wandering, discursive discussion of our department needs in a way that the dean would "buy" our argument and give us the fiscal support we needed.

Put yourself in the reader's place to see if you can understand what a particular reader needs to learn from the text. That may be your focus.

Angle of Vision

When writing, the writer invites the reader to stand at the writer's side so the writer can point out the view and comment upon it. The place the writer stands gives focus to the text.

Often the writer moves the point of view or angle of vision, taking the reader along as the view changes and their understanding of what they're seeing increases. It is where they stop and where they walk, that keeps the writing in focus.

There are many other ways to focus your writing. You will discover them naturally as you write and as you keep account of what the act of writing is teaching you.

The Importance of Distance to Focus

A key element in writing that is rarely discussed in teaching writing is distance. As is true of many important ideas, it is obvious once you know it. Distance is the space between the subject and the writer/reader.

The danger in not understanding the importance of distance is not that the writer will not use it because every piece of writing includes the distance between writer/reader and subject. The danger is that the writer uses distance unawares and therefore ineffectively or inappropriately.

Many writers always write close up; others always stand back at the same distance. Movies and television have made all of us sophisticated users of distance if we understand what we are doing.

Move in close up and we see in detail. The lens frames the revealing action, response, or object. We gain immediacy and intensity but can lose context, what the detail means.

Stand way back and each detail is in context. Pun intended, we see the big picture. The frame extends so that we have a broad view but we lose intensity, reader/writer are detached.

The trick—craft is a matter of tricks—is to stand at a variety of distances, each appropriate to what is being said. The writer moves in close to increase intensity, moves back to put what has been seen in context; the writer stands back to establish context, then moves in close to make the reader see, feel, think, care.

What is close? What is standing back? Ah, that depends. Depends on what? The writer? The genre? The reader? Yes, I suppose, but most of all on the subject. There is no ideal distance apart from subject. The craft is to always be at that distance that helps the reader see, feel, and understand.

The skillful writer uses a zoom lens, adjusting the distance so that the reader experiences intensity without losing context; has enough detachment so that the reader has room to respond; is close enough so that the reader is forced to respond.

Play with distance as you focus and draft, to see how it will help you explore your subject and communicate it.

Experimenting with Form: The Reflective Narrative _____

"Write what you know," we command and so you produce the personal-experience paper and then many English teachers scorn it. I think that scorn is misplaced. The writers I have read in class who impress and teach me, almost always impress me with an honest, specific, and moving personal-experience paper.

It is true, however, that many personal-experience papers seem just that, an account without significance, a piece of writing that does not demonstrate the critical thinking central to an education.

That is why I prefer to call this fundamental form of writing the *reflective essay*. The writer explores a subject the writer knows that concerns the writer. The experience or issue or idea is described and thought about. The writer *reflects* on the subject.

In the reflective essay, the writer ruminates, considers and reconsiders, examines and studies the subject. The topic is put in perspective and given meaning.

That meaning may be thought out in considerable detail before the first writing. This is likely to happen when the writer attempts to explore a traumatic subject such as the death of a brother because that topic has been rehearsed, thought over and over in the writer's mind. It may also be the cognitive style of the writer to turn a subject over and over in the mind before writing.

The meaning, however, may be entirely discovered in the writing. The writer may be obsessed with a subject and have no understanding of it until the shape of the draft, what is in the act of being said and how it is in the act of being said, reveals the meaning to the reader. This often happens to me. I plunge in, hoping that meaning lies on the blank page—or the blank screen—and it usually does, revealed in the words I do not expect to write.

Most times, meaning comes in a combination of prethinking and drafting. We have a hint, a clue, a sense of what we *may* discover and then the writing defines and redefines, qualifies and clarifies that idea, gives it fullness and meaning.

In writing the reflective essay, you discover and develop the skills of critical thinking. The writer moves in close and then stands back. There is immediacy and detachment, close examination and the placing of event in perspective, there is compassion and judgment, feeling and thought.

An effective reflective essay is often personal, but it is not private. The reflective essay allows the reader to discover the subject—and the meaning of the subject—with the writer. The reader is invited to think along with the writer and to think against the writer, discovering in the act of reading the reader's own meaning in the essay.

A Writer's Case History: "Scenes Frozen in Memory" ____

This reflective essay that became a column began in the classroom. I was conducting a workshop for teachers conducted by Dave Roberts at Samford University in Birmingham, Alabama, on my way from New Hampshire to Arizona, and when I work with teachers we write, then talk about writing. And I write under the same conditions they do.

I felt the same panic they did. What was I going to write about. The well is empty. I have nothing to say, and then, in my daybook in which I was writing in class I find the line: "Why I'm not going to Tullahoma."

That is private language. No one can read that and know what it means. More important, I cannot read it and know what it means. But I can imagine that behind the why is a reason I have not yet articulated.

We wrote in bursts of between two and four minutes. First I wrote:

When we were driving through Tennessee, I saw the road to Tullahoma where I was trained as a paratrooper 45 years before.

For a moment I decided to turn west to Tullahoma but I kept on the highway south to Birmingham. Over sixty, I knew Tullahoma would be there, not my Tullahoma.

That last sentence isn't a sentence. But I am not worried about grammatical problems. I am exploring for meaning and I have begun to spot it. I dropped a couple of lines down the page and scribbled:

It was easy to kill and easy to die.

More private writing filled with potential meaning for me. In the next burst of inclass writing, I wrote:

How many Tullahomas do I have? Places that are no longer what they were.

And were never what they were. The good old days weren't. The experience and in the immediate recovery of that experience, it is changed. We distort experience into our own meanings. These are necessary lies.

This was writing about writing, the writer talking to himself. It may be essential to the writing, but it would never be published in this way. I went on talking to myself and then went to listing:

Unrelatived
Ian and his war stories
He tells the same story different ways
I want to go back to specifics:
> Tullahoma
> NH woods
> Maine Beach
> Boston
> UNH student
>> teacher

There is more. I don't even know now what most of it means—unrelatived???—but that isn't important. I was an explorer following paths that faded and disappeared, but I was exploring not knowing what I would discover.

Several weeks later, I wrote the following reflective essay, 978 words, about the length of a typical Freshman English paper, and here it is as it was published under the headline "Scenes Frozen in Memory":

1   TEMPE, Arizona - We didn't go to Tullahoma, Tennessee, on the way out here.

2   I thought we'd turn right at Chattanooga on our way west and I'd show my wife the area where I took my parachute training in World War II, the towns where I served as an MP and shot at my first human being—a fellow soldier who had just killed a bartender.

3   But then I realized that the South I remembered, the small towns, the taxi driver bootleggers, the smell of magnolias on a summer evening as I sauntered around a town square, the waitresses who refused to serve a "Damnyankee"—which was always one word—were gone.

4   I could not find the old roadhouses filled with sin out beyond the county line, show her the red clay mud roads that made jeep driving a toboggan thrill, the square miles of treetops and the speck of field where we were to jump to from the C-47, the world of the old Army where we lined up for chow by rank—sergeants, corporals, privates first class, privates like myself last—the alien culture of a small-town South I feared and enjoyed and hold, frozen in memory.

5   I have heard rumors of industry in Tullahoma and I was sure there would be malls with the same stores I visit in the Newington Mall near home. People would dress pretty much the same as home and act as if they watched the same TV shows. We are becoming more the same, and as one who was on duty during a military race riot in the segregated Army, I will not say progress is bad and old style bigotry quaint, but I am sure the

Tullahoma of my memory exists only there. We turned south, away from the places—and times—we could not visit.

6   Over sixty I have constant double vision. I see right through Boston's concrete and brick temples of politics to the Scollay Square of the Old Howard, Sally Keith and her tassels that went in opposite directions, Joe and Nemo's hot dogs, and the Casino Burlesque where you could see women older and fatter than your mother dancing without clothes.

7   When I dropped out of North Quincy High School to work on the old Record-American, one of my jobs was to go to the afternoon show at the Casino, sit in the back row and wait until they had collected enough money—less than $10 I believe—to pay for the next day's advertisement. I would call in the authorization to run the ad and strut back to the office remembering what I had seen on the stage. Each step away from reality, the dancers grew younger, more graceful, thinner—but not too thin—than the tired performers I had seen moments before.

8   We remember the good times, and if they weren't so good, we need to dress them up a bit. I will never, for example, climb Mount Chocorua again.

9   When I last climbed it I was fourteen and the peak then was higher than Everest and it was there I had my first experience with responsibility in a situation of utter physical terror.

10   A fat kid from New York had frozen in fear on a path five inches wide. The mountain rose thousands of feet in sheer ledge above us and the drop below was at least a mile—to a tiny stream edged with sharp rocks.

11   I was acting assistant counsellor and bringing up in the rear. When the chubby New Yorker hung on to the rock face with terror and refused to go on or turn back, the counsellor yelled, "Murray, get out here with me so we can pry him off that rock."

12   I looked around. He meant me. The great Hillary or even Linda and Boyd Allen of Amesbury never faced such a challenge in the Himalayas. We pried him off the ledge and I grew strong with that rescue, often built on it in combat, and I will never go back to that real ledge which might be a bit less hazardous than I imagine.

13   A few years ago I was invited to go to James Bay in Northern Quebec and I was delighted. When I was twelve or thereabouts and sickly I lay in bed and studied a National Geographic map of the Far North I had pinned to the ceiling. I explored Labrador, the Yukon, the Mackenzie River, but I always kept returning to James Bay.

14   I explored that world by canoe, snowshoe, and dog sled; hunting, fishing and, although I wouldn't go near a trap with a dead mouse in it, I was for weeks at a time a trapper living in a log cabin (in a land where there were no logs).

15   Now I was going to the mysterious land I had imagined fifty or more years before. And then the deal fell through. I was disappointed, but soon realized that the Far North of my imagination would always be more exciting than anything I could visit.

16   Later I learned that a Japanese conglomerate bought furs from the Indian village where I had planned to stay, and in an intricate deal for the

furs, established a plastic canoe factory where the Indians could work off-season. My imagined canoes were hand sewn from animal skins and they leaked gloriously.

17   So much for James Bay. We will continue to travel to places where we haven't been, but we will not return to those lands of memory and imagination that are our true reality.

18   On the way home I will see again the highway to Tullahoma but I will not take it. As I drive on I will, however, swagger down the streets of memory, a forty-five on my hip, an M.P. leaner, harder, meaner, tougher than I ever was.

Now let's read it through together while I tell you something of what I was trying to do as I wrote it, the problems I saw and how I tried to solve them.

Remember that I am reading this with you *after* it was published and, most of the time, not recreating my thoughts while I was writing. I write instinctively, consciously thinking about the text as I revise and polish.

1 TEMPE, Arizona - We didn't go to Tullahoma, Tennessee, on the way out here.

I hope this lead establishes a tension or question in the reader's mind that will make the reader go on: What's in Tullahoma? Why didn't you go there?

2 I thought we'd turn right at Chattanooga on our way west and I'd show my wife the area where I took my parachute training in World War II, the towns where I served as an MP and shot at my first human being—a fellow soldier who had just killed a bartender.

I answer the reader's questions but spark a new one: Hey, wait a minute, what's that about killing a fellow soldier?

This paragraph, I realize, clearly builds up to the important point of emphasis at the end.

You may have been taught to construct fully developed paragraphs and I hope I do that but in a newspaper column, each typewritten line doubles when it is reproduced in column width. The five-line paragraph becomes ten lines and that begins to be a lot of gray type for the busy reader.

3 But then I realized that the South I remembered, the small
   towns, the taxi driver bootleggers, the smell of magnolias on a
   summer evening as I sauntered around a town square, the
   waitresses who refused to serve a "Damnyankee"—which was
   always one word—were gone.

I go back and set up
my memory of the
South, what made
me consider
returning to
Tullahoma, but
reflecting on it I
realize that South is
gone. I give the
reader specific
evidence of the
South I knew as a
Yankee soldier. And
I continue the
documentation
below, all aimed to
lead the reader
toward the focus of
the piece—you
can't go back to the
real/imaginary
worlds of your
memory.

4 I could not find the old roadhouses filled with sin out beyond
   the county line, show her the red clay mud roads that made
   jeep driving a toboggan thrill, the square miles of treetops and
   the speck of field where we were to jump to from the C-47, the
   world of the old Army where we lined up for chow by rank—
   sergeants, corporals, privates first class, privates like myself
   last—the alien culture of a small-town South I feared and
   enjoyed and hold, frozen in memory.

At the point of
emphasis in the
paragraph, I add
some tension, the
contradictions in my
memory.

5 I have heard rumors of industry in Tullahoma and I was sure
   there would be malls with the same stores I visit in the
   Newington Mall near home. People would dress pretty much
   the same as home and act as if they watched the same TV
   shows. We are becoming more the same, and as one who was
   on duty during a military race riot in the segregated Army, I
   will not say progress is bad and old style bigotry quaint, but I
   am sure the Tullahoma of my memory exists only there. We
   turned south, away from the places—and times—we could not
   visit.

I reinforce the focus
by saying how all
places have
changed, how we
have become more
alike, mourn the
erasing of
difference and then,
thinking of my
friend and colleague
Les Fisher, who is
black, I remind
myself that
nostalgia isn't the
same for blacks in
the South and
adjust my
memories. I hope I
have been able to
contain such
complexities in a
relatively short
paragraph.

6 Over sixty I have constant double vision. I see right through
   Boston's concrete and brick temples of politics to the Scollay

Now a turn where I
put what I've been

Square of the Old Howard, Sally Keith and her tassels that went in opposite directions, Joe and Nemo's hot dogs, and the Casino Burlesque where you could see women older and fatter than your mother dancing without clothes.

doing in a larger context: the double vision of the over sixty. And I lighten the weight of the piece with the kind of memories I have of staid old Boston.

7 When I dropped out of North Quincy High School to work on the old Record-American, one of my jobs was to go to the afternoon show at the Casino, sit in the back row and wait until they had collected enough money—less than $10 I believe—to pay for the next day's advertisement. I would call in the authorization to run the ad and strut back to the office remembering what I had seen on the stage. Each step away from reality, the dancers grew younger, more graceful, thinner—but not too thin—than the tired performers I had seen moments before.

But I support my focus or thesis by showing how I almost immediately romanticized— nostaliaized???—my memories at the time I was having them. I could not, in a sense, even then go back to the imaginary strippers I had created on the walk back to the office. I move easily and instinctively back and forth in time, making use of whatever pops into my head *under the guidance of my focusing idea.*

8 We remember the good times, and if they weren't so good, we need to dress them up a bit. I will never, for example, climb Mount Chocorua again.

Now I document my focus again, with another story. I hope the readers will relive their own stories as they read mine. I know as a writer that the more specific I am about my own memories, the more specific their memories will be. The reader and I are creating a text that is not what I have written on the page and not what they had not articulated before they read my piece. It is a text that we create together and exists about halfway between writer and reader if we are lucky.

9 When I last climbed it I was fourteen and the peak then was higher than Everest and it was there I had my first experience with responsibility in a situation of utter physical terror.

> I tell the reader the meaning to me of that remembered experience. The cliché is show, don't tell, but actually we usually show *and* tell, tell *and* show.

10 A fat kid from New York had frozen in fear on a path five inches wide. The mountain rose thousands of feet in sheer ledge above us and the drop below was at least a mile—to a tiny stream edged with sharp rocks.

> I hope I have written this in such a way that the reader knows I'm exaggerating, reporting on what I remember, not what was actually there.

11 I was acting assistant counsellor and bringing up in the rear. When the chubby New Yorker hung on to the rock face with terror and refused to go on or turn back, the counsellor yelled, "Murray, get out here with me so we can pry him off that rock."

> Although I am writing an essay, I use narrative techniques of description, scene, dialogue. I want to make the reader observe, or better yet, share my experience.

12 I looked around. He meant me. The great Hillary or even Linda and Boyd Allen of Amesbury never faced such a challenge in the Himalayas. We pried him off the ledge and I grew strong with that rescue, often built on it in combat, and I will never go back to that real ledge which might be a bit less hazardous than I imagine.

> Who are the Allens? Friends of mine who are real mountain climbers. I'm having fun but making a point. Now I tell the reader, again, how important that real/imaginary experience was to me and make it clear how my memory has exaggerated or changed reality, a main point that runs through the essay that reflects on experience.

13 A few years ago I was invited to go to James Bay in Northern Quebec and I was delighted. When I was twelve or thereabouts and sickly I lay in bed and studied a National Geographic map of the Far North I had pinned to the ceiling. I explored Labrador, the Yukon, the Mackenzie River, but I always kept returning to James Bay.

> I show how what I have learned about imaginary places helps me deal with places I've always wanted to go and now, like my Over Sixty readers, begin to realize I never will.

14 I explored that world by canoe, snowshoe, and dog sled; hunting, fishing and, although I wouldn't go near a trap with a dead mouse in it, I was for weeks at a time a trapper living in a log cabin (in a land where there were no logs).

In editing, I discovered how stupid it was to have said log cabin, then realized that documented what I was saying and left it in.

15 Now I was going to the mysterious land I had imagined fifty or more years before. And then the deal fell through. I was disappointed, but soon realized that the Far North of my imagination would always be more exciting than anything I could visit.

My focus is again restated, refined and expanded.

16 Later I learned that a Japanese conglomerate bought furs from the Indian village where I had planned to stay, and in an intricate deal for the furs, established a plastic canoe factory where the Indians could work off-season. My imagined canoes were hand sewn from animal skins and they leaked gloriously.

I liked the gloriously. It would not be romantic to be in a real leaky canoe in the Far North but it would be romantic in my imaginary Far North. The real subject is too serious to be written about in an end of dreams, despairing, heavy tone. There is something sad but also funny about my focus, how we romanticize the past and our dreams.

17 So much for James Bay. We will continue to travel to places where we haven't been, but we will not return to those lands of memory and imagination that are our true reality.

Okay, what have I learned from my reflections and what I am going to do with what I have learned?

18 On the way home I will see again the highway to Tullahoma but I will not take it. As I drive on I will, however, swagger down the streets of memory, a forty-five on my hip, an M.P. leaner, harder, meaner, tougher than I ever was.

I end on a note of humor that supports my focus. I will, by God, have my fantasies even if I know I've made up my own history. My dreams are silly but they are mine and it's ok for me—and for my readers—to have their own silly memories as long as they don't try to go back and find them in the real world.

A Student's Case History: Anne Campbell _____

This account of a student writing a personal essay is especially interesting for several reasons. The student picked a global subject as many students do. The feelings the student chose to explore were typical of many college freshmen: sincere, painful, and very hard to nail down. The instructor, an excellent writer herself and coauthor with Donald H. Graves of *Write from the Start* (Dutton, New York, 1985), is a master teacher. Her account of what happened will touch every teacher and is worth students' careful study; they may not realize how delicate and difficult our task is, at least the job of those of us who teach by conference. How much is enough or too much, what is helpful and not helpful, what do we intend and how are we perceived? Her essay is worthy of study as a fine example of the essay form. And I am impressed with her openness, courage, and candor in being willing to share her experiences with us.

Finally, the paper didn't work for me. In conference, I would be able to use the word "failure," but I worry about using that word in print. It seems final. It seems to say that the writer is a failure. Not at all. In my course, I think the students would know that failure is essential, as natural a part of the writing process as failure in experiments are a natural part of the scientific process. We learn little from our easy successes that have been rehearsed in our subconscious, but we can learn a great deal as we attempt a difficult subject, as this student has, and work at it again and again, discovering weaknesses and strengths in each draft. This is an instructive piece of work—to the writer and to us.

The Instructor's Account by Virginia Stuart

A Matter of Distance

1   Many people consider the personal narrative to be the easiest kind of paper to write—all you have to do is write about yourself, the subject you know best. Both students and teachers soon discover, however, that writing about the subject you know best can be more difficult than they thought. The emotions surrounding a past experience may motivate a writer. It is the emotional or psychological insight, after all, that makes a good personal narrative gratifying to read and to write. But emotions can also get in the way, clouding the vision of both student and teacher. It's a problem of distance. At some point in the process, the writer must be able to stand back and see the material from a reader's point of view. And the teacher, while responding as a reader, must also be able to stand back and see the material from the writer's point of view. When all goes well, the writer can then make his or her own discoveries, and the reader benefits from those discoveries. Both Anne and I struggled to keep our distance from the material in "Some Things Don't Change." We didn't always succeed, but we both learned some lessons in the process.

2 From the beginning, Anne showed a sensitivity to her readers' need for details that would both prove her point and keep their interest. Thus she rejected her first two leads, which were filled with sweeping statements about her friendship. Instead, she chose to open with a scene describing her romantic canoe ride with a boyfriend under the stars. Her friend Kristin came along to paddle. This concrete example not only showed how close the two girls were, but it also contained the seed of their conflict. The last line of the paragraph introduced the tension, the promise of a problem, that would keep readers reading. When she came to discuss her prewriting with me, Anne told me that lead had shown her a way to write the whole paper. And, indeed, the first half of her first draft continued in the same vein, piling up image after image that revealed the closeness of their friendship plus a hint of the conflict to come.

3 But when she brought her first draft to me, Anne said that she was disappointed with the second half of the piece. She found that she had lost the strong voice and momentum that carried the first half. I agreed. It seemed that she was not announcing her feelings with bald statements rather than allowing readers to share those feelings through details. But I also thought there was something more missing as I finished reading. I wasn't sure what she had made of her experience, what she wanted it all to add up to—a perfectly normal state of affairs for a first draft. I asked her several questions that had occurred to me as a reader and waited to see what the next draft would bring.

4 When she returned with a second draft, she was quite satisfied with it. But, in fact, the new draft was very close to the first. I told her that I wasn't quite sure what the point was. She, like many freshmen, questioned whether a point was needed. Wasn't the experience in itself enough? All her friends had liked it. Unfortunately, it is a rare friend who can be honest enough and impolite enough to say, "So what?" And that is often the hardest part of writing a personal narrative—realizing that this wonderful or terrible thing that happened to you may have some entertainment value as "just a story" shared in conversation, but that readers need more. They need answers to questions like "So what? Why are you telling me this? What makes the story of your accident or your friendship different from everyone else's? What have you learned that I can learn from?" Of course, the writer benefits from struggling with these questions. For the readers' questions are really a mirror image of the writer's own questions: "What is the pattern here? What is the meaning, the significance, of this experience? Why am I telling this story?"

5 One of my own writing teachers has said that it is during revision that "sight becomes insight." Anne found that when she looked hard enough, she did find meaning in her experience. Revision had become not just a cosmetic touch-up but a genuine re-seeing. In short, she had found a focus. Actually, she found two, and that was my own vision as a teacher became blurred.

6 The development of her first idea can be traced through the journal

she kept while writing her paper. After she had written her first draft, she wrote in her journal, "It's hard to look back and see things the way I saw them at the time and then try to figure out how they really were.... There has to be a way to show how close we were but also to show how separate we were." I found her strongest statement of this theme not in a draft but in her second attempt at free writing. She described her confrontation with Kristin thus: "Looking back on it a year later, I'm still not over it, and our relationship is different because of it. It was like somehow in that day, we lost something that I'm not even sure was there in the first place." But throughout Anne's writing there had appeared a second theme—the reaffirmation of the girls' friendship in spite of their conflict. At the end of her third draft, she wrote in her journal, "The ending is not necessarily happy, although it does show that Kristin and I are still close, which is what I think the whole point is." In other words, some things—like friendship—don't change.

7   Any piece of writing has many different potential ideas or focuses. In this case, Anne had found two, and neither one was "right" or "wrong." There are very few rights or wrongs in writing. But there are betters and worses, and to my mind Anne's first focus was better than her second. Her confrontation with Kristin had induced her to see their relationship—her own behavior, a whole chapter in her life—in a new light. The realization wasn't pleasant, but it struck me as a significant idea on which to build her paper. Readers might learn from Anne's experience, perhaps re-seeing some of their own relationships as a result. This insight of Anne's rang true for me. More important, the insight seemed to be honest and true in view of many things Anne had written. In her very first free-writing session, she wrote, "It has never been the same although Kristin is still my best friend." In her second free write, she said, "We never bring that time up—it's better that way because when I think about it I still resent her." Similar references are sprinkled throughout her pre-writing and drafts. As I saw it, some things don't change, but this relationship had. Permanently.

8   Nevertheless, Anne chose her second option—the idea that friendship conquers all. I think the reasons for her choice are numerous. In one sense, at this stage she may have been overly conscious of her readers. From the start, she knew she would show the piece to Kristin, and she mentioned several times that she feared the early drafts sounded too "vindictive." But even without Kristin peering over her shoulder in spirit, I suspect, she would have chosen to put the best possible face on this unpleasant experience.

9   Students often resist the idea of writing something that seems "negative," even when it's more honest and more original than a positive sentiment. Last semester, I had a student who wrote a piece called "A Rushed Decision." It gave an excellent description of the negative aspects of pledging a sorority—the pressure, the falseness of conversations, the lack of genuine information with which to make a decision on either side, the pain of rejection. But the writer summed up her paper with a paragraph on the

delights of sisterhood and concluded that, once it was over, rush really didn't matter. It didn't even matter who was chosen. Any group of young women chosen at random would develop a sisterly bond just in the course of living together. When asked what she had intended as her main idea, the writer referred to her last paragraph. Whether she was motivated by a fear of betraying the sorority or by a desire to avoid appearing "negative," she seemed unwilling to recognize the strength of the emotions, the ideas— even the writing—that made up 90% of the paper.

10   Of course, that last paragraph contained a significant, original idea of its own. But the main idea of a paper cannot be attached to the end at the last minute like a caboose. It must be a part of every car from the locomotive to the caboose, as well as the couplings in between. It must be a part of every paragraph, every sentence. To support her intended idea, my student would have had to write a new paper showing how living together made the girls sisters. In the end, she chose to leave her paper as it was. She didn't want to write the second piece, but she still couldn't acknowledge the meaning of the piece she had written.

11   I believe Anne found herself in a similar predicament, further complicated by the intensity of the emotions surrounding her experience—and the freshness of the hurt. In a journal entry written shortly after the first draft, Anne wrote, "I'm not far away from the subject yet. Maybe I picked the wrong time to write this paper." She expressed a similar sentiment on other occasions, and I had to agree. Yet at the same time she felt compelled to write the paper then.

12   Our differing views of the paper became clear during our conference on her third draft. I think our recollections of the talk differ, and I suspect that in her brief essay on the process of writing her paper she tends to give me more "credit" than I deserve or care to accept. But there's no denying the result. Anne's journal reveals that she left my office convinced that her idea of the focus was not "the real focus." And she went back to her room to write "what I think she wants."

13   Had I had an opportunity to read Anne's journal, I would have known then that I had, in a sense, lost the semester in my attempt to win the paper. I work very hard to show my students that there are very few questions of right or wrong, black or white, in writing. I want them to see that there are always many options available to them and that the more options they can find, the more likely they are to choose a good one. But in the process of trying to help Anne write a better paper, I had instigated, or reinforced, a serious misconception—the idea that each paper has only one "right" focus.

14   Ironically, I had lost the paper at the same time, because as soon as Anne went home to write "what the teacher wanted," the paper was no longer hers. Now, several months later, I read the third draft and I hear a vitality, a voice, there that is lacking in the ending Anne wrote "for" me in her final draft. In the third draft, Anne had found a strong, original metaphor in the clocktower that told the wrong time. That image encompassed

all that she wanted to say about the friendship—including both the falseness she had uncovered and the hope that she still harbored. With some tinkering, she could have made that metaphor a little more subtle as well as apt. In her final draft, her only figures of speech were cliches—eggshells underfoot and looks cutting through people like knives. Even her images were no longer her own in that draft.

15   For me the art of teaching lies in knowing when to speak up and when to shut up, when to push and when to wait. I had felt safe in expressing my own preference between her two focuses because I knew that both ideas were hers, not mine. The realization that there can never be a friendship in which the friends are like two bodies with one head came out of Anne's experience and reflections. It came out of her own pen on a number of occasions. What I didn't realize was that by pushing her to focus on an idea she didn't want to face, I was taking control of the paper as surely as if I had given her the idea and the words to express it. My protestations that I didn't want her to write anything that she didn't want to say undoubtedly sounded hollow.

16   Of course, the art of writing lies in part in knowing when to listen to a reader's advice and when to reject it. Ideally, I would want my students to stand by their own intents and preferences on certain issues and let the grades fall where they may. Some of my students have done that, and I have respected them for it. Often, the writing comes out better as a result. At the same time, I realize how difficult it is for students to overcome twelve years' practice at figuring out "what the teacher wants," especially when the teacher is still handing out grades.

17   In retrospect, I might have done a number of things differently, beginning by urging Anne to choose a different experience to write about for the time being. But, most important, I would not have made clear my preference for one of her ideas over the other. I would have helped her to say what she wanted to say better rather than trying to get her to say something else.

18   Both Anne and I have learned from our experience with this piece. Like Anne, I learned much in retrospect, in the process of writing and rewriting about what happened. The lessons did not come easily nor were they pleasant. And in one sense our lessons were one and the same: Friends and teachers should allow people to paddle their own canoes.

19   There is no pat ending to this piece or the process it came out of. (Anne says one of the things she learned from the experience was the never-finished quality of writing.) No easy answers for student or teacher. But her paper has elicited strong reactions from everyone who has read it. Students could discuss the different endings and talk about where they might have ended the story. They might explore the issue of trying to put a pleasant face on unpleasant things. And they could discuss the practice of trying to write "what the teacher wants" as opposed to what you want to say or what you believe will make the best piece of writing.

The Student's Account by Anne Campbell

1   In the past I have always written without thinking about it, and I was fairly successful too, although I didn't know what I was missing. In English this semester I was introduced to the book *Write to Learn,* and although I read what was in it, I never paid enough attention to what it could mean to my writing. When I took the time to try some of the methods outlined in the book, I found them to be incredibly useful. I had never thought of writing as such a logical process.

2   As it says in the book we learn when we write; for me this was very true. The subject that I wrote about was something very close to me. Kristin was a very difficult topic though, because the incident described in the paper was something that I have chosen not to think of very much. I had also never analyzed the experience in my mind so thoroughly. In the beginning stages of freewriting and brainstorming I was not really that surprised by what I wrote. I took a fairly shallow look at what had happened. As I became more involved in the paper, I learned more about what I really thought of the experience. I kept trying to put a happy ending on the paper, until I realized that it was much more valuable to analyze how I saw our friendship differently in light of what had happened.

3   Freewriting was a great discovery for me also; it was difficult at first to get used to the idea of writing knowing that most of it wouldn't work anyway, but it was a great way to see what I was thinking, and to simply clear my mind. Brainstorming helped me to remember things that I wouldn't really think relevant. I would never have thought of the canoeing experience as something that would be relevant to a paper, but when I looked at the list and thought about it, it became a major part of the paper.

4   The most trouble I had with this paper was with the focus. I wrote the first draft without even realizing that I should be aware of it, and it came out with a sketchy focus. Virginia noticed this right away, and through asking me questions about how differently I saw things after Kristin talked to me that day, she got me to think more about the focus. In my third draft I decided what I thought the focus should be—that Kristin and I went through a dramatic change in our relationship, but that we had remained friends. I was satisfied with this, and I liked the third draft the way it was. Virginia still had trouble with it, and wanted to know how differently I saw things as a result of it. I was very frustrated because I thought we saw things so differently, but I tried to write it the way I thought she would like it. I reflected on the changes that happened, and left the ending without it being happy. I wound up liking it better that way, because I had been using the ending that I had written to please Virginia; not because I wanted to please her, but because it worked better that way. Her help was invaluable, because without it I wouldn't have looked any deeper, and even though I was frustrated at times, her prodding made my paper better.

5   This was all new to me, working through my thoughts so carefully. I

would never have known how much can be learned from writing if I hadn't had to try it this way. This paper is a result of a lot of hard work and thought. I still think that it could stand improvement, but I never would have thought that before. Revising was a fairly foreign notion to me because once something is written down it seems so permanent to me, but now I see that there is always something that can be improved if you just look hard enough. If I had just written things down the way they came to me I would have missed out on some important discoveries that came through the various steps I used from the book.

Here is an example of Anne's brainstorming and her free writing, which she did at several times as she searched for her way into the paper.

```
Anne C mpbell
Brainstorming

    First list:
Kristin
my best friend
inseperable
center of the group
too close?
my perverbial sidekick
same interests
same grades
different personalities
another four years?
first kiss
first beer
college trip
two halves
Anne and Kristin is one word
McDonalds and All my Children
Licorice and cherry soda
turkey sandwiches on Weds.
8th grade english teacher
tall, thin , curly hair
short, chubby, straight hair
like her mother
college acceptances
could we live another four years?

    Second list:
canoeing at eaglesmere
visiting Bill
when I was n the hospital
invitations as one
haircuts together
grounded from each other
Todd and Chris freshman year
acting drunk off half a beer
spying on Steve and Bill
babysitting together
sharing lockers
Washington D.C.
camp
paper route
were in the play
writing for the paper
new year's eve
Florida
Biff and Steve
```

Anne Campbell
Freewriting

What is this paper supposed to be about? I guess that's
my problem, I think I'm trying to do something in it that is
irrelevant to anyone else--how do I make it interesting to
other people that Krisitn and I were best friends? I'm
frustrated because I don't think I know how to make the
reader care. I think there are too many examples in it noe,
maybe the part about getting grounded is enough. I think
it makes the statement that I want to make. So what is the
rest of it about????
    Kristin and I didn't go to college together because she
told me that I would ruin her life if I did. It wasn't so
much that decision that changed our relationship, but what
came out in that fight that changed everything that I had
taken for granted and counted on for five years. She was
the biggst part of my life, despite boyfriends, family and
everything else. She was the most stable part of my life,
and then everything changed, I had seen everything through
rose colered glass. Looking back on it only a year later,
I'm still not over it, and our relationship is different
because of it. It was like somehow in that day, we lost
something that I'm not even sure was there in the first
place. O.K., so how is it different? It's not really as
much fun. We were so fun-loving when we were younger, the
things we did were so silly, out relationship was something
that other people marveled about, and it gave us an identity.
I felt as if w3 lost that, and that everything became much
more serious after that fight. I didn't know how to act
around the person I felt most comfortable with. But she was

What follows are some trial leads.

Anne Campbell
Trial beginnings for my paper

April 15 is a fairly important day for everyone, but
especially to a high school senior aspiring to go to college.
On April fifteenth my fate was determined for the next four
years, and I also went through a dramatic realization about
my personality. I never thought that I wouldn't get into
Tufts.

Kristin is my best friend. She is a vital part of me.
I can hardly remember a day in the last five years that I
haven't seen Kristin. She came on vacations with my family,
worked with me in the summer, played the same sports that I
did, and we had the same friends. My teachers in high school
refered to her as my perverbial sidekick, our friends thought
of us as one person, and I thought of her as an extension
of myself. No one knows me better than Kristin. Kristin
and I looked a t colleges together during the spring break
of our junior year. It was great, our first taste of in
dependence--a car, lots of money, and three full weeks to
go wherever we wanted.

It's hard when you're seventeen to know what is best
for you.

When I was fiftenn and I visited my boyfriend's summer
home for a week my best friend Kristin came with me. When
he and I went for a romantic excursion in a canoe late at
night under the stars, Kristin rowed the boat. When he and
I broke up Kristin let me cry on her shoulder. Kristin has
been there for me every time I have ever neede her. She
was someone to laugh and cry with , but best of all she was
someone to sit in silence with. I mean comfortable silence
where words aren't needed and you know what the other
person is thinking so you don!t feel alone. I never thought
there would come a day when Kristin couldn't help me
through a problem ,and I never dreamed that she could become
the problem.

No one in the whole world is as close to me as Kristin,
my best feiend. All through high school we were inseperable.

The author is talking to herself in her journal as a way of seeing what she has done, what she needs to do, and what it means.

Anne Campbell
Journal entries

  I've written a rough draft of my paper, it really helped
me put the whole thing in to perspective. I now have a
vague idea of how I want to say everything. I really liked
the beginning and the ending. The beginning really surprised
me, it came out of nowhere and it sounds perfect to me.
The draft helped me to organize my thought sif nothing else
because I don't like it very much. Now, I can learn about
what I know I don't like and try to keep the threads of what
I do like for the next draft. It's something that I usually
wouldn't turn in or even let anyone see. Everyone ina while
there is a sentence that I like, but for the most part
I'm frustrated because I don't know what to do next. Revising
is the hardest part because once you see something written
it seems so final.

  I think I know what I shoul try and do in this paper,
find a way to demonstrate how Kristin was my perverbial side
kick, but the point is so subtle that I hadn't really noticed
it myself. I've never really thought about it a lot, it's
hard to look back and see things the way I saw them at the
time and then try to fugure out how they really were, I'm
not far away from the subject yet. Maybe I picked the wrong
time to write this paper. There has to be a way to show how
close we wer but to also show how separate we were.

  I have written a second draft which isn't that much
better than the first, it doesn't go much further than the
first one. I am confused as to the focus, Virginia is too.
What I thought was the focus is either not clear or not
sufficient. Now, I am wondoring if I can do this a t all.

  I wrote a third draft, I really like ti and I think
it says what I want to say. I'm excited. The ending is
not necessarily happy although it does show that Krisitn and
I are still close which is what I think the whole poin it.
Virginia does not agree with me, she doesn't think that is
what the real focus is anyway. I don't know what to do,
I think that it is good, and she thinks that it should be
better. I'm not sure that I know how to make it better because I like what is already there. Throughout this whole
thing I have had the most trouble with revising things.

  I wrote what I think she wants. The ending isn't really
an ending and it doesn't say what I think about the outcome
of everything. I think it is important to note that we are
still as close as we wer even though things are very different
and I have learned something about myself that I'm not sure
I wanted to. Yes, the things I said in the las t ending
are true, bu t I feel as if there is more to it than that.
I don't know what I will do in the end. I'll wait until
I talk to Virginia on friday.

Anne also tried sample endings. Here is an example.

Anne Campbell
sample ending

    I guess there really is no end to it. I knew, even
then, that our friendship was not over. For a long time
I would be walking on eggshells wondoring if I was overshadowing Kristin. I'm not sur how much things have changed
since then.

    We walked downtown that afternoon after I told her
that I wouldn't go to F&M. I knew that we would miss each
other, but I guess there is a time when you have to go on.
For us it was the best thing, through all of my confusion
I knew that she was right. That's the hardest part, she
taught me something about myself that I don't think I wanted
to know. It made everything that was so constant and simple
seem confused and unsure. While we were sitting on the green
eating licorice and drinking soda I realized with some sadness, that I wasn't sure I could change things. I hadn't
appreciated how simple everything about us seemed then. I
guess no one ever does.

    In a lot of ways I miss the way things used to be, I
wondor if she does--somehow I don't think so. I had stuck
by Kristin through some bad times, and we've been through
things that will always hold us together. The sun was setting behind the stores on main street, and Kristin and I
hadn't spoken yet. It was odd because I realized that
I didn't really know what she was thinking. Maybe I never had.
We kept sitting there, not saying anything and it became
dark. I wanted to say something to make everything all right,
but I couldn't find the words. We wer there together, that must
mean something--the fact that we were together was always good.

The author attempted some sequences and some titles.

```
Anne Campbell
Sequences--p.98 Wrive to Learn


Bill, Eaglesmere lake, breaking up, Kristin always there.
  --never thought she could become the problem.


bi-line in the newspapre
party freshman year
grounded from each other
worst punishment possible

Our rituals together
cherry sodas and licorice on the green
first beer together
turkey sandwiches from the barvarian pastry shop on Weds.

Our ability to be together and yet flourish with other oeople
she was my perverbial sidekick
it wasn't conscious, it's just the way it was

College trip
similar aplications
I never thought it would come to that

Real disapointment
Kristin wasn't there for me
she was concerned about herself, and what my decision would
do to her life

She didn't want me to go to F and M, but she did want our
friendship.  She was living in my shadow

If I went to F&M she would resent me forever.
If I didn't go, I wo uld rsent her for forcing me not ot,
and for not being able to be her own person around me.

I made the choice for her to save our friendship.  I'm happy
where I am and so is she, we are still best friends, but many
things have changed.  Friendship is hard, but it is worth it.
```

Anne Campbell

Titles

My perverbial sidekick

Even my Best Friend wasn't there for me

College is a chance to Start over agin

What are friends for?

Kristin, my best Friend

Some things stay the Same

Some Things Don't Change

There are far too many student drafts for us to reprint them all here but you should
be able to empathize with the student in her struggle to discover what she felt and
what it meant, then to share those discoveries with the reader. On Draft 3, Anne
Campbell was still making crucial decisions.

Anne Campbell
English 401d   Draft #3
Virginia Stuart

              Some Things Don't Change

      I ran home from Kristin's house furious. Actually,

I don't know whether I was more hurt or angry. I was

crying, sniffling, and sobbing and all that I could think

forget this / it doesn't do anything for the paper

of was that I hoped no one would see me that way. I don't

know how it came to that; one minute I'd been rejected

by my first choice college, and the next thing I knew Kristin

and I were screaming at each other like we had never done

before, and it seemed like there was no way to save our

relationship.

      Kristin is my best friend. When I was fifteen and I

visited my boyfriend's summer home for a week, Kristin

came with me. When he and I went for a romantic excursion

in a canoe late at night under the stars, she rowed the

boat. When he and I broke up, Kristin was right there for

me. She let me cry on her shoulder and she listened to

my irrational misery for as long as I wanted her to; and

when I wanted to be left alone, she left me alone. I couldn't

remember a time when Kristin wasn't there for me. She

was someone perfect for laughing with or crying with; but

best of all she was someone I could sit in silence with.

I mean comfortable silence where words aren't meeded to

communicate--because she usually knew what I was thinking

anyway. I never thought there would be a time when Kristin

couldn't help me through a problem, and it never even crossed

my mind that she could become the problem.

Here is Anne Campbell's final draft.

SOME THINGS DON'T CHANGE
Anne Campbell

1   Kristin is my best friend. When I was fifteen and I visited my boyfriend's summer home for a week, Kristin came with me. When he and I went for a romantic excursion in a canoe late at night under the stars, she rowed the boat. When he and I broke up, Kristin was right there for me. She let me cry on her shoulder and she listened to my irrational misery for as long as I wanted her to; and when I wanted to be left alone, she left me alone. I couldn't remember a time when Kristin wasn't there for me. She was someone perfect for laughing or crying with; but best of all she was someone I could sit in silence with. I mean comfortable silence where words aren't needed to communicate—because we usually understood each other without words anyway. I never thought there would be a time when Kristin couldn't help me through a problem, and it never even crossed my mind that she could become the problem.

2   All through high school we were inseparable—Kristin shared every aspect of my life. At thirteen we snuck a beer from her parents' supply in the basement. We split it and thought that we were drunk; little did we know that the grownup carefree feeling it gave us was all in our minds. Our parents found out and we were grounded from each other for a month. Supposedly this was the worst possible punishment for the two of us, and we would be reminded of the seriousness of our delinquency every time we felt the urge to see one another. We snuck phone calls late at night, and actually looked forward to going to school so that we could see each other again. When we were together, we spent the time scheming against our parents. We thought of suicide, running away, shaving our heads, and finally we came up with the ultimate solution. We decided that we would literally stop speaking to anyone except each other in order to prove to our parents that life meant nothing to us without each other. The plan lasted about three hours, and before we could put another one into action, the month was over and we were back together again the way it was supposed to be.

3   When we were too young to go out on summer nights, but too old to play kick-the-can with the kids in our neighborhood, Kristin and I used to walk into the village and buy cherry soda and a yard of red licorice. We'd sit on the village green in the twilight with the crickets chirping in the background, and talk about the things we would do when we got into real life. When I thought of the future, of getting my driver's license, graduating from high school, falling into love, or getting married, I always saw Kristin standing right beside me—sharing everything with me.

4   I started writing for the school newspaper during my sophomore year. In the beginning of my junior year I was asked to write what I thought was a really boring article. Kristin helped me write the article—it turned out to be really funny, and at the same time informative; she helped me so much that I put both of our names on the article. She always was better at that kind of stuff than I was anyway. From that day forward, Kristin and I wrote humor articles for the paper in every issue. I suppose that it is usually hard for people to write together and have an even amount of input, but Kristin and I were different—we seemed to complement each other perfectly.

5   So we drifted through the years together and saw each other through changes, but one thing always remained the same; Kristin was always by my side. Teachers referred to her as my proverbial sidekick. A friend once said that we were like two bodies with one head, and to me she was the most constant and stable part of my life.

6   The years gave way to uncertainty for Kristin and me and the question of college seemed to take away the simplicity I'd loved so much. When that question first came up, neither one of us considered it very seriously. Naturally we looked at colleges together, but I knew that I was going to Tufts and Kristin to Franklin and Marshall—regardless of our other applications. When I didn't get into Tufts I was devastated. I had never really considered any other options, but I had been accepted to Franklin and Marshall, and so had Kristin. I figured that I would discuss it with Kristin and see what she thought. Before I opened my mouth, she made my decision for me. She told me that she didn't want to go to college with me, that college was a chance for her to start all over again, on her own. She said that she didn't want to live in my shadow any more, that she wanted to live her own life. I was lost, never, in five years, had she told me how she felt.

7   I left her then, for a lack of anything better to say or do. Walking home with tears streaming down my face, I thought the world seemed still—the way it does after a violent summer storm. A gap developed in our relationship that day that I don't think has ever mended. For a long time I would be walking on eggshells, wondering if I was overshadowing Kristin. It's funny, because when I stood myself next to her I was always looking up. I always thought of her as a better person.

8   We walked downtown the next afternoon, and I told her that I wouldn't go to Franklin and Marshall. The relief in her eyes shot through me like a knife, but I knew that she was right. That was the hardest part; she taught me something about myself that I never wanted to know. I suppose it was my idea to have that beer, and I suppose that I dragged her along with Bill and me that night. I suppose that I had instigated a lot of the things we'd done together—maybe even talked her into doing things that she hadn't wanted to do. She never told me though—there was nothing I could have done. As we were sitting on the green, I realized that even now, since she had told me, I wasn't sure how things could be changed. The strength I had always seen in our friendship wasn't there any more because I had always

thought of us as two halves of the same thing. Now it was she and I—two very different and separate people. I wondered if I would ever feel whole again.

9   The sun was setting behind the stores on Main Street. Kristin and I hadn't spoken the whole time; we were in comfortable silence. I thought it was odd because I could guess what she was thinking, but I didn't know for sure—maybe I never had. It began to get dark. I wanted desperately to say something that would make everything all right again, but I couldn't find any words; there were no words. We were sitting together in our old and familiar spot. I figure that must mean something. The fact that we were together would always be good.

Focusing for the Reader

Readers do not like to be confused. In fact, they won't be confused; they'll just stop reading. It is essential that the readers know, in the beginning, in the middle, and in the end that the writer has a focus, that everything that is being said relates to and develops a main point.

The focus of the piece of writing is the North Star the writer uses during everything else that follows. It is normal for the writer to have found more material than can be used. It is also normal for that material to be interesting. But it cannot be used in the piece of writing unless it has a significant relationship to the main point.

Sometimes writers rush ahead and choose the genre and develop the structure before they have a potential focus. Other times, writers will even produce an entire draft, and then try to figure out what it means. That may be a good technique for fiction or the personal narrative, but even there it is an inefficient way of writing. Experienced writers anticipate the reader's needs and delay ordering or drafting a piece of writing until they have found a focus.

The focus may change, however, as the ordering or drafting educates the writer. That's a natural process. It would be nonsense to stick to a focus regardless of what's happening during the writing of the piece. Military history is full of generals and admirals who stuck to a good plan regardless of what was happening. They weren't winners.

Put yourself in the reader's place and imagine what you would need to be served by the writer. What one thing do you need or want to be taught by the piece of writing?

Questions about Focusing

• *What if what I want to say has been said before?*

It probably has, but don't worry about it. It hasn't been said by you. Your own particular background and way of thinking and speaking may make it different.

But the difference isn't the important thing. The important thing is to have a well-explored subject, a piece of writing that is so well made it will stand up and speak to a reader.

And remember that at this stage you can't be sure just what you're going to say. You may have a focus—you know the island you want to explore—but you haven't done the exploration yet. A good piece of writing will almost always be different when it is finished from what the writer thought it would be when the writing process began.

- *What's more important?*

What the reader needs to know or what you would need to know if you were the reader.

- *What if what I think is most important isn't what the teacher thinks is most important?*

You have to be able to support your idea of what's important with convincing evidence. That evidence will be lined up and presented to the reader during the next stages of the writing process. But, of course, this depends on the teacher. Some teachers believe there is only one right answer, and you may have to find that answer to pass the course, but most college teachers are willing to be persuaded if you have a specific focus supported by concrete evidence.

- *Everything seems equally important.*

Ah, that's the challenge. You have to find the key, or just decide arbitrarily for this piece of writing that one element is most important. You can write about two or three things that are equally important, but then you have to find a way of making the combination of them most important—for example: "Most law school professors agree that there are three qualities an effective courtroom lawyer needs," or, "There are four equal forces that came together and led us into the Vietnam War."

- *My focus seems too personal.*

Most good writing does start from a personal point of view. The writer thinks and cares. The writing, however, shouldn't sound too personal. You need to get out of the way and let the evidence speak for itself.

The reader is persuaded by information, not by being told what to think (remember how long it was since you really enjoyed the sermon?). As you move from focusing to clarifying, you will be providing the information for the reader. The starting point may be personal, but in many cases the final draft will be written in such a way that the reader will be convinced by the objectivity and the fairness of the prose.

• *I think I'm too close to the subject.*

Then stand back. Role-play someone who doesn't know the subject. The most obvious things about the subject may be the most important.

• *I'm too far away from the subject. I guess I don't care about it.*

Then find a new subject that you do care about, or at least want to explore.

• *But it's an assignment—I don't have any choice.*

You have to find a way to make the assignment your own. Get in and do the research, root around the information, see what connections you can make with your own experience. Professional writers learn how to take assignments and adjust them so that they write on their own territory. For example, a football player faced with an abstract assignment on ethics may be able to write a strong essay about the issues he faced when a coach taught him, as one of my coaches taught me, how to make illegal blocks and get away with it.

• *What if my focus isn't the right one?*

There isn't usually a right one, and that's something that's hard for most beginning college students to accept. William Perry of Harvard has done studies that show college freshmen want to find an absolute right or wrong. That's natural, but college is not a place where you get precise answers; it's where you discover how to ask good questions. We live in a complicated and complex world, and although for some of us there are absolute wrongs (if I were president, I would make it a capital offense for anyone to eat a smelly, gooey, soft-boiled, poached, or sunnyside-up egg in a public place—but I would face pressure from egg lovers, the police and courts who would have to enforce the law, and the egg lobby), most issues are complex.

In writing there ain't nothing that is absolutely right or wrong. I just used incorrect English, on purpose, to make a point and get attention, and therefore it became correct. In writing what works is right. You can write correctly and produce unreadable prose. You can write incorrectly and communicate. This is one of the things that makes writing hard—and fun.

Focusing Activities _____

1. Circle your subject, performing each of the activities listed in the chapter, or picking out those that spark your interest.
2. Go back to Chapter 2 and look over the collecting techniques to see if there are one or two you want to try to help you find a focus.
3. Collaborate with another student to see if he or she can help you find the focus. You can, for example, try out potential focus or describe your subject to see what interests that test reader.

4. Think back to the techniques you've used in other areas of your life—on a job, playing a sport, resolving problems with people, studying a subject—to find out what methods you used to focus on what was important. Try that method to develop a focus on your subject.

5. If you've kept a process log or daybook, go back through it to see those words, facts, or ideas that keep recurring. They may tell you where the focus of the subject is. I find that certain ideas will keep coming up, sort of like a whale that surfaces from time to time. When I spot that recurring information or thought it may become the focus for the piece I'm going to write.

6. Make lists in answer to the following questions about the area you are exploring through writing.

   ▶ What surprises you?
   ▶ What made you mad?
   ▶ What made you laugh?
   ▶ What made you curious?
   ▶ What information could you make use of?
   ▶ What would you like to know more about?
   ▶ What forces are in the material?
   ▶ Where do those forces intersect?
   ▶ Where do they work together?
   ▶ Where do they work against each other?

   Make up your own questions, and ask them of yourself.

7. Put away your notes and write in one sentence the most important thing about the subject you're exploring. Be specific. Nail it down.

8. Make believe you're the reader. Tell you, the writer, what you'd like to know about the subject.

9. Tell someone about your subject. Listen to what you say to see if you reveal the focus.

10. Study the student case history. Compare how the student focused her paper with how she might have done it. Decide what works and doesn't work for you. Why? What might have been done differently?

11. Imagine the piece you are going to write after it has been published in a journal or magazine or book or newspaper. Describe it to yourself. What would the title be like? The ending? The length? The approach?

12. Take a football game or a scientific experiment or a legislative decision and talk with the people involved to discover the most important moment in the series of actions, discoveries, and decisions that occurred. Practice looking for such key moments as you watch a game, a movie, a governmental hearing, or work on an experiment.

Chapter 5

ඣ Explore Your
Subject: ORDER

Has a drinking song ever been written by a drunken man? It is wrong
to think that feeling is everything. In the arts, it is nothing without
form.

GUSTAVE FLAUBERT

Prose is architecture, not interior decoration.

ERNEST HEMINGWAY

Because I'm interested in structure, I must sound mechanistic. But it's
just the opposite. I want to get the structural problems out of the way
first, so I can get to what matters more. After they're solved, the only
thing left for me to do is tell the story as well as possible.

JOHN MCPHEE

129

Wait. Don't write yet.

Well, it may be the time to write. Don't pay too much attention to me. You may have collected a pile of information, found a focus, and feel you're ready to plunge ahead. Try it. It may work. You may write so fast you will feel you're on automatic pilot, with everything falling into place without conscious effort. The writing may be writing itself.

It's wonderful when that happens. Follow the text to the end. Do not interrupt the flow of prose. But more often, we find we have flown into the side of a mountain, smiling with confidence right up to the moment of impact. Other times, the plane suddenly starts to wobble and then heads into a nosedive.

Most of the time we write too soon, and run into problems that could have been solved in advance, or lose our way and have to waste time starting over again and again and again, hoping that by shooting in the dark we'll hit the target. Virginia Woolf told herself in her diary, "As for my next book, I am going to hold myself from writing it until I have it impending in me; grown heavy in my mind like a ripe pear pendant, gravid, asking to be cut or it will fall."

As you move through the writing process, you move closer to the reader, and it may be appropriate to become more aware of the reader's needs. You'll feel most comfortable doing this if collecting and focusing have made you feel confident of your material and its significance. You may feel less comfortable confronting the reader if you're still deeply in the process of discovery. There is no right or wrong to this. Sometimes you'll want to be aware of the reader, and that awareness will help you order the piece; other times you'll have to ignore any reader but yourself and use the ordering techniques to help you understand the pattern of meaning within your subject.

Many a battle is lost because the general follows the plan regardless of what happens on the battlefield. A writing plan is not an order or a binding contract. It is a sketch, a guess, a hunch, a suggestion—"Hey, let's head for the beach." When you write you may not get to the beach, you may stop along the way, decide to go to the mountains, run into some interesting people and spend time with them. The picnic may be eaten in a restaurant or the restaurant food taken out on the rocks. But it helps to have a plan, to have a sense of destination, and that is what planning writing gives you. And most of the time you do go to the beach.

The Effective Design

Most people think that writing appears magically as if a wand passed over a blank piece of paper. And there are those precious moments when the writer feels that way too. For a few minutes, every ten or twelve years, that happens. It isn't worth waiting for. And when it does happen there's a good chance that what seemed magical the night before is anything but magical in the morning.

Built. Constructed. Planned. Made. Designed. Those are the words that writers use over and over again, talking to each other, and most of all, talking to themselves at the workbench.

I have a physical feeling about a good piece of writing. I can shove it, pick it up and drop it, kick it, jump up and down on it (and I am a sumo class writer), and it will hold its shape.

That is important, because the form of a piece of writing, in a way, is the meaning of a piece of writing. A lyric poem says that there is a song to be sung. An argument implies argument, a proposal means there is something to propose. Opinion. Report. Such words contain their own design, and that design is an expression of what they mean. A story, for example, implies a beginning, a middle, and an end, and characters, place, and dramatic action between the characters, that grows out of the past and ignites a change.

There is a danger in this, and all writers should be aware of it. Journalists begin to see the world through the lens of a news story. That can be a clarifying or a blinding vision; the important event may be spotted or missed. We tend to write in those forms with which we have had success in the past, and to be able to do it we may try to pour experience into that structure, even if the facts do not fit it. We may, for example, like to write biography, and so we see history as caused by individuals, when some history is caused by forces that are not manmade, or if manmade are not the result of an individual action. Our designs give order to the confusion of our lives, but we should never forget that simplification of confusion always has the danger of oversimplification.

Still, it is the writer's need and purpose to bring order from chaos. It may be, as Robert Frost said, "a momentary stay against the confusion of the world," or what Saul Bellow describes as "the achievement of stillness in the midst of chaos. A stillness which characterizes prayer, too, and the eye of the storm. I think that art has something to do with an arrest of attention in the midst of distraction."

We must create designs that reveal and communicate meaning, but we must never think that there is one design, or that a design can always hold its shape against new experience. Still, the creation of design is at the center of the play of writing. It is a way that we make sense of our lives, and it is so important that we should never take it too seriously and work rigidly, but always sketch out designs so that they can be not only filled in, but changed or discarded through the process of drafting and developing our meaning.

The Elements of an Effective Design

Designs that contain meaning, and more than that, become meaning themselves so they can travel into teachers' minds and be understood, usually have similar elements.

• *Walls.* A design includes and excludes, it limits the subject; it supplies a unity by bringing together those things that belong together, and leaving out those other elements, no matter how interesting, that do not belong in this particular piece of writing.

• *A point.* This is a point of emphasis, a focal point, a central hub in one design, the point of an arrow in another, the top rung of a ladder in still another. Think of it as a room. The point may be the fireplace, the view outside, the arrangement of chairs to encourage conversation, the location of the TV set that prohibits conversation, the well-lit chair for reading, the darkened chair that will discourage reading. Each effective design has a main point.

• *Energy.* Most people forget this, and they create an outline or order that is flat and static. A successful design flows, and some interesting designs are called flowcharts for that reason; they lead the eye and the mind through a series of actions. A good design stimulates the writer to think. It is not just a reflection of what has been thought, but a catalyst to cause continued thought.

• *Relationships.* "Only connect," said E. M. Forster. It is the job of the designer–writer to relate facts, details, ideas, quotations, people, events, theories, principles, observations, reflections—all the various elements of the world that is being designed, so that they relate to each other, and through that relationship reveal meaning.

• *Resolution.* The effective design has a sense of completion, not perhaps a final theological sense of Absolute Truth, but that moment of stillness, that momentary stay, that educated guess. The reader and the writer both need to have their sense of order satisfied, at least for the moment, to have a vision of meaning or truth with a small *t* that they can consider and reconsider as they start to construct a new design.

Look at other writers' designs and your own. Decide what are the elements of design that worked for you, so that you develop a mental checklist that will help you as you sketch out the meaning that you will develop in a draft.

Primary Technique for Ordering Your Writing: The Promising Opening

Effective writing opens with a promise to the reader.

And the nature of that promise solves many of the writer's problems.

We usually think of the opening—beginning or lead—of a piece of writing in terms of the reader—and we should. Readers are in a hurry, they have many distractions, we have seconds—no more—in which to catch and hold the reader's attention.

The opening promises information the reader wants or needs. It promises clarity, grace, and surprise, just a bit more than the reader expects. It promises, however, to satisfy the reader's expectations; a narrative tells a story, an argument makes one. It provides a tension that produces the energy that drives the story forward. The opening promises a closing, a sense of completion.

The writer must be aware of the promises made in the opening if they are to be fulfilled. And therein lies the importance of the opening for the writer.

Joan Didion reports, "What's so hard about the first sentence is that you're stuck with it. Everything else is going to flow out of that sentence. And by the time you've laid down the first *two* sentences, your options are all gone." Elie Wiesel adds, "With novels it's the first line that's important. If I have that the novel comes easily. The first line determines the form of the whole novel. The first line sets the tone, the melody. If I hear the tone, the melody, then I have the book."

An effective opening solves most of the problems the writer would face in the first draft and solves them efficiently, ahead of time, when the writer is not trapped in a tangle of prose. Let's list what the opening establishes:

► The focus
► The context
► The form
► The evidence
► The voice
► The writer's authority
► The audience
► The length
► The pace
► The order
► The closing

Whew. It *is* a long list but it can also be a checklist for drafting and revising an opening that will make the writing go quickly and go well. Some of the items on the checklist will take time, others may be dealt with in a matter of seconds.

How to Write an Effective Opening

I *never* proceed without an opening that I think will produce a good piece of writing. That's the only never in my personal tool box. That opening may not produce a piece of writing that works and I may have to start over; what I discover in the writing may require a new opening; but I know only one place to start: at the beginning.

The search for the opening begins when I receive the assignment or when I realize I have a piece of writing that must be brought to paper. Sometimes the idea for a piece of writing comes to me in the form of the line or sentence or paragraph that is the opening.

In every case, I play with potential openings all during the research and planning process. I note possible openings in my head, in my daybook, in my file on the computer for that topic.

When it is time to write I play with openings. Play is important. I must be free to make discoveries, free enough to allow what I am writing to tell me what I need to say and how I need to say it.

I used to write at least fifty to seventy-five openings for every article or book I wrote. After fifty years of writing, I am not that compulsive and I don't keep count. Once every couple of years an opening will come to me that seems just right the first time, but most of the time, my openings are a product of careful, logical play. Let's use that checklist to reveal some of the tricks I practice to find an effective opening, one that will attract readers and solve my writing problems.

• *The Focus.* I look for surprise and tension expressed in a line. By line, I mean the force released when one word runs into another. I am writing a book that began when I wrote in my daybook that, "I had an ordinary war." But what terrible events become ordinary in combat! That line had surprise, it made me realize what horrors I had accepted while at the front, and it had tension between the words ordinary and war. In drafting openings, I look for what I have learned during the researching, thinking, and planning and I look for the point of conflict or tension where energy may be released by writing. This part of the opening writing process may take time, but it is never wasted. Unless I have the focus, I will waste time writing.

• *The Context.* The surprise and tension must have significance. It must be more than an isolated fact—few college men wear boxer shorts. The focus must exist in a context, it must illuminate a matter of some importance—or interest— to the reader.

• *The Form.* The draft opening makes me aware of the form or genre that will develop what I have to say. Unless the form has been assigned, I find in drafting the opening that I am writing an essay, a short story, an argument, an academic article, a humorous newspaper column. The opening tells the reader the form to expect and the writer knows how to deal with those expectations.

• *The Evidence.* Statistics, quotations, revealing details, description, academic documentation, all the forms of evidence are implied by the opening. In choosing a particular opening, I am choosing the forms of evidence that will make the writing believable.

• *The Voice.* I read the openings I draft over and over, listing to the music of the evolving text. Yes, my writing has my voice but, more important, it has its own voice, my voice tuned to the subject, its treatment, its audience. The music of the text supports and reveals the meaning of that text, first to the writer and later to the reader. And the music—melody, beat, tone—established in the opening must be used throughout the draft.

• *The Writer's Authority.* Most writers have only a moment or two to establish their authority, their right to be listened to by a reader on this subject. A few writers have a reputation and that means the reader *may* read a few paragraphs before deciding to read on or put the text aside. I look at every opening and ask, "Would I believe this guy?" If not, I rework the opening, usually making the information more specific and the tone of voice more confident.

• *The Audience.* An effective opening has a specific reader in mind. In my columns, for example, I aim for the person who is over sixty. I hope others will read the columns and they do, but I am speaking to a special audience. The opening should appeal to a target reader.

• *The Length.* The length is usually implied in the opening. It tells the reader, for example, that the piece is an exhaustive treatment of an entire subject or a detailed examination of one part of the larger subject.

• *The Pace.* I use the opening to check the pace as quickly as I check the length. The opening signals the reader that this will be a leisurely stroll through the subject or a hard hitting argument, fact on fact.

• *The Order.* The opening often establishes the sequence or structure the writer will use to develop the text. The opening may make the reader expect a logical construction, a process of problem-solving activities, an accumulation of detail. I check my opening to see if it predicts, even controls, the order of what I am going to write.

• *The Closing.* The end must connect with the opening. What has been promised must have been delivered. Read the opening over to see what closing it implies.

Checklist

After you have written your final opening, read it again to make sure your opening is:

• *Quick.* The reader will decide to read on—or not to read on—in a matter of seconds.

• *Accurate.* The reader who spots a tiny error will refuse to believe anything you write.

• *Honest.* Don't hoke up an opening to tease the reader, because you must deliver what you promise.

• *Simple.* Cut back the underbrush. Use proper nouns, active verbs, and concrete details whenever possible.

• *Packed with Information.* The effective opening gives the reader information, and that information makes the reader want to read on.

• *Heard.* The reader should hear an individual writer speaking directly to the reader.

Categories of Effective Openings

It may be helpful to take a piece of paper and list the kind of openings you have in your writer's toolbox. Most of us have many more ways of beginning a piece of writing than we realize. Some of the openings in my toolbox are:

• *News.* Tell the reader what the reader needs to know in the order the reader needs to know it. Check the five Ws—who, what, when, where, why.

• *Anecdote.* This is a brief story that captures the essence of what you will be dealing with. It is the most popular magazine opening, but watch out—if it's a good story but doesn't aim the reader in the direction you want the reader to go, the whole piece may be lost.

• *Quotation.* A quote is a good device, for it gives additional authority and an extra voice to the piece. Like the anecdotal opening, however, it must be right on target.

• *Umbrella.* This is an opening that covers several equal, or almost equal, elements in the story. "The Second World War, according to Morison, was caused by three events."

• *Descriptive.* The writer sets the scene for the story. Remember to use specifics.

• *Voice.* Voice is an important element in every opening, but in some it is the most important element. It establishes the tone of communication between reader and writer. Read aloud and make sure that the voice is communicating information.

• *Announcement.* This lead tells the reader what you are going to say. Most of the time you just want to say it. Get out of the way. Do not write an introduction.

• *Tension.* This opening reveals the forces in the story in action. They are coming together on a collision course, or pulling against each other. The opening contains the forces, and makes the reader feel the tension between them.

• *Problem.* The opening establishes the problem that will be solved, or not solved, in the piece.

• *Background.* The writer first gives the reader the background of an event, argument, conflict, issue, or action.

• *Narrative.* This opening establishes that the story will be told in narrative form. Be careful not to start too early. Start as near to the end as possible to involve the reader in the story.

• *Question.* This sounds like it should work, but it rarely does. The writer usually knows the answer to the question and so it sounds patronizing, like the nurse who says, "Now we would like to take our medicine, wouldn't we?"

• *Point of View.* The writer establishes the position from which the reader will be shown the subject.

• *Reader Identification.* The inexperienced writer tries to do this by speaking directly to the reader in the second person, saying, "you . . ." That doesn't usually work. The reader identifies best with a "he" or a "she," best of all with a specific name.

• *Face.* A character is revealed in action. The reader becomes interested in the person and then the issue.

• *Scene.* The writer establishes a scene that is central to the meaning of the piece.

• *Dialogue.* The reader hears one person speak and another react. It's not often you can use this opening, but when it's appropriate, it is dramatic and provides a lot of energy.

• *Process.* A process central to the story is shown in action, and the reader is carried forward into the story.

These are not all the ways to write openings. They are samples from my own toolbox. Make a list of the openings you like to write, and then look through periodicals and books to see other ways of writing them. Steal them. And also pay attention to the beginnings you see in movies and on television. Those were all written too, and we can learn from each other.

Additional Techniques for Ordering Your Writing: Titles _____

Most writers don't write titles. They let editors do that, and then complain that the title doesn't fit the article. I never wrote titles until, as a junior editorial writer, I got to work by myself on Sunday. I was my own editor, and I was able to write my own titles. Then I started writing the titles first, and found it greatly improved my writing.

In writing the title, I captured the direction of the story, a glimpse of its limitations and pace. Most of all, I discovered its tone. Now when I write an article, I take the time to brainstorm many titles. I average about 150 titles before I settle on one. The one may be the second or third or thirteenth title, but I don't know it's the right one until I see the others that don't work.

It doesn't take much time to write a title. In fact, it's something that can be best done in small chunks of time—while waiting for a class to begin or for a friend to come out of the store, or sitting in a car when the drawbridge is up, or waiting for a string of commercials to get off the tube. As in all brainstorming, you have to be willing to come up with silly titles, even stupid ones, to get to those that may work.

When I begin to brainstorm titles, some are just labels—"War," "A Day at the Beach." Others are too long or vague or weak. A good title has a strong sense of voice; it's specific; it catches the reader and draws the reader into the article—"When I Found I Could Kill," "Bikinis, Sand Fleas, and the Undertow."

But to find those good titles, I have to write a lot of bad ones. I don't like doing it, but it seems to be part of the process for me, and I know that the time spent fishing for titles will make it possible for me to write a draft that works in a much shorter period of time than if I didn't mess around with titles first.

I start by brainstorming titles, putting down my combination of words that might become a title, making the censor stand over in the corner while I am silly, stupid, dumb, clumsy, awkward because I usually have to be all of those to finally become articulate.

When I finish brainstorming titles, I often feel a sense of disappointment, even failure. Sometimes a really exciting title leaps off the page, but usually I have a rather ordinary list and I have to look back to see if anything is happening.

I play with my list, circling a few that seem to have possibility, connecting ones that are related with arrows, editing titles into new forms, adding new ones, fooling around with the central ideas in the piece of writing, and, of course, in doing that, I begin to see the piece of writing more clearly.

I'll keep coming back to these titles and putting new ones into my daybook. The title I'll end with may look spontaneous, but it probably will be worried into place. As Phyllis McGinley said,

> There is such a thing as inspiration (lower case) but it is no miracle. It is the reward handed to a writer for hard work and good conduct. It is the felicitous word sliding, after hours of evasion, obediently into place. It is a sudden comprehension of how to manufacture an effect, finish off a line or

stanza. At the triumphant moment this gift may seem like magic but actually it is the result of effort, practice, and the slight temperature a sulky brain is apt to run when it is pushed beyond its usual exertions.

When the title does, magically (and usually after hard work), seem just right, notice how much it helps you control and direct the piece of writing. The title leads to the opening and becomes the focus for the piece of writing. It reveals its tone, limits, direction. Titles can be the greatest help you will have in finding your way toward an effective piece of writing.

Closings _____

The end is a beginning.

John Irving says, "I don't know how far away the end is—only what it is. I know the last sentence, but I'm very much in the dark concerning how to get to it." "If I didn't know the end of a story, I wouldn't begin," says Katherine Anne Porter. "I always write my last line, my last paragraph, my last page first," Eudora Welty agrees. "I think the end is implicit in the beginning. It must be. If that isn't there in the beginning, you don't know what you're working toward. You should have a sense of a story's shape and form and its destination, all of which is like a flower inside a seed."

Many good writers know where they want to end before they begin to write. It gives them a sense of destination. Sometimes they just have the closing in mind, but often they write the end first. They know, of course, that the closing may change after the piece is written, but it still helps during the writing to have a closing in sight.

Only rarely in effective writing is the closing a formal summary or conclusion in which the writer repeats in general or abstract terms what has already been said. The most effective closings are usually the same devices that make effective openings: specific detail, quotation, anecdote, scene, and all those other tools listed in the section on openings.

Asking the Reader's Questions _____

There's a myth that popular writers write down to the reader, that the reader is a slob with a fifth-grade education who picks his teeth with a beer can. Not so. The reader is an intelligent person who may not know the subject, but is no dope.

The reader will ask good, intelligent questions of any piece of writing, and the experienced writer will answer those questions, not by writing down but by writing across to the reader, using a tone of voice the writer would use to an equal.

Sometimes it helps me to imagine sitting across from my desk, sprawled in an armchair, a skeptical, surly doubting Thomas. I make a statement, and my reader snarls, "Who says?" And I stick in an attribution. I say something else, and the reader asks, "How come?" I stop and tell the reader how come. I write another paragraph and the reader says, "What's that mean?" I tell the reader what it means. The reader snarls, "Who cares?" And I make sure the reader knows the importance of what I'm saying.

Other times I imagine a specific person, an individual who is not all impressed by me or what I know about the subject. And by writing to that person I make my draft clear.

Sometimes we have to write for several different readers. In that case, I pick one of them and write for that person. In the revision process, I will read and revise for each of the other readers. But I must focus on a single reader at a time.

Good writing is a conversation between an individual writer and an individual reader. The writer has to anticipate where the reader is in that conversation and deliver the information the reader needs when the reader needs it.

Sometimes the reader asks so many nasty questions I can no longer write. I get mad at this surly, overly critical baboon who makes me feel dumb and inadequate. When that happens, I send him out of the room. I'll deal with him later, after the draft is done, during the last stage of the writing process, when I have to invite him in anyway. He isn't polite about leaving. Sometimes he even makes obscene gestures, and wears that all-knowing sneer that says, "I'll get you later." Fair enough. I'll have to deal with him later, but when I do, there will be a text we can read together. If I don't get him out of the room there will be no text at all.

After I have drafted the questions the reader will ask, I put them in the order the reader will ask them. That's always predictable and I have begun to outline my article.

~ Outlines _____

Outline is a nasty word for many students, and I was one of them, for it is often taught in such a rigid manner that it doesn't work. An outline is not a formal blueprint that has to be followed precisely; it is not a contract, and you can't be sued if you break it. An outline is a sketch, a guess, a scribbled map that may lead to a treasure.

Outlines are written by experienced writers with the knowledge that the writing will change the structure and the meaning of the writing. Writers may create outlines and then not refer to them during the writing, for what they learned by making the outline allows them to get on with the writing. Sometimes it is also helpful to make outlines in the middle of the writing to see where you've gone and where you might go, and at the end of the draft to see what you have discovered through the writing and how you have organized your material.

There are many ways to outline, but I will list ten here to show how different outlines can be. None of these is *the* way to outline. Develop your own system of outlining. Outline only if it helps you, and then outline in a way that provides that help.

Outline 1

We have already created my favorite form of outline in this chapter:

▶ Title
▶ Opening
▶ Ask—and answer—the Reader's Questions
▶ Closing

Outline 2

The formal outline may be appropriate for a formal, very structured subject. It uses arabic and roman numerals and capital and small letters to break down a subject into categories and subcategories in a logical sequence. There are also numerical outlines that are popular in some disciplines and many computer software programs have a formal-outline pattern built in.

The most formal outline requires a full and complete sentence for each entry, but most people just use fragments, as signals for what will be said. I would urge you to be careful of the formal "Harvard" outline because it may inhibit the search and discovery of meaning that should come during the writing.

Outline 3

A writer friend of mine, Donald H. Graves, uses this outline form. He lists everything that might be included in the piece of writing in the left-hand column; then he moves items to the columns marked Beginning, Middle, End.

Some of the things don't get moved, of course, and others come to mind as the outline is being made and go right into the appropriate column. Some things in the left-hand column are not used. It's a brainstorming list, and it becomes an inventory of material that may be used. And some items that are not on the list come to mind when the writer is working on the right-hand columns. The items are ordered—by number—within the columns after the writer has finished. Then the writer is ready to write.

Outline 4

A way to use the outline to dramatize the importance of certain parts of the piece of writing to the reader is to make a box outline in which the size of each box represents the importance of each part. The first paragraph, for example, is much more important to the reader than the pages that follow and might be two inches by four.

The subject of the next four pages is indicated in a phrase contained in a box only a quarter of an inch by two inches.

A main turning point might be in a box one inch by three and then the rest of the piece in another tiny box. Finally, the closing might be in a box as larger—or larger—than the first paragraph.

This outline really forces me to face up to the importance of the opening and the ending—to the importance of what I'm going to say and how I'm going to say it. It also forces me to see the structure of the piece in stark, efficient terms.

Outline 5

A fine way to outline, especially on a complicated subject, is to brainstorm the questions the reader will ask and then put them in the order the reader will ask them.

This is a repetition of what we have said but it is such an effective outlining technique by itself, I am including it again. It has saved the day for me—and hundreds of my students—when we have faced an especially complicated topic.

There will usually be five questions—sometimes three or four, sometimes six or seven, but most likely five. You don't want to use the questions in the text, but simply give the answers. The questions are in the reader's mind; the writer anticipates and answers them.

Outline 6

The writer can adapt outline forms from other disciplines. I often find it helpful to use a flowchart, similar to those used in systems engineering and in business-organization study. These charts are designed to show how a factory works, how a material flows from a natural resource to a manufactured product, how power flows into a corporation. Using this device I can often spot a movement or force that can order my piece.

Outline 7

A related outline form I find useful I've borrowed from computers. Computer users have developed a number of different forms of outlining that break down complicated subjects into their sequential parts. Most of these outlines flow from left to right.

At the left I ask a question: "How Can I Teach Writing?", then I give two extreme answers, one above the question and over to the right—by allowing students to write first—another below and over to the right—by telling students what and how to write first.

I break down every answer this way until I see a pattern of potential meaning emerging.

Outline 8

In many effective pieces of writing, fiction as well as nonfiction, each chunk of writing—a paragraph, a page, a scene—answers a question and asks a new question. For example, will they get married? Yes, but will they be happy? Or, will the product sell? Yes, but will it bring a profit?

Outline 9

Many fine writers, such as John McPhee and John Gregory Dunne, use a card technique to outline. This is the most popular technique of movie script writers.

Each element in the writing is put on a card, sometimes using cards of different colors for different characters, or different kinds of material in nonfiction. Then the cards are pinned to a cork board and moved around so the writer can see the pattern of the entire piece—book, movie, or article.

Outline 10

A way to see how a piece of writing is shaping up is to make file folders for each topic within the piece of writing. This is helpful on a large project. You can renumber and move the file folders around, and you can put all your raw material right into a folder—clips, photocopied articles, notes, photographs. When a folder is full, it may have to be divided. When it has nothing in it, you may have to drop that topic, or do more research.

Try out these outline forms, and then try to make up others that fit the way your head works. There's no way to outline, and no ten ways to outline. But you should find some way of preseeing what you may write.

Yes, there are writers who say that they do not outline, but if you interview them, as I have, you find that most of them have outlined in their head, sometimes without being aware they were doing it. That happens to me sometimes, I just know where the writing is going and how it is going there. It seems like a feeling, even though it's probably a very organized intellectual act.

What do you do if you feel that way? I write. I don't outline unless I feel the need to outline. But I do find that most of the time my drafts collapse unless I have outlines in my head or on paper.

Of course, when you outline you may realize that you need more information, or that you need a different focus, and you have to go back through one or both of the earlier stages of the writing process. That isn't failure. You haven't made a mistake. That's one of the big reasons to outline, so that you will see the information you need to have before you write the draft. You will see, by outlining, if you have the information to develop the focus.

Experimenting with Form: Analysis _____

Analysis is as important to the writer's toolbox as the wrench is to the mechanic. Analysis helps us take apart an idea, an event, a feeling, a text to see how it works, to discover what it means.

Analysis is a work of the mind more than the emotions even though we analyze emotional matters as I do in the writer's case history that follows.

We have to be close enough to what we are analyzing to be able to examine it but distant enough to be critical. We analyze by questioning what is under study. That makes many people uncomfortable. We are taught it is not nice to question; it is even dangerous, to some people, to doubt, be skeptical, to question.

Graham Greene once asked a profound question: "Isn't disloyalty as much the writer's virtue as loyalty is the soldier's?" The writer is cursed with this disloyalty. We question ourselves, family, friends, neighbors, strangers. We question the world.

Writers are takers apart. We dissect, x-ray, analyze, looking for causes and effects, theories, patterns, systems. The only defense of our lonely trade is that we are also putter-togetherers.

We construct in our analyses new buildings of meaning that bring order, sense, and reason. And these new constructions of ours will face analysis from others as the intellectual world struggles to understand.

The principal elements of effective analysis include a clear and *fair* statement or description of what is to be taken apart, a logical process of dissection complete with evidence at each step of the way, a tone or voice that is appropriate and convincing, and a conclusion that constructs a new meaning.

A Writer's Case History: "Living after Her Leaving" ____

I didn't want to write this article. My daughter's death is the worst thing that has happened to us; nothing else in my life compares to it. It is twelve years and the pain is immediate when I remember her—and I remember her many times every day. But I received a letter from a reader discussing his pain at losing a son and asking for any help I could give him from my experience.

I tried—and tried and retried—to write him a letter. I couldn't. I couldn't get any words down that made sense. I wandered all around the subject, mouthed clichés; I couldn't even explore what I wanted to say.

I needed structure. I needed form. I needed discipline. I needed a familiar order. I needed rhetoric.

I decided to write a column and told myself I would not publish it. The subject would be too private, but by using the familiar structure of the column I might be able to write something I could turn into a letter.

Now my writing task was clear: a column of analysis in which I would try to think back and discover what I had learned from this terrible experience: What had I done? What had I learned? What did it mean? What counsel did I have for someone going down the same road?

I was going into emotional territory but I was armed with rhetoric tradition, with the limitations and experience of column writing. I had a discipline that made it possible for me to write.

The writing didn't go easily. The material was too painful for that. It was the hardest thing I had ever written and when it was done I was able to send it to the man who had written me along with a letter I could now write.

And I decided to publish it. My personal assignment in the column was to cover aging as I experienced it in the belief that others were experiencing the same thing. The death of a child is something, unfortunately, that many people over sixty have suffered.

I offered it, tentatively, to my editor, Evelynne Kramer, who found it painful to read but said it was important to publish it, and the letters I received after publication from readers over and under sixty justified our decision to publish.

Here it is as it was published under the title, "Living after Her Leaving."

1   A reader who noted in a column that we had lost a daughter at 20 writes to ask me for comfort and counsel as he walks the same road.

2   Comfort I can offer. The lonely comfort that each of us must suffer in our own way. That each loss is individual. And that we must accept. We have no choice.

3   Counsel? I have not looked back at myself to see what I may have learned. Perhaps, as we come up to the 12th anniversary of Lee's sudden leaving it is time. I worry about being too personal at times in this column but the readers' response in the past has reminded me that we can, at times, connect and help each other.

4   I do know that those who are Over Sixty who have had a child leave ahead of them experience a special, continuing sense of loss.

5   I can only speak honestly and directly of what I did and do. I cannot speak of what her mother does and her sisters. We are together—and alone.

6   Each of us has to understand and accept each other's individual loneliness. We reach out to comfort each other but we, each in our own way, grieve alone.

7   I wept openly and frequently. My wife could not—then. She felt guilty at times about that. No reason she should. I did not feel guilty about my manly tears, she should not feel guilty about her womanly silence. There is no measuring stick to grief and should not be.

8   These are some landmarks in my own landscape of grief and remembering:

9   • I do not forget Lee—and I will not forget Lee. When I am asked how many children I have, I say three. I can remember being critical of people who spoke of the dead as if they were living, who kept pictures on the mantle of those who are gone. It made me uncomfortable.

10   I am no longer critical. I will not push her aside or exclude her. I talk of her, and with her. She was with me in intensive care, she sits in the rocker nearby as I write this.

11   • Worth repeating. We grieve in our own way. Only by accepting feelings and dealing with them, only by accepting our loneliness and dealing with it, can we make ourselves ready to reach out to others.

12   After Lee's death one of the hardest things I had to do was to drive alone in the car. More than once I stopped by the side of the road and howled. Like an animal in grief and loss. It was a primitive and essential comfort.

13   • I could never forget that I was not the only one she left. I tried to reach out to my wife, her sisters, her boyfriend [who, with his wife, are our friends today], her friends. It was a comfort to comfort them, to reach out and do for the living what we cannot do for her. In her memory— and for our own needs.

14   And my wife, Minnie Mae, and Lee's sisters, Anne and Hannah, in those cruel days at the hospital, the weeks afterwards, and the years since, have taught this combat veteran a hundred lessons in strength and courage.

15   • And I who always wants to drive, to be in control, to give, learned something about accepting. The night we came home from the hospital, Phyllis Heilbronner knelt by my chair and fed me, bite by bite. The Lindens held us in their arms as did Hans Heilbronner; the Clarks and others kept walking by the house to make sure there were not too many people visiting; the Graves, Father Joe Desmond, the Swifts, the Robin-

sons, the Griewanks, the Ladds, the Mertons, the Milnes, and dozens of other friends and neighbors cared for us and still do. Karen Mower's letter, and all the other notes, meant so much. They all taught me to receive as well as give, never to apologize for my needing their love.

16   • I had to accept Lee's death from Reye's Syndrome. Most survive; our daughter did not. We had to remove extraordinary means—our beautiful Lee looked as if she were asleep but she was brain dead—and I had to execute her family's decision. I still have day visions and night dreams of her hopping up, laughing, saying it was a joke.

17   It was not. And I have to realize that her death, and my grief, is simply a condition of my life, as much a part of me as the nearsightedness, the funny walk, the sense of humor she and I shared. My grief was not going to go away. It was there, to be lived with, made part of me.

18   • And I've learned to avoid. Our favorite instrument was the oboe and we had a large collection of oboe recordings. Lee had just been accepted at the New England Conservatory to study oboe when she died. I know it makes her unhappy, but we cannot listen to those soaring melodies. Not yet.

19   • But we can celebrate life. In fact, my life seems, in some strange way, a gift from Lee. After the days in the hospital, after her burial, after I had begun to get through parts of days instead of parts of hours, I remember walking home from work and realizing that I had done what I had to do, for Lee, for her sisters, for my wife. I was 53 years old and I made, in that moment, the first step in accepting myself. I was far from what I wanted to be, from what I thought the world thought I should be, but I had made it. I wasn't so bad after all.

20   • Lee's death reminded me not only to accept myself but to appreciate the life I have left. My private memorial, never mentioned to anyone before, is to take pleasure in small things. Perhaps the submarine sandwich with everything on it Lee liked so much, certainly the Handel organ concerto that is playing on the hi fi this moment, the pattern of sun and shadow on my hands as I write this that is different from yesterday because the leaves have begun to unfold this late spring. She would want me to appreciate such moments of life. When I get busy and forget, Lee reminds me. I stop. I celebrate, for her, the life she celebrated but left so early.

21   Lee, I'm sure, was with me the other morning when I whistled at a bird and it whistled back. For a quarter of a mile the bird and I continued our conversation. Lee was listening—and laughing.

22   And I reach out, as I have tried to here, believing that if we are honest and open to each other, that pain can be shared, and if not healed, at least accepted and survived.

Now let me re-read this essay with you, pointing out the specific problems I faced in the writing and discussing my way of attempting to solve them.

1 A reader who noted in a column that we had lost a daughter at 20 writes to ask me for comfort and counsel as he walks the same road.

Not a great opening, but at least it is direct and it sets up the pattern of the essay for the reader—and for me.

2 Comfort I can offer. The lonely comfort that each of us must suffer in our own way. That each loss is individual. And that we must accept. We have no choice.

Here I state a theme that runs through the piece and it is a theme that makes it clear to the reader that I do not expect everyone to react as I do. It is important to give readers room, especially in a piece such as this, to respond in their own way.

3 Counsel? I have not looked back at myself to see what I may have learned. Perhaps, as we come up to the 12th anniversary of Lee's sudden leaving it is time. I worry about being too personal at times in this column but the readers' response in the past has reminded me that we can, at times, connect and help each other.

I am allowing the reader to explore the subject with me. I also face the discomfort I feel in being personal, in worrying that I am exploiting my daughter's death, by sharing my discomfort with the reader, by raising the problem I see and responding to it. We can make the reader an accomplice to our writing.

This essay brings up the whole question of writing about personal or painful topics. I have found that the more personal the writer is, the more honest and direct, the greater readers identify and are helped by the writing and the more therapy the writer experiences. Still, I have my doubts.

A few weeks after Lee died, we had to

return to the hospital for a session I dreaded but that turned out to be good therapy. The first thing Dr. Shannon, who knew I was a writer, asked was if I was going to write about this. I was horrified and said "No." I was guilty because, as a writer, I had been making mental notes and even rehearsing what I might write. He said, "You have to," and my wife, Lee's sisters, and her boyfriend agreed.

4 I do know that those who are Over Sixty who have had a child leave ahead of them experience a special, continuing sense of loss.

5 I can only speak honestly and directly of what I did and do. I cannot speak of what her mother does and her sisters. We are together—and alone.

The writer can establish his or her authority to write on the subject and place limitations on that authority.

6 Each of us has to understand and accept each other's individual loneliness. We reach out to comfort each other but we, each in our own way, grieve alone.

I repeat that theme that seemed to be developing as I wrote, a theme that echoes what Dr. Shannon taught in telling me I had to write, that was my way of dealing with this tragedy. And it was all right. It was normal, natural— for me.

7 I wept openly and frequently. My wife could not—then. She felt guilty at times about that. No reason she should. I did not feel guilty about my manly tears, she should not feel guilty about her womanly silence. There is no measuring stick to grief and should not be.

Here I document what I have been saying. Yes, when I write about my family, I check with them before submitting what I have written for publication.

8 These are some landmarks in my own landscape of grief and remembering:

I had not found a simple pattern of

development, a clear sequence of what I had to say, so I use this device to bring some order to what I have to say. The items in these notes are not random or presented just as they came in the writing. I have moved them around so that they will best serve the reader and finish on a strong note.

9 • I do not forget Lee—and I will not forget Lee. When I am asked how many children I have, I say three. I can remember being critical of people who spoke of the dead as if they were living, who kept pictures on the mantle of those who are gone. It made me uncomfortable.

I confess my own feelings in the past that may also be the reader's feelings in reading this essay. I understand that, I am saying, and that's all right, just as crying or not crying is all right.

10   I am no longer critical. I will not push her aside or exclude her. I talk of her, and with her. She was with me in intensive care, she sits in the rocker nearby as I write this.

I worry that I am being too sentimental here, but it is the way I feel and I stick with it.

11 • Worth repeating. We grieve in our own way. Only by accepting feelings and dealing with them, only by accepting our loneliness and dealing with it, can we make ourselves ready to reach out to others.

12   After Lee's death one of the hardest things I had to do was to drive alone in the car. More than once I stopped by the side of the road and howled. Like an animal in grief and loss. It was a primitive and essential comfort.

The reader accepts repetition for purpose especially if you let the reader know you are repeating and if the repetition adds something to the reader's knowledge.

13 • I could never forget that I was not the only one she left. I tried to reach out to my wife, her sisters, her boyfriend [who, with his wife, are our friends today], her friends. It was a comfort to comfort them, to reach out and do for the living what we cannot do for her. In her memory—and for our own needs.

This was a surprise to me: that it was comforting to comfort others.

14 And my wife, Minnie Mae, and Lee's sisters, Anne and Hannah, in those cruel days at the hospital, the weeks afterwards, and the years since, have taught this combat veteran a hundred lessons in strength and courage.

> We need both to give and to receive. It is important to accept help. A transition to the next point.

15 • And I who always wants to drive, to be in control, to give, learned something about accepting. The night we came home from the hospital, Phyllis Heilbronner knelt by my chair and fed me, bite by bite. The Lindens held us in their arms as did Hans Heilbronner; the Clarks and others kept walking by the house to make sure there were not too many people visiting; the Graves, Father Joe Desmond, the Swfits, the Robinsons, the Griewanks, the Ladds, the Mertons, the Milnes, and dozens of other friends and neighbors cared for us and still do. Karen Mower's letter, and all the other notes, meant so much. They all taught me to receive as well as give, never to apologize for my needing their love.

> Of course I am thanking my friends and neighbors in print, but their acts can tell the reader how to behave as well as reinforce the importance of accepting help.

16 • I had to accept Lee's death from Reye's Syndrome. Most survive; our daughter did not. We had to remove extraordinary means—our beautiful Lee looked as if she were asleep but she was brain dead—and I had to execute her family's decision. I still have day visions and night dreams of her hopping up, laughing, saying it was a joke.

> The reader needs to know how Lee died and this seems the natural place to tell the reader since it supports an important point.

17 It was not. And I have to realize that her death, and my grief, is simply a condition of my life, as much a part of me as the nearsightedness, the funny walk, the sense of humor she and I shared. My grief was not going to go away. It was there, to be lived with, made part of me.

> This is one of the most important things I had to say. This grief, this loss stays with you, it becomes part of you. Sometimes people want you "to get over it." Impossible.

18 • And I've learned to avoid. Our favorite instrument was the oboe and we had a large collection of oboe recordings. Lee had just been accepted at the New England Conservatory to study oboe when she died. I know it makes her unhappy, but we cannot listen to those soaring melodies. Not yet.

> Admit what you cannot do and don't feel guilty about it.

19 • But we can celebrate life. In fact, my life seems, in some strange way, a gift from Lee. After the days in the hospital, after her burial, after I had begun to get through parts of days instead of parts of hours, I remember walking home from work and realizing that I had done what I had to do, for Lee, for her sisters, for my wife. I was 53 years old and I made, in that moment, the first step in accepting myself. I was far from what I wanted to be, from what I thought the world thought I should be, but I had made it. I wasn't so bad after all.

> I do want to have something positive to say and I discovered in writing that I did. Writing of this growth of understanding reinforces it. The writing of this essay, although painful, was constructive and helpful.

20 • Lee's death reminded me not only to accept myself but to appreciate the life I have left. My private memorial, never mentioned to anyone before, is to take pleasure in small things. Perhaps the submarine sandwich with everything on it Lee liked so much, certainly the Handel organ concerto that is playing on the hi fi this moment, the pattern of sun and shadow on my hands as I write this that is different from yesterday because the leaves have begun to unfold this late spring. She would want me to appreciate such moments of life. When I get busy and forget, Lee reminds me. I stop. I celebrate, for her, the life she celebrated but left so early.

I discovered the depth of this in writing it. I knew it on one level but had not realized how extensive it was. I hope my sharing of this isn't embarrassing to the reader but helpful. Of course I'll never know. We do not own the text we create. Each person reads such a piece, as you have, with your own autobiography. If you have not suffered the death of anyone you love, you will read it differently from those who have lost a child, a parent, a brother or a sister, a friend, a grandparent—and each of those readers will create their own texts reading mine.

We write to communicate, yes, but just as important, to allow—inspire— readers to articulate their own unread thoughts and feelings.

21 Lee, I'm sure, was with me the other morning when I whistled at a bird and it whistled back. For a quarter of a mile the bird and I continued our conversation. Lee was listening—and laughing.

I worried about this. Speaking directly to Lee, although I do it, might seem hokey or fake to a reader. The editor helped me tone this paragraph down a bit. I don't have my first draft, but this is the toned-down version.

22 And I reach out, as I have tried to here, believing that if we are honest and open to each other, that pain can be shared, and if not healed, at least accepted and survived.

This was added in my early revisions. I still think it might have been better

to drop this paragraph. It seems preachy, to wrap up everything too neatly. It tells the reader how to think and feel and I don't like to do that. I prefer to close in a way that will cause the reader to do the thinking and feeling alone. You decide.

A Student's Case History: Rebecca Durost _____

One of the most common academic tasks for students is to analyze a piece of writing and write a critical essay about it. Sometimes it is difficult for instructors to be patient as the student struggles with the critical stance. Many students merely repeat what the original writer said and find it hard to stand apart from that text and comment upon it. This critical stance, however, is a basic position for the intellectual. We think not just by absorbing a text, but by thinking about it.

Teaching writing, we teach, above all, thinking. The writer's advantage—and often our discomfort—is that writing eventually makes one stand apart and examine what is being written about. Language and rhetoric are tools of distance. In the most personal pieces of writing, the writer receives therapy because of that distance. The writer escapes, for a moment, the experience, and that casting out, that distancing, is therapeutic.

The writing we emphasize in school is as healthy for the mind as personal writing may be for the emotions. Writing allows us to make use of experience and combine it with the experience of others. It is the way people share experience and its meaning. Language and the larger structures of composition are the ways that most of us make meaning. We understand life through what we hear others say to us and through what we say to ourselves in the privacy of our minds.

When we take that private discourse and put it on paper, we gain further distance and, usually, the very act of writing teaches us things we didn't know we knew. If we share our writing with an audience—classmates and an instructor and who are all writing—we find our own thinking clarified and, by observing others thinking, we learn to make meaning in the head and on the page.

The instructor's essay gives us a chance to understand one teacher's writing environment that encourages each student to develop a meaning that answers the student's own questions and, then, may also answer the reader's questions. We can see, in this case study, how the student develops her own draft and her own thinking until there is a text worthy of being shared with readers who are not familiar with the essay that she is discussing. She is not just reviewing a piece of writing, she uses the piece of literature to ignite thought.

The Instructor's Account by Barbara Tindall

Trotting behind Becky:
A Workshop/Response Ritual

1 My writing, said William Faulkner, "... begins with a character, usually, and once he stands up on his feet and begins to move, all I do is trot along behind him with a paper and pencil trying to keep up long enough to put down what he says and does."

2 Teaching writing isn't so different. Once Becky stood up on her own feet, I jumped out of her way, to allow her to find her own reasons for writing. And like Faulkner, I merely trotted along behind, trying to understand what she said and did.

3 Becky wrote "Finding a Permanent Home" to resolve her own questions about Eisley's essay. (A search for meaning lay at the center of each successive draft.) No matter how fine my suggestions to her about writing technique and process, I had to give Becky the room to discover her own questions and to teach me about why she wrote.

4 Small group workshops are the best area I have found to provide students the freedom they need to discover their own reasons for writing. In my absence, they are invited to admit what it is they do not know, to ask questions and hypothesize with their peers. The focus of the small group workshop is a classroom of individual writers questioning and identifying their own meanings.

5 The small group workshop rids my students of me, but only momentarily. Like Faulkner trotting behind his characters, I want to know where the workshop has taken them. Their written workshop responses fill me and teach me how I can best teach them.

The Ritual and the Rules

6 Every two weeks, my students join their workshop group of three or four colleagues in writing. Although they are free of me, they carry with them my four rules of the workshop:

1. Each writer shares a draft in progress;
2. Copies are provided so that all eyes may follow the text as the piece is read;
3. Each writer is given equal time; and
4. Writers define the help they want.

7 These rules define the structure of each group meeting but not the content, the questions each student needs addressing. As students grow accustomed to our biweekly ritual, they become more interested in preparing themselves for each workshop session, reading their drafts more closely

and identifying the questions they want answered. My structure remains the same for the course of a semester; their content shifts and develops and provides the element of surprise.

8 The workshop response, collected at the following class meeting, holds each student responsible for answering two questions:

1. What are my reactions as a writer: and
2. What are my reactions as a reader?

9 The questions are purposefully general. Although I want students to see themselves in the reciprocal roles of reader and writer, more importantly, I want them to find their own reasons for responding. Early workshop responses may only be a summary of what happened. In time they learn to react to their discussions, to make the process of writing the response one that they can learn from.

10 The workshop responses are valuable documents to me, almost as valuable as their weekly drafts. A draft is frequently opaque, not always allowing the reader to see inside the writer's mind to the alternative weighed and the decisions made. The responses make student thinking overt about their own and others' writing.

11 Writing the response helps students to reconsider and think through the feedback their colleagues have offered them. Often the response is a first step for future revisions. But they also serve another purpose: from them I am instructed in the progress and needs of the class as a whole and each student individually. As the responses accumulate week after week, I read them in a variety of combinations: by student, by group, and by student and group over a period of time.

12 For my students, workshops are the focus of our classroom activities. For me—who ought not be present at these sessions—workshop responses provide the focus for my classroom and conference teaching. These responses instruct my student and me in a number of ways.

Initiating Response to a Text

13 My inexperienced writers frequently have difficulty initiating a response to their drafts, particularly before their teacher. They have little distance from their writing; it just "is." When students, however, can ask the first question or make the first statement about their drafts, I can begin teaching. When students recognize problems and successes in their writing, notions of better and worse arise from the students' own knowledge and not as willy-nilly dictates from their teacher.

14 The workshop-response ritual invites students to discover the meanings and questions their drafts raise before coming face to face with their teacher. Frequently, the issues a student raises in the response is the point at which our conference begins.

15 Just as frequently, however, the responses remind me that students' insights into their own and others' drafts can be better than my own. Stu-

dents do not always need my questions or opinions intruding upon their thinking. A response may let me know that a student is well on her way to envisioning a future draft.

Watching the Group Interact

16   Reading the responses for a single group over a period of time provides clues about the developing dynamics within the group. I look for the kinds of interaction each student finds helpful or destructive. In conference, we talk about the kinds of questions this writer can ask to get the feedback she needs. I look for potential teachers in each group and how other students respond to these leaders. In conference, we talk about how this writer can best help other writers.

17   Although the skills of asking for and giving help may seem a step removed from teaching the specifics of writing, they are skills which have a life far beyond my classroom. The emphasis on question asking shifts the locus of authority from the teacher as the bearer of right answers, to the student as problem finder and problem solver. The ability to ask questions and to seek out answers on their own should far outlive their reliance on me as their teacher of writing.

Watching Development Over Time

18   Teachers know that weekly student drafts infrequently make a steady progress up a ladder of "better writing." This frustrates students and me, when I hear their frustration.

19   The writing group responses, however, provide both my students and me with a developing chronicle of their changes as writers. Because their thinking about writing is the very subject of the responses, students recognize the subtlest changes in the questions they bring to their own and others' pieces.

20   Students save their workshop responses in folders along with their weekly drafts. Periodically, they use their folders as the basis for self-evaluation. Through an analysis of their old responses, they witness changes that they fail to recognize in their daily struggle with the blank page.

Giving Back Possession

21   Becky didn't bring "Finding a Permanent Home" to her workshop for help. She took on the assignment at semester's end. Still, asking help from a colleague was an important part of Becky's process. Through talk she clarified her purpose in writing.

22   Writing her essay, "... from the first word at the first draft to the final period," Becky wrote, "consisted of a search for the right question." The right question didn't come from me or even from my classroom but from

real talk at home with her sister. Workshops invite this kind of talk in the classroom.

23   When teachers assign questions, Becky continued, "... the student has to find a way to take possession of the question—to find some angle which relates to his or her personal knowledge." Unlike Becky, not all my students know what it means to take possession of their writing. They look for signs from me to clarify the purpose of their drafts. Workshops allow my students to take possession of their drafts with an audience of peers, before I have the chance to steal possession from them.

24   Workshops do not mean, however, that I have relinquished control over my students' learning. Rather, the workshop-response ritual requires my students to teach me first how best to teach them.

The Student's Account by Rebecca Durost

1   I first wrote about "The Brown Wasps" as a short reading-log entry, but the essay remained in my mind. I remember I felt that I hadn't quite caught it, hadn't quite grasped the essence of what Eiseley was saying. I was still intrigued, so when asked to do a literary criticism essay, I chose "The Brown Wasps" as my subject. Now all I had to do was find a topic.

2   I began by reading the essay again and asking myself questions like: What did I like about the essay? What bothered me? What was its thesis? I tried to relate the essay to myself in order to better understand it. Then ... I chickened out. My first draft was superficial, dealing mostly with Eiseley's use of language. I remained distant—like someone looking down on a field from an airplane. It was only in the last paragraph that I described my personal reaction, but it was this paragraph that felt the most important. My teacher agreed with me, so I set out to do another draft.

3   My goal in my second draft was to analyze more of Eiseley's meaning, and combine this with my personal experience. First, I wanted to pin down just what Eiseley was trying to say. I reread the essay several more times, and saw that it was a lot more complicated than I had first thought. I felt that to understand the essay I had to see it in smaller parts, so I picked out quotes that seemed to sum up the meaning of different sections. I looked at each quote separately, and made notes on what I thought they meant. Now my head was bursting with ideas, so much that I felt almost overwhelmed. Here, it was like I was walking through that field, only now all I could see were the blades of grass. I didn't know where to begin, so I showed the whole mess to my "best editor"—my sister. She always gives me helpful feedback. In fact, she helped me find the idea that later served as the focus for my essay. I was trying to think of an example in myself that proved Eiseley's idea that people need to hold onto certain memories. She asked me, "Why do people feel the need to hang on?" Because they feel like they're going to lose something. "Have you ever felt that sense of loss?" There it was. I *had* felt it. I finally understood what Eiseley was talking about.

4   By my second draft, however, I hadn't realized that this idea was the key. The essay still lacked a clear focus. I discussed it with my teacher, and she pointed out the ideas that seemed the most prominent. I still had to narrow it down to one idea. This meant editing out a lot of information because by then I knew a lot more about Eiseley's essay than the person who read mine would. In a way, this was a painful process, because I wanted to fully express my understanding of a complicated and fascinating essay to someone who had never read it.

5   Finally, in my third draft, I found a focus—the "thread" that ties the essay together. I related each part of Eiseley's essay to one idea—the sense of loss. Then I discussed how this feeling related to my own life. To me, this was the proof that Loren Eiseley's thesis was valid. By finding echoes of it in myself, I could communicate my understanding to a reader.

6   In writing this essay I went through three drafts, each quite different from the others. Each draft had its own mint-process of thinking: collecting and organizing information, writing and re-writing; but the overall process, from the first word of the first draft to the final period, consisted of a search for the right question.

7   Sometimes when students are assigned a literary criticism essay the teacher also gives them a question to answer. In this case, the student has to find a way to take possession of the question—to find some angle which relates to his or her personal knowledge and understanding of the work in question. In my case, all I had to start out with were personal feelings. Instead of imposing them on a question that already existed, I had to search them to find one. When I found the right question and asked it of myself, the answer would be a focused, meaningful essay.

8   Of course, at the time, I didn't realize that this was what I was doing. When I write, I don't consciously follow any one process. Each essay is different. I simply have a general goal in mind, some feeling for where I want to go, and then I just do what seems necessary to get there.

Becky marked up a photocopy of the essay she was going to discuss. Here is a page from Becky's reading log with the instructor's comments in the margin.

Eiseley Durost
3 reading Logs ?

Responding to quotes from "The Brown Wasps"

"You want your place in the hive more than you want a room or place where the aged can be eased gently out of the way."

Wasps & Men
the bench is
like a boulder
in a stream. You
climb on top
are not swept
away, get you
can dabble
your feet in the
water and touch
the river.

— The derelict old men and the brown winter-wasps are dying, but they cling to life as long as possible. If no one remembers you, then you almost might as well be dead. The place, the hive and the sheltering benches are symbols — the tangible, touchable thing you hold on to that stands for the statement, "I am alive. I have a share in all these |journeys|." The wasps and men are not looking for a place to die — they following a desire for life. "It is life that you want, that bruises your gray old head with the hard chairs; a man has a right to his place."

"But sometimes the place is lost in the years behind us. — Sometimes we are taken away, swept away from that place that, for whatever reason, symbolizes our place *for us* in life. The place has reality in our minds, and thus in never changes in time. It remains permanent when everything else is |transitory| Eiseley's tree sym-

neat
contrast

the "place"
|connection|
in a world
that is largely
transitory

bolizes for him his place in life. When he and his father planted it they were making a statement, saying, "We are buying stock, taking an interest in this place, this section of life." At times when you may have no |connections| with the rest of life that flows around you, when you have no share in anyone else's |journey| this memory, this home in your mind is a place-holder for when you can. As you get older you need this place to be tangible. You |fear death| and so you must assert your life. This is the reason for Eiseley's journey back to the tree. I hadn't thought of it this way the child isn't faced w/ death — only sees the transitory world ✓

We have reproduced the first page of Becky's third draft that shows her thinking in writing.

In his essay, "The Brown Wasps," Loren C. Eiseley explores the idea that, "...all living creatures...can survive only by fixing or transforming a bit of time into space or by securing a bit of space with its objects immortalized and made permanent in time." ~~When he is saying~~ *He says* that people and animals have an overwhelming need to hang on to specific places or times ~~both~~ memory. These "places in time" remain permanently ~~in the midst~~ *removed outside the stream* of life which is always changing.' When we compare this mind image with the reality of now, we see how quickly life ~~moves~~ *has moved,* *So* ~~our~~ our lives are ~~always~~ tinged with a sense of impending loss, that just makes us cling all the harder.

It is this sense of loss which tinges the whole of Eiseley's essay. ~~Through it~~ *Beneath the words* there runs the feeling, though this is never stated, that life is an uncontrollable stream that sweeps us along. We ~~must~~ *can only* hold onto the permanence of our memories ~~to hold onto~~ *to* keep from drowning. To illustrate his point Eiseley uses four main examples. *Each example shows a different kind of loss, but each victim has the same desire to hold on.* The first describes a resemblence that Eiseley has seen between the behavior of dying wasps clinging to their hives into the winter, and derelicts clinging to benches in a railway station. Both are afraid of losing their "place in the hive." For the brown wasps and the old men, the physical objects they cling to are symbols of their place in life. All creatures have a need to be involved in life, to share in the journeys of their fellow creatures. The dying ones are afraid that they will be passed by, so they cling to a place which proves that they are still a part of things. But, "sometimes the place is lost in the years

How much of Eiseley's essay to put in?

Condense?

Each example demonstrate different type of loss.

loss? why important?

Finding a Permanent Home
Rebecca Durost

1   In his essay, "The Brown Wasps," Loren C. Eiseley explores the idea that, "... all living creatures ... can survive only by fixing or transforming a bit of time into space or by securing a bit of space with its objects immortalized and made permanent in time." He says that people and animals have an overwhelming need to hold on to specific places or times in memory. These "places in time" remain permanent—removed from life which is always changing. When we compare this mind-image with the reality of the present, we see how quickly life has moved. So our lives are tinged with a sense of impending loss that just makes us cling all the harder.

2   It is this sense of loss which flavors the whole of Eiseley's essay. Beneath the words runs the feeling, though never stated, that life is an uncontrollable stream that sweeps us along. We must hold on to the permanence of our memories to keep from drowning. To illustrate his point Eiseley uses four main examples. Each shows a different kind of loss, but each victim has the same desire to hold on.

3   The first example describes a resemblance the author has seen between the behavior of dying wasps clinging to their hives into the winter, and derelicts clinging to benches in a railway station. Both are afraid of losing their "place in the hive." For the old derelicts and the brown wasps, the physical objects they cling to are symbols of their place in life. All creatures have a need to be involved in life, to share in the journeys of their fellow creatures. The dying ones are afraid they will be passed by, so they cling to a busy place which proves that they are still a part of things. But, "sometimes the place is lost in the years behind us. We cling to a time and place because without them man is lost, not only man, but life." The place does not have to exist in the real world anymore. Its reality is in our memory only, and thus, can never be lost.

4   The next two examples are of animals who, dispossessed of their familiar homes, continue to carry the memory of them in their minds. At least, this is what their actions suggest to Eiseley. In this case, the sense of loss causes the animals to recreate their memories after the destruction has taken place.

5   First, a mouse exiled from his field by a bulldozer, tries to recreate his home in a flower pot in the author's apartment. "I could visualize what had occurred. He had an image in his head, a world of seed pods and quiet, of green sheltering leaves in the dim light among the weed stems. It was the only world he knew and it was gone." But the mouse refused to accept the loss. Eiseley describes how, each night when he returned home, the burrow has been redug, but the mouse is nowhere in sight. He identified with the mouse's struggle because it is trying to keep things the same. It is trying to stop time, and that is something people often wish they could do. "About

my ferns there had begun to linger the insubstantial vapor of an autumn field, the distilled essence, as it were, of a mouse brain in exile from its home." Eventually, the mouse disappears, but its example starts Eiseley thinking about all the dispossessed animals that wander the world, carrying these dreams of home with them. "Every day these invisible dreams pass us on the street, or rise from beneath our feet, or look out upon us from beneath a bush." The world is full of dreams, humming in the air like radio waves, people living out of suitcases, exiled animals, all carry the essence of their lost homes in their minds.

6   The next example illustrates this mind attachment. Eiseley describes a flock of pigeons who depended on an old elevated railway, its crowds and peanut vending machines, until it was replaced by a subway. The pigeons orbit around the deserted station for awhile, and then disappear. However, when men return to tear down the station, the same flock of pigeons reappear. "It was plain that they retained a memory for an insubstantial structure now composed of air and time."

7   Finally, as a human example, Eiseley describes his own experience. "... I have spent a large portion of my life in the shade of a nonexistent tree...." He describes going back to a house he once lived in, to see a tree that he planted with his father. Through the years, the tree has taken on a great significance in his mind as a symbol of things that are permanent. Now he is old, perhaps sensing his own death, and like the animals, feels the need to make the dream tangible. "After sixty years the mood of the brown wasps grows heavier on one." When he finally arrives the tree is gone ... but it doesn't matter.

8   "Life disappears or modifies its appearances so fast that everything takes on an aspect of illusion...." We know that everything is either already lost or soon to be lost. This knowledge makes us cling (futilely) to an unreality. But often this unreality seems more concrete than transient life.

9   Eiseley says, "In sixty years the house and street had rotted out of my mind. But the tree that no longer was, that had perished in its first season, bloomed on in my individual mind, unblemished...." When a curious little boy sees Eiseley standing there he asks, "Do you live here Mister?" Eiseley answers, "Yes." because, in a sense, that is where his life is. "It was from this tree that ... my memories led away into the world."

10   The conclusion that Loren Eiseley finally comes to is that the attachment people feel to a "place in time" is more than just an animal's fixation with a familiar place. He says, "... it was part of our morality." What Eiseley means by this is that by fixing a place or time in mind, we are saying that we care about that little bit of life that is connected to it. At the times when we have no connections with the people around us, because life is sweeping us past them too quickly, this memory proves that at least once we had the ability to care. It says that at one time in our lives we were more than just disinterested observers. We cared enough about one time or place to want not to lose it. We cling in vain but without this caring we would not be human.

11   My first reaction after reading Eiseley's essay is to wonder, do I hold on to such a "place in time"? In probing my mind to find one, I search for that sense of impending loss which, at the time, would have prompted me to fix such a thing in my memory. But I am only 19, and I have lived in the same house in the same small town all my life. The necessity of holding on to a place in memory is hard for me to understand, and yet I do find that sense of loss, that desperate clinging feeling is there in me. It has to do with a time in my life when I was afraid of growing up. I looked at the adult world and didn't like what I saw, but at the same time I felt life inexorably carrying me towards it. So I tried to cling to my old self. Ideas are slippery, so I stuck to physical things. Even now I can't bear to throw away the things that defined me as a little girl—worn stuffed animals, almost illegible scribblings in an old diary, crayon sketches of imaginary horses. Even at the time I made them I must have been afraid of losing them or they would have been discarded long ago. For now, they are my permanence. Eventually I will move away from here, and then the place will become the important thing.

12   I see this happening in other people. Tena, an old friend of the family, loves to tell of her girlhood in Canada. Gently prodded by my questions, she spills out the details of growing up 80 years ago on a farm in Nova Scotia. I can see that the images are crystal clear in her mind, preserved and "permanent in time." In all her long life it is this place which she kept with her, the one she cared for most, the "most home." I think that sometimes she would like to go back, like Loren Eiseley to his tree, but she is afraid. Over 80 years many things change and are destroyed.

13   As for me, I suppose I must already carry it with me—the seed of the "place in time" I will always hang on to. I can't feel it there now, but someday there will come a great lurch in my life, and afraid of drowning, I will throw out a hand and grasp the memory that comforts me and keeps my head above water. But as yet, I am too young to have to be carrying my home around in my mind.

Ordering for the Reader ———————————————

The form of a piece of writing—the genre or type of writing it is—serves the reader by being an island of meaning in an ocean of confusion. It provides the reader with an intellectual unit, which represents what the writer has to say. The writer picks a form—an argument, a story, a literary analysis, a review, because it will represent an area of thought the writer and the reader can explore together. The writer expects it—the form—to contain enough experience that meaning can be found in it.

The reader has similar expectations. Each genre, as we have pointed out earlier, implies certain things—a story implies a story, events structured chronologically. The writer can play variations on that expectation, but the writer had better be aware of what the reader expects when choosing a genre.

The order or structure of a piece of writing is designed to lead the reader on a trip of exploration. Sometimes it is effective to arrange what the reader sees or is given to think about in such a way that the reader is unaware of the trail. Other times the reader needs road signs. Some road signs are there all the time— the title, the lead, the end. But it may be helpful to use cross heads, for example, to point out the stages in the evolution of an argument, or the categories of evidence to be presented in a proposal.

One of the most effective tricks of ordering is to anticipate, then order the reader's questions, so that the piece of writing answers those questions as they occur to the reader. If the subject is complicated and important for the reader to understand, for example, a brochure urging people to pay attention to the symptoms of diabetes, or one given to patients after diabetes has been disagnosed, it may be helpful to include the questions in the text, so that the trail that the reader should follow in exploring this island of meaning is explicit and well marked.

Often we have to consider the element of pacing in helping a reader. If we move the reader along too fast, the reader has no time to absorb new information and apply it to what comes next. If we move the reader along too slowly, the reader will fall asleep and never make the trip with us.

Questions about Ordering

• *What if I'm working on an opening and I think it might make a closing?*

Make a note in the margin beside it "close?" Or make a note in your "closing" file. This often happens, and you shouldn't let the idea get away. Good beginnings often make good endings, and the other way around.

• *What if the draft openings won't come?*

Switch around and try titles or outlines. Try closing. Plunge in and start to write the text. Put someone's name on it and start it as a letter. Try any of the other ordering strategies. You can outline first and then go back and write titles or openings. Closings can come before beginnings. Go with what works.

• *I do all this stuff in my head—why do I have to write it down?*

You don't. If you do it in your head and your writing is well organized, don't do it. There are people who never write down outlines, and others who only do it when they face a new and difficult writing task—writing about a complex, unfamiliar story; trying to appeal to a new audience; writing in a different form from what they are used to. If your writing works well, follow the process that is succeeding. If you're having problems writing well, then try some of the techniques proposed in the text.

• *I had a teacher who taught me to remember CUE as a way of reminding me of coherence, unity, and emphasis. How is that different from the stuff you have on design?*

I had a teacher who used the same device, and it is one of the few pieces of teacher advice I remember as I write. It's pretty good stuff. I've gone on to develop it a bit, but in doing that development I've probably paid attention to coherence, unity, and emphasis.

● *How can I do all this planning when I've got to write the paper tonight?*

Planning helps you write more efficiently and more quickly. If you have an hour, take five or ten minutes to collect the information with which you'll be writing. Take a few more minutes to make sure you have the focus, and then a few minutes to put the information in order. If you take ten minutes for each of those tasks, you'll only have invested half an hour. You'll have twenty minutes to write and ten minutes to check over what you've written. The planning will make your draft quicker, often longer, and better.

● *Do you have to follow the outline?*

Of course not. It isn't a legal contract; it's merely a sketch or a plan. It is a tool to help you. Writing isn't completed thought written down; writing is thinking. The draft should change under your hand. It will teach you about the subject. When you're writing best you are often writing what you did not expect to write. Remember John Fowle's counsel: "Follow the accident, fear the fixed plan— that is the rule."

Ordering Activities

1. Look through half a dozen magazines and write down the article titles that made you want to read. Do the same thing with book titles in a library or bookstore. Work alone or in a group to decide what the qualities of a good title are.
2. Share your idea for a piece of writing with another person in the class or with a small group; then write titles for each other. Write new titles for textbooks or pieces of literature you are reading.
3. See how many titles you can write for the piece you're working on. Do at least twenty. Do them quickly, in small chunks of time.
4. Find ten openings for articles, stories in magazines or newspapers, or chapters in books, that make you want to read. Share them with others and decide what elements they have in common.
5. Collect by yourself or with others fifty to a hundred good openings and list the different techniques used by these successful opening writers.
6. Write ten new openings, taking no more than five minutes each, for something you've just read.
7. Write at least twenty-five openings for the piece you're working on.

8. Look back at pieces of writing you've read recently or that you consider good and list the techniques the writers used.
9. Share the idea you're working on with others and draft endings for each other.
10. Take a piece of writing you've read and see how many different ways you can close it.
11. Draft as many closings as you can—at least twenty-five—for the piece of writing you're working on.
12. Take a piece of writing you like and write down the three to five principal points that are made in it.
13. Share your subject with someone else and write down, for each other, the main points that will be made and the order in which they'll have to be made.
14. Sketch out ten different sequences that might be used to get you from one of your leads to one of your endings. (What if the sequence reveals you need a new opening, a new closing, or both? Good. That's one of the reasons to play with sequence.)
15. Design your own outline form and share it with others who are sharing theirs with you.
16. Outline your piece at least five different ways.
17. Study the case history to see just how the piece is organized. Try to reorganize it. Do the same thing with a page or two of this text, of another text, of your own text, or your classmate's.

Chapter 6

ꙮ Explore Your Subject: DEVELOP

There are some kinds of writing that you have to do very fast, like riding a bicycle on a tightrope.

WILLIAM FAULKNER

I try to write without consulting my material; this avoids interruption and prevents me from overloading my text with quotations. In this way, I establish a comfortable distance from the mass and pressure of data. It helps the narrative flow; it is a guard against irrelevancy.

LEON EDEL

The language leads, and we continue to follow where it leads.

WRIGHT MORRIS

You've found your subject, collected an abundant inventory of information, developed a point of view, created a structure, now—*write !*

Gulp.

It is the moment of truth, a time of revelation. You will expose yourself on the page, show what you know and what you do not know. It is appropriate to gulp. Hesitate. Start. Stop. Gulp again.

The Write Attitude

Beginner and old timer are alike at this moment of terror. But the writer is the one who has developed an attitude that allows pen—pencil, typewriter, computer—to begin a draft.

The attitude that allows me to start writing includes several elements. I have to remind myself to:

Lower My Standards

I carry the poet William Stafford's advice with me at all times. He says: "I believe that the so-called 'writing block' is a product of some kind of disproportion between your standards and your performance. . . . One should lower his standards until there is no felt threshold to go over in writing. It's easy to write. You just shouldn't have standards that inhibit you from writing."

He has also said, "I can imagine a person beginning to feel he's not able to write up to that standard he imagines the world has set for him. But to me that is surrealistic. The only standard I can rationally have is the standard I am meeting right now." Stafford continues, "You should be more willing to forgive yourself. It doesn't make any difference if you are good or bad today. The *assessment* of the product is something that happens *after* you've done it."

He says it all.

Write Badly to Write Well

My closest writing friend, to whom I always turn when I'm stuck, reminds me that we have to "write badly to write well." When I start to write I want it to be perfect but that isn't possible; it isn't even desirable. Slick, glib writing should not be the goal; I should be seeking writing that is turning up unexpected, undeveloped meanings. My early drafts should be filled with accident, awkwardness, possibility, potential.

166

Remember That a Draft Is a Draft

Especially the first one. I am writing to discover what I may have to say. There will be other drafts before the final one. I will have time to redevelop, refine, shape, revise, edit. All writing is an experiment in meaning—and most experiments fail.

Study what attitudes you had when the writing went well. Hold to those attitudes and develop them so that it becomes easy to write.

Primary Technique for Developing Your Subject: Fastwrite _____

Write fast. The faster the better. Language should carry you forward toward meaning. At times it will almost feel as if you are out of control. William Faulkner described this feeling when he said, "A writer writing is like a man building a chicken coop in a high wind. He grabs onto any board he can and nails it down fast." When the writing is going well, it is almost automatic for me. I hack away at the computer with two wildly dancing fingers that do not seem to belong to me.

I'm not aware, consciously, of what I've just said or what I'm going to say. In fact, I'm not really aware of what I'm saying. I'm just moving forward as fast as I can. I am not thinking about writing, I am writing.

Not everybody writes this way, and not everybody should write this way. There are writers who carve their copy out of stone, making each word, line paragraph, and page right before they move on. But they're in the minority. Most of us have to write fast to write well.

It's a good idea to write without notes. Put your notes aside before you start to write the draft. You've done the collecting and the focusing and the ordering. The important thing now is what's in your head, not what's on the paper. Too often writers become bound by their notes, and they write a draft that is really a transcription of their notes. It is usually a dull prose that is clogged with excessive, indiscriminate information.

When I worked on *Time Magazine* and came to a statistic or a quote that wasn't handy I put in the capital letters "TK" to indicate that information was to come. I had left blanks for the Stafford and Faulkner quotes in this chapter, for example. I don't have a good memory; I remember enough to know I want to use the quotes, but I certainly can't quote them accurately, so I leave a blank. I'll fill them in later. I don't want anything to stop the flow of prose.

Write fast to outrun the censor. Write uncomfortably fast so that you will have accidents of diction, grammar, rhetoric, logic, content, meaning. Fastwriting will cause accidents and it is through accident that we produce lively, insightful writing.

Speed is as essential to writing as it is to riding a bicycle. It is the velocity that makes it possible. Speed inspires the mind. Writing fast you remember things you didn't know you knew. Writing fast, you make unexpected connections between fragments of information and those collisions give off ideas. Writing at top speed produces accidents of language and voice that are essential to an attractive and persuasive style.

Of course, you'll go back to consider and reconsider what has been rushed to the page. But the text worthy of careful reconsideration and development is usually the result of fastwriting.

The more you are afraid to write fast, the more you should try it. Outrun the censor. Put down on the page what comes. Discover that you do not know what you have to say, but in saying what you do not know, you discover what you will have to say.

Additional Techniques for Developing Your Subject: Layer _____

Most writing by beginners is underdeveloped, thin, lacks texture. The writer fears saying too much or knows the subject so well that the writer imagines a few general words will give the reader the same full vision they spark in the writer.

Another reason for undeveloped writing, by both experienced and inexperienced writers, is that writing doesn't usually come all at once. It comes in spurts: The writing produces the writing. I do not know what I will write or how I will write it until I draft. Then the evolving text instructs me, telling me what I have to say and hinting at how I may say it. And with this comes an increasing awareness of audience as we write in the beginning for ourselves and, later, for others.

One technique I've been using, especially in writing the novel, is to layer my writing. Once I did quite a bit of oil painting and my pictures were built up, layer after layer of painting until the scene was revealed to me and a viewer. I've been writing each chapter of the novel the same way, starting each day at the beginning of the chapter, reading and writing until the timer bings and my daily stint is finished. Each day I lay down a new layer of text and when I read it the next day, the new layer reveals more possibility.

There is no one way the chapters develop. Each makes its own demands, struggles toward birth in its own way. Sometimes it starts with a sketch, other times the first writing feels complete [next day's reading usually shows it is not]; sometimes I race ahead through the chapter, other times each paragraph is honed before I go on to the next one. I try to allow the text to tell me what it needs.

I start reading and when I see—or, more likely, hear—something that needs doing, I do it. One day I'll read through all the written text and move it forward from the last day's writing; another time I'll find myself working on dialogue; the next day I may begin to construct a new scene [the basic element of fiction]; one time I'll stumble into a new discovery, later have to set it up or weave references to it through the text; I may build up background description, develop the conflict, make the reader see a character more clearly; I may present more documentation, evidence, or exposition, or hide it in a character's dialogue or action.

I've adapted the same process to my writing of nonfiction or poetry, but the layer technique is rarely recognized or taught. One reason is that it is confused, when done, with revision. I am guilty of that as well, doing one thing at my desk and calling it something else in my writing. But this is not revision of an existing text but the production of a complete and fully developed first draft.

The layer technique is ideally suited for the computer as it is easy to write over what you have written, but it can be done with typewriter or pen and paper as well. Part of the technique involves, of course, developing inserts that can be written or pasted within sentences or paragraphs, between paragraphs or sections, at the end, in the middle, or even before the beginning. Remember there are no rules; the text leads and you follow.

The best way I know to get the feel of layering is to write a paragraph—perhaps of description—then to start again on a new page and write it again without reading the first one or, at least, only reading it loosely. Write easily. Relax. Let the text lead. Then do it a third time, a fourth, perhaps a fifth. Does that mean you should always do it five times? No. The text may call for three layers—or seventeen. Let me demonstrate that exercise:

1. When I think of North Quincy High School, I think of corridors more than classrooms. I expect to think of classrooms. Say elementary school and I think of the huge classroom clocks with Roman numbers and waiting for the last clicks in the afternoon. Three minutes. Two. One. Escape.

2. North Quincy High School. Not classrooms but corridors jammed with the hourly flood of teenagers. Beer jackets and saddle shoes, letter sweaters and girls with mysterious blooming sweaters. Sweater girls. Shouts and laughter, "swell" and "neat," the harsh, ugly south of Boston accent and the fastracingyankeetalk, the slamming of locker doors and the bells summoning the prisoners for lock up.

3. I heard myself say, "Everybody's alienated in high school" and was surprised I saw North Quincy High School and long, empty corridors. I would have expected to remember classrooms, hours that felt like whole lifetimes, clocks with huge roman numerals with hours between the click of the minute hand, teacher voices that used sarcasm like the flicking end of a bull whip. Or the flood of students between classes, beer jackets and sweater girls, "swell" and "neat," the slam of locker doors, peanut butter and jelly sandwiches, the perfume of sneakers and gym shorts. But what I remember, with something close to nostalgia, is the long empty corridors with the classroom doors closed.

4. We were talking about high school the other night and I heard myself say, "Everybody's alienated in high school" and was surprised I saw North Quincy High School, long, empty corridors and something that felt like nostalgia. High School was not a good time for me. I dropped out twice and flunked out at the end. I would have expected anger, perhaps bitterness, even embarrassment, not nostalgia.

I would have expected to remember classrooms, hours that felt like whole lifetimes, lectures on physics or algebra in which I lost any sense of meaning, clocks with huge roman numerals with hours between the click of the minute hand, teacher voices that used sarcasm like the flicking end of a bull whip. Or the flood of students between classes, beer jackets and sweater girls, "swell" and "neat," the slam of locker doors, peanut butter and jelly sandwiches, the perfume of sneakers and gym shorts. But what I remember, with something close to nostalgia, is the long empty corridors with the classroom doors closed.

The floors gleamed with wax and the green locker doors were silent. The walls, I think, were stucco and light fixtures hung from the ceiling. Inside the glass doors of the classrooms I saw the tired gestures of the teachers and numbed faces of the students, faces that seemed drugged by information they did not want to know and would never understand.

5.   My wife and daughters and I were talking about high school the other evening—none of us wanted to return—and we laughed at someone who was still angry at being unappreciated and alienated in high school and I heard myself say, "Everybody's alienated in high school." As I spoke I was carried back to North Quincy High School, long, empty corridors and something that felt like nostalgia.

I was surprised. I have never felt nostalgic about high school before. It was not a good time for me. I won no letters, retained a virtue I desperately wanted to lose, dropped out twice and flunked out at the end. I would have expected anger, perhaps bitterness, even shame, not nostalgia.

And I would have expected to remember classrooms, those educational cells to which I had been sentenced with hours that felt like whole lifetimes, lectures on physics or algebra in which I lost any sense of meaning, clocks with huge roman numerals with hours between the click of the minute hand, teacher voices that used sarcasm like the flicking end of a bull whip. Or the flood of students between classes, beer jackets and sweater girls, "swell" and "neat," the slam of locker doors, peanut butter and jelly sandwiches, the perfume of sneakers and gym shorts. But what I remember, with something close to nostalgia, is the long empty corridors with the classroom doors closed.

The floors gleamed with wax and the green locker doors were silent. The walls, I think, were stucco and orange bulbed light fixtures hung from the ceiling. Inside the glass doors of the classrooms I saw the tired gestures of the teachers and numbed faces of the students, faces that seemed drugged by information they did not want to know and would never understand. And I was alone in the corridor. I had escaped.

Of course, I remember those corridors with nostalgia. Just the other day I found stacks of forged corridor passes, stored away in case I get returned to high school. I worked on the newspaper and the yearbook; I learned the system and then how to work it. I escaped homeroom and study hall, sometimes even class. I possessed the loneliness I had learned at home and the delicious egotism of alienation. I was an outsider, a writer before

I knew I would become a writer, an almost man with forged corridor passes, documentation that I would escape high school, learn new systems and how, as a loner, to manipulate them. Those aged slips of paper were, I now realize, my diploma, and oh how I have used that education in the years since, walking so many corridors by myself, alienated and smug.

That was fun—and totally unexpected. The conversation took place and the image of the empty corridors came to mind but I didn't begin to understand them until I completed this hour [53 minutes] of layering, putting down text on top of text, revising to produce a first draft.

In reading over these versions I teach myself what I have done. I was not aware of doing these things. They are instinctive with me, but it is helpful to articulate and, therefore, reinforce instinct. Let me walk you through these drafts and show you what I think I learned.

1. When I think of North Quincy High School, I think of corridors more than classrooms. I expect to think of classrooms. Say elementary school and I think of the huge classroom clocks with Roman numbers and waiting for the last clicks in the afternoon. Three minutes. Two. One. Escape.

2. North Quincy High School. Not classrooms but corridors jammed with the hourly flood of teenagers. Beer jackets and saddle shoes, letter sweaters and girls with mysterious blooming sweaters. Sweater girls. Shouts and laughter, "swell" and "neat," the harsh, ugly south of Boston accent and the fastracingyankeetalk, the slamming of locker doors and the bells summoning the prisoners for lock up.

I was trying to get into the text faster and, most of all, to develop the scene in my mind, to flesh it out with detail.

3. I heard myself say, "Everybody's alienated in high school" and was surprised I saw North Quincy High School and long, empty corridors.

I got into it slower so I could put it in context.

I would have expected to remember classrooms, hours that felt like whole lifetimes, clocks with huge roman numerals with hours between the click of the minute hand, teacher voices that used sarcasm like the flicking end of a bull whip.

I transposed the material from elementary school. We had the same clocks in high school and I waited for their clicks with the same desperation.

Or the flood of students between classes, beer jackets and sweater girls, "swell" and "neat," the slam of locker doors, peanut butter and jelly sandwiches, the perfume of sneakers and gym shorts.

I added detail, paced it a bit differently. All this detail I hoped would take me back to high school and lead me to meaning.

But what I remember, with something close to nostalgia, is the long empty corridors with the classroom doors closed.

I develop the key image, the picture that haunts my memory.

4.   We were talking about high school the other night and I
heard myself say, "Everybody's alienated in high school" and
was surprised I saw North Quincy High School, long, empty
corridors and something that felt like nostalgia. High School
was not a good time for me. I dropped out twice and flunked
out at the end. I would have expected anger, perhaps
bitterness, even embarrassment, not nostalgia.

In the previous and
the following
paragraphs, I
continue to develop
with more detail,
setting up the
situation in the first
paragraph,
revealing the world
of the school in the
second.

I would have expected to remember classrooms, hours
that felt like whole lifetimes, lectures on physics or algebra in
which I lost any sense of meaning, clocks with huge roman
numerals with hours between the click of the minute hand,
teacher voices that used sarcasm like the flicking end of a bull
whip. Or the flood of students between classes, beer jackets
and sweater girls, "swell" and "neat," the slam of locker doors,
peanut butter and jelly sandwiches, the perfume of sneakers
and gym shorts. But what I remember, with something close
to nostalgia, is the long empty corridors with the classroom
doors closed.
        The floors gleamed with wax and the green locker doors
were silent. The walls, I think, were stucco and light fixtures
hung from the ceiling. Inside the glass doors of the
classrooms I saw the tired gestures of the teachers and
numbed faces of the students, faces that seemed drugged by
information they did not want to know and would never
understand.

Now I have placed
myself—and,
therefore, the
reader—in the
lonely corridor. As I
distance myself
from those locked
into the classrooms,
teachers and
students alike, I am
unknowingly taking
a big step toward
the meaning the
next layer of text
will reveal.

5.   My wife and daughters and I were talking about high
school the other evening—none of us wanted to return—and
we laughed at someone who was still angry at being
unappreciated and alienated in high school and I heard myself
say, "Everybody's alienated in high school." As I spoke I was
carried back to North Quincy High School, long, empty
corridors and something that felt like nostalgia.

In the first
paragraph, I am
extending the
context a bit, setting
the scene more
completely. In these
first paragraphs I
am instinctively
establishing, mood,
tone, pace; tuning
my language to the
evolving voice of
the piece that will
reveal meaning to
me and will reveal
and support
meaning to the
reader.

I was surprised. I have never felt nostalgic about high
school before. It was not a good time for me. I won no letters,
retained a virtue I desperately wanted to lose, dropped out
twice and flunked out at the end. I would have expected anger,
perhaps bitterness, even shame, not nostalgia.
        And I would have expected to remember classrooms,

With the word
escape, the text has
revealed the
meaning to me.

those educational cells to which I had been sentenced with hours that felt like whole lifetimes, lectures on physics or algebra in which I lost any sense of meaning, clocks with huge roman numerals with hours between the click of the minute hand, teacher voices that used sarcasm like the flicking end of a bull whip. Or the flood of students between classes, beer jackets and sweater girls, "swell" and "neat," the slam of locker doors, peanut butter and jelly sandwiches, the perfume of sneakers and gym shorts. But what I remember, with something close to nostalgia, is the long empty corridors with the classroom doors closed.

The floors gleamed with wax and the green locker doors were silent. The walls, I think, were stucco and orange bulbed light fixtures hung from the ceiling. Inside the glass doors of the classrooms I saw the tired gestures of the teachers and numbed faces of the students, faces that seemed drugged by information they did not want to know and would never understand. And I was alone in the corridor. I had escaped.

Of course, I remember those corridors with nostalgia. Just the other day I found stacks of forged corridor passes, stored away in case I get returned to high school. I worked on the newspaper and the yearbook; I learned the system and then how to work it. I escaped homeroom and study hall, sometimes even class. I possessed the loneliness I had learned at home and the delicious egotism of alienation. I was an outsider, a writer before I knew I would become a writer, an almost man with forged corridor passes, documentation that I would escape high school, learn new systems and how, as a loner, to manipulate them. Those aged slips of paper were, I now realize, my diploma, and oh how I have used that education in the years since, walking so many corridors by myself, alienated and smug.

In the last paragraph, I have explored, developed, examined, and extended that meaning—playing with it, turning it over, moving back to the slips, seeing their significance, delighting myself with the surprise of "smug" which gives me an insight about my lifetime of proud alienation. I have maintained the private illusion and arrogance of alienation even when I have earned awards, promotion, title, tenure. It is true I still feel alienated although I may be seen as alienated and it is true I am smugly alienated, secretly feeling superior to those around me. Too true, at times, not all the time, I hope. This writing which I did just to document a point has put me on the couch, revealed myself and made me squirm and made me feel I deserve a couple of good squirms. And in reading all this over I am struck by my patience. Once I would have wanted to know the meaning right away—or even thought I should have known the meaning before I wrote the first word. I would have sought meaning, panted after it. Now I am patient—and confident. Experience has taught me that if I keep writing, meaning will come. I will not think meaning. I will watch meaning arise from my page. The painter William de Kooning once said, "I can't paint a tree but I can find a tree in my work" and Pablo Picasso testified, "To know what you want to draw, you have to begin drawing. If it turns out to be a man, I draw a man. If it turns out to be a woman, I draw a woman." They are patient, and I have learned patience as well. And I have learned it by rereading these drafts.

You will see other things I have done—good or bad—or should have done. And you may make your own discoveries, comfortable and uncomfortable as you live my drafts. Mark them all down on my text, try them on yours.

Layering is just one technique of many I use, but it is a valuable one to me. Try it and I think you'll see how it can give your writing a greater depth and texture than before.

And what will I do with the version number 5? I don't know. Play with it perhaps. See if it grows into a column or a short story. It may pop up in the novel I'm drafting or turn into an academic article on layering, may even shrink to a poem. Most likely it will remain what it is, a piece of writing that was fun to do because it captured an important part of my life and allowed me to examine it and come to some understanding I did not have before.

Write Outloud

Even the most experienced writer speaks a thousand times more than he or she writes. When drafting, we should consciously use this oral sense and listen to what we are saying as we say it.

When I visit a newspaper's city room as a consultant on writing, I look around and then I guess who the best writers are. More often than not, the editors think I've made good picks. What did I look for? I looked to see which writers' lips were moving as they wrote. Most writers read aloud when they're writing. Sometimes they speak right out, but usually they have taught themselves to speak under their breath. Their lips, however, betray them.

Conscious reading aloud is especially helpful on the most difficult passages, as the speaking voice tells the writing voice how to make the prose flow.

Writing is not speaking written down, as anyone who has been tape-recorded knows. Effective writing, however, creates the illusion of speech. The flow and music and pace and rhythm and individuality and intimacy and experience of speech has to be created with the written word.

Readers appreciate writing they can hear, writing that is coming from an individual, writing that plays the music of language, supporting and extending the text's meaning through human song.

Develop

Most beginning writers underwrite. They assume the reader will know what they know. It is better to overwrite, to turn out a draft that has an abundance of revealing detail.

Effective writing is built from concrete, accurate information. Too many beginning writers think that writing is made with words and literary flourishes that are detached from meaning. Good writing is not a collection of colorful balloons that bob aimlessly against the ceiling. Good writing—poetry as much as nonfiction—delivers information to the reader.

During the writing of the draft, the writer should be conscious of the information that is being delivered to the reader, and the writer should try to make that information as abundant and specific as possible. Words, after all, are symbols for information. Words that have no information behind them are as valuable as checks drawn on an account with no money in it.

Readers hunger for information, and the writer should satisfy this hunger by constructing a piece of writing with solid chunks of information.

One important way to develop is contained in the old counsel to "Show, don't tell." I prefer reveal and tell or tell by revealing. The skillful writer usually does not tell the reader *about* the subject, but instead reveals the subject to the reader.

It isn't easy for a writer to learn how to get out of the way. Most beginning writers call attention to themselves rather than the subject. The reader should see the subject and then have the room to make up his or her own mind about it. The most quoted, remembered, and probably influential parts of the Bible are the parables, little stories that tell by showing.

George Orwell said, "Good writing is like a windowpane." The effective writer knows how to get out of the way and let the reader see the subject. When I wrote editorials, I often played a secret game. I imagined I was a defense attorney and my client was charged with murder. In my summation to the jury I wanted to be able to say, "I'm not going to tell you how to vote. I'm just going to remind you of the evidence." My editorial was the evidence, as unadorned as possible. I just wanted to reveal the information so that readers would absorb that information and think for themselves—what I wanted them to think.

The inexperienced writer tries to jam all the information that has been collected into the story. This is not the way a good prose is created. When I was at *Time*, an editor there used to say, "You can tell a good story by the amount of good stuff that is thrown away."

When a student is asked to write a short paper, the student, naturally, tries to compress. And the result is what I call the garbage-compactor story. All the information is jammed together into a tiny, unreadable little block.

Brevity is achieved not by compression so much as by selection. The writer has to select the information the reader needs, and then develop it properly. Each anecdote, definition, argument, description—whatever needs to be said— has to be set up and developed adequately so that the reader can experience that part of the story at an appropriate pace, a pace that will allow the reader to absorb the information.

Each fully developed text grows according to its own needs. One text needs descriptive specifics, another needs dialogue and action, another demands a carefully explained process, another a detailed history, but all texts need a de- livery of information that satisfies the reader. Such a text has texture and depth. It doesn't just slide over the surface.

Let the text go. Err on the side of abundance. Write too much. It may feel like too much but not, in fact, be too much. Remember you can cut what is there but you cannot cut, revise, polish, develop, shape what is not on the page.

Document

And document each point.

The reader needs evidence to support each point. Sometimes the statement can be so specific it carries its own evidence within it, but most times a statement needs to be backed up with an example, a statistic, a quotation, a reference to authority that will convince the reader.

Unfortunately, most of us write with the evidence we feel most comfortable using. One writer will always make the point with a quotation from an authority; another will salt the page with statistics; a third will back up each assertion with an anecdote; still another writer will walk on stage and use an "I" to speak directly to the audience. We have to watch out that we don't always choose the form of evidence with which we are comfortable, instead of using the form of documentation that will most effectively persuade the reader.

Twenty-six Ways to Defeat Writer's Block ⎯⎯⎯⎯⎯⎯⎯⎯

It never gets easier to write. All writers are masters of avoidance. If there are no interruptions, they create them. They make phone calls, travel far on unnecessary errands, cut wood in July, buy a snow shovel in August. When it is time to write, writers read, attack the correspondence and the filing, sharpen pencils, buy new pens, change the typewriter ribbon, shop for a word processor, make coffee, make tea, rearrange the furniture in the office. When writers get together, they often, shamefaced, share new ways to avoid writing.

But some of that avoidance is good. E. B. White reminds us, "Delay is natural to a writer. He is like a surfer—he bides his time, waits for the perfect wave on which to ride in. Delay is instinctive with him." This waiting is purposeful, for most writers discover that starting a draft prematurely causes a total collapse three, five, or seven pages along, and it's harder to pick up the pieces and repair a train wreck of a draft than to start one along the right track.

Writers, of course, being writers, are never sure whether they are allowing their subject to ripen properly or are just being lazy. This waiting is often the worst part of writing. It is filled with guilt and doubt, yet it is essential.

And then comes the time—commanded by the deadline—when there can be no more delay, when the writing must be done. Here are some ways to overcome inertia and start writing

1 nulla dies sine linea. Never a day without a line. Make writing a habit. Sit in the same place with the same tools every day and write until it becomes uncomfortable *not* to write. Then writing will come as a matter of course.

2 Make Believe You Are Writing a Letter to a Friend. Put "Dear ⎯⎯⎯⎯⎯⎯" at the top of the page and start writing. Tom Wolfe did this on one of his first New Journalism pieces. He wrote the editor a letter saying why he couldn't write the piece he'd been assigned. The letter flowed along in such a wonderful, easy fashion that the editor took the salutation off and ran it. It established a new style for contemporary journalism.

3 Switch Your Writing Tools. If you normally type, write by hand. If you write by hand, type. Switch from pen to pencil or pencil to pen. Switch from unlined paper to lined paper, or vice versa. Try larger paper or smaller, colored paper or white paper. Use a bound notebook or spiral notebook, a legal pad or a clipboard. Tools are a writer's toys, and effective, easy writing is the product of play.

4 Talk about the Piece of Writing with Another Writer, and Pay Close Attention to What You Say. You may be telling yourself how to write the piece. You may even want to make notes as you talk on the telephone or in person. Pay attention to words or combinations of words that may become a voice and spark a piece of writing.

5 Write Down the Reasons You Are Not Writing. Often when you see the problem you will be able to avoid it. You may realize that your standards are too high, or that you're thinking excessively of how one person will respond to your piece, or that you're trying to include too much. Once you have defined the problem you may be able to dispose of it.

6 Describe the Process You Went through When a Piece of Writing Went Well. You may be able to read such an account in your journal. We need to reinforce the writing procedures that produce good writing. A description of what worked before may tell us that we need to delay at this moment, or it may reveal a trick that got us going another time. We should keep a careful record of our work habits and the tricks of our trade, so that we have a positive resource to fall back on.

7 Interview Other Writers to Find Out How They Get Started. Try your class-mates' tricks and see if they work for you.

8 Switch the Time of Day. I tried to write this chapter just before noontime. Nothing. Well, not nothing, just the first paragraph and a feeling of total help-lessness. Now it is early morning the next day and writing is perking. Sometimes writing at night when you are tired lowers your critical sense in a positive way, and other times you can jump out of bed in the morning and get a start on the writing before your internal critic catches up with you.

9 Call the Draft an Experiment or an Exercise. All my courses are experi-mental, so I don't have to worry too much about failing as a teacher—failure is normal during experiments—and I'm ready to try new ways to teach. Good writing is always an experiment. Make a run at it. See if it will work. The poet Mekeel McBride is always writing "exercises" in her journals. Since they are just exercises and not poems she doesn't have to get uptight about them, but of course if an exercise turns into a poem she'll accept it.

10 Dictate a Draft. Use a tape recorder, and then transcribe it from that. You may want to transcribe it carefully, or just catch the gist of what you had to say. No matter how experienced we are as writers, we are a million times more experienced as speakers, and it's often easier to get started writing by talking than by writing.

11 Quit. Come back later and try again. You can't force writing. You have to keep making runs at it. Come back ten minutes later, or later that day, or the next day. Keep trying until the writing flows so fast you have to run along behind it trying to keep up.

12 Read. Some writers read over what they've written, and they may even edit it or recopy it as a way of sliding into the day's writing. I can't do that; I despair too much, and when I read my own writing I feel I have to start over again; it's worthless, hopeless. If you don't feel that way, however, it may be a good device to go over the previous day's work and then push on to the new writing, the way an experienced house painter will paint back into the last brush stroke and then draw the new paint forward.

13 *Write Directly to a Reader.* The too-critical reader can keep us from writing, but we can also get writing by imagining an especially appreciative reader, or a reader who needs the information we have to convey. If we can feel that reader's hunger for what we have to say, it will draw us into the text. Sometimes, as I have been writing this book, I must confess, I've imagined the enjoyment I expect Don Graves, Chip Scanlan, or Nancie Atwell to feel at an unexpected turn of phrase, a new insight, or a different approach. I read their faces as I write the way I read and speak to friendly faces in an audience.

14 *Take a Walk, Lift Weights, Jog, Run, Dance, Swim.* Many writers have found that the best way to get started writing is by getting the blood coursing through the body and the brain. As they get their physical body tuned up, their brain starts to get into high gear. Exercise is also the kind of dumb, private activity that allows the mind to free itself of stress and interruption and rehearse what may be written when the exercise is done.

15 *Change the Place Where You Write.* I write in my office at home, but I also write on a lap desk in the living room or on the porch. I like to take the car and drive down by Great Bay, where I can look up from my lap desk and watch a heron stalk fish or a seagull soar—the way I would like to write, without effort. Some writers cover their windows and write to a wall. I like to write to a different scene. Right now, for example, I'm looking at the green ocean of Indiana farmland and a marvelously angry gray sky as I drive west and write by dictation. In the 1920s, writers thought the cafés of Paris were the best places to write. I don't think I could work on those silly little tables, but my ideal writing place would be in a booth in a busy lunchroom where nobody knows me. Yesterday morning, I started writing in a Denny's in a city in Michigan; it was a fine place to write. When my writing doesn't go well, I move around. I imagine that the muse is looking for me, and if it can't find me at home I'll go out somewhere where I may be more visible.

16 *Draw a Picture, in Your Mind or on Paper.* Take a photograph. Cut a picture from a magazine and put it on your bulletin board. When small children start writing, they usually first draw a picture. They do on paper what experienced writers usually do in their mind—they visualize the subject. Last summer, I started my writing sessions by making a sketch of a rubber tree that stands on our porch. I wasn't writing about the rubber tree, but the activity of drawing seemed to help me get started and stimulated the flow of writing.

17 *Free Write.* Write as hard and as fast and free as you can. See if language will lead you toward a meaning. As I have said before, free writing isn't very free, for the text starts to develop its own form and direction. But the act of writing freely is one of the techniques that can unleash your mind.

18 *Stop in the Middle of a Sentence.* This is a good trick when the writing is going well and you are interrupted or come to the end of the day's writing during a long project. Many well-known writers have done this, and I've found that it really helps me at times. If I can pick up the draft and finish an ordinary sentence, then I am immediately back into the writing. If I've stopped at the end of a sentence or a paragraph it's much harder to get going. And if I've stopped at the end of a chapter it may take days or weeks to get the next chapter started.

19 *Write the Easy Parts First.* If you're stuck on a section or a beginning, skip over it and write the parts of the draft that you are ready to write. Once you've got those easy, strong pieces of writing done, you'll be able to build a complete draft by connecting those parts. A variation on this is to write the end first, as I've suggested in other parts of the text, or to plunge in and grab the beast wherever you can get hold of it. Once you have a working text, you can extend it backward or forward as it requires.

20 *Be Silly.* You're not writing anyway, so you might as well make a fool of yourself. I've numbered the day's quota of pages and then filled them in. One of my writer neighbors loves cigars, but he won't let himself have a cigar until he finishes his daily quota. Reward yourself with a cup of coffee or a dish of ice cream, or a handful of nuts. It is no accident that some writers are fat; they keep rewarding themselves with food. Do whatever you have to do to keep yourself writing. Jessamyn West writes in bed the first thing in the morning. If the doorbell rings she can't answer it; she isn't up and dressed. Use timers, count pages, count words (you may not be able to say the writing went well, but you'll be able to say "I did 512 words," or "I completed two pages"), play music, write standing up (Thomas Wolfe write on top of an icebox, Ernest Hemingway put his typewriter on a bureau), start the day writing in the bathtub as Nabokov did. Nothing is silly if it gets you started writing.

21 *Start the Writing Day by Reading Writing that Inspires You.* This is dangerous for me, because I may get so interested in the reading I'll never write, or I'll pick up the voice of another writer. I can't, for example, read William Faulkner when I'm writing fiction: a poor, New Hampshire imitation of that famous Mississippian is not a good way to go. The other day, however, when I couldn't get started writing, I read a short story by Mary Gordon, one of my favorite authors. Reading a really good writer should make you pack up your pen and quit the field, but most of us find reading other writers inspiring. I put down Mary Gordon's short story and was inspired to write.

22 *Read What Other Writers Have Written about Writing.* I may not write as well as they do, but we work at the same trade, and it helps me to sit around and chat with them. You may want to start a "commonplace book," an eighteenth-century form of self-education in which people made their personal collections of wise or witty sayings. I've collected what writers have said about writing in my commonplace book, which has grown to twenty-four 3-inch-thick notebooks. Some of my favorite quotes from that collection appear before each chapter in this book as well as in the text. I find it comforting to hear that the best writers have many of the same problems I do, and I browse through these quotes as a way of starting.

23 *Break Down the Writing Task into Reasonable Goals.* A few years ago, I watched on TV as the first woman to climb a spectacular rock face in California made it to the top. It had taken her days, and as soon as she got over the edge, a TV reporter stuck a microphone in her face and asked her what she'd thought of as she kept working her way up the cliff. She said she kept reminding herself that you eat an elephant one bit at a time. You also write a long piece of writing one page, or one paragraph, at a time. John Steinbeck said, "When I face the desolate impossibility of writing 500 pages a sick sense of failure falls on me and I know I can never do it. Then I gradually write one page and then another. One day's work is all I can permit myself to contemplate." If you contemplate a book, you'll never write it, but if you write just a page a day you'll have a 365-page draft at the end of a year. If you're stuck, you may be trying to eat an elephant at one gulp. It may be wiser to tell yourself that you'll just get the first page, or perhaps just the lead done that day. That may seem possible, and you'll start writing.

24 *Put Someone Else's Name on It.* I've been hired as a ghostwriter to create a text for politicians or industrialists. I've had little trouble writing when someone else's name is on the work. Most of the time, when I can't write, I'm excessively self-conscious. Sometimes I've put a pseudonym on a piece of work and the writing has taken off.

25 *Delegate the Writing to Your Subconscious.* Often I will tell my subconscious what I'm working on, and then I'll do something that doesn't take intense concentration and allows my subconscious mind to work. I walk around bookstores or a library, watch a dull baseball game or movie on TV, take a nap, go for a walk or a drive. Some people putter around the house or work in the garden. Whatever you do, you're allowing your mind to work on the problem. Every once in a while a thought, an approach, a lead, a phrase, a line, or a structure will float up to the conscious mind. If it looks workable, go to your writing desk; if it doesn't, shove it back down underwater and continue whatever you're doing until something new surfaces.

26 *Listen.* Alice Walker says, "If you're silent for a long time, people just arrive in your mind." As Americans, we are afraid of silence, and I'm guilty too. I tend to turn on the car radio if I'm moving the car twenty feet from the end of the driveway into the garage. One of the best ways to get started writing is to do nothing. Waste time. Stare out the window. Try to let your mind go blank. This isn't easy, as those who have tried meditation know. But many times, our minds, distracted by trivia, are too busy to write. Good writing comes out of silence, as Charles Simic says. "In the end, I'm always at the beginning. Silence—an endless mythical condition. I think of explorers setting out over an unknown ocean. . . ." We have to cultivate a quietness, resist the panic that the writing won't come, and allow ourselves to sink back into the emptiness. If we don't fight the silence, but accept it, then usually, without being aware of it, the writing will start to come.

These are some ways to get writing. You will come up with others if you make a list of techniques from other parts of your life that may apply here. A theater major may have all sorts of exercises and theater names that can spark writing. A scientist will be able to apply techniques of setting up experiments to setting up the experiment of writing. Art majors know how to attack a white canvas, and ski team members know how to shove off at the top of a steep slope.

Keep a record of methods of starting writing that work for you. The more experienced you become, the harder it may be to start writing, but you will also have developed more ways of getting words down on a page.

Experimenting with Form: Argument _____

Am I going to tell you about argument, you who started manipulating adults about the age of three months and knew a hundred argumentative strategies before you went to first grade?

No. I am going to *remind* you about argument. And the secret of argument: audience.

To argue effectively, the writer has to empathize with the reader the writer wants to persuade, to get inside that reader's head and discover what arguments will convince that particular reader.

This takes imagination and a dose of reality. All of us like to believe that we are right and our rightness will shine so strongly it will blind and convince the reader. It is not so. We can not simply raise our voices and persuade.

Think back to the arguments you have won—to drive the car, to go on a coed camping trip, to stay out all night—and list the strategies that worked and did not work. Write your own manual on argument.

A Writer's Case History: "Please Raise My Taxes!" _____

One reason I took a month long teaching job in Arizona one February was to experience the winter retirement world of the desert. I have spent time in Florida and written about it for my column, now I wanted to go to the desert. And we also wondered if we might want to retire there ourselves.

Writing makes you especially sensitive and, I suppose, critical of the world around you. That can make you a discomforting family member, friend, or neighbor I suppose, but it does keep you alive. I was bored in high school but I have never been bored since. When things are boring I sit back and observe. If that pales, I write in my head. Writers see more than most people and see it again when they write about it.

Since retirement is the goal of so many people, where people go and the world they create there makes a powerful comment on our society. If we can look we can see America's dream.

To me that dream was a nightmare and this column is my way of dealing with it. I did not expect to write an argument when I started making notes. I tried to be as fair and nonjudgmental as possible but, of course, I see the world as everyone does, through the eyes of my own heritage, experience, and prejudices.

My daybook has random fragments:

► to someone from NH, Arizona is west but I discovered it was east California

▶ she sat on his lap in the restaurant waiting room, grooming him

▶ the retired, busy at golf, pass my window

▶ I am surprised to find my home guarded by a cactus (Cacti??), dragged in from their lonely existence in the desert and given suburban duty.

▶ the land of bumper sticker Christians

▶ ostentatious wealth and unconcern

▶ living behind walls

These are about all of the notes I can find spread over four weeks in my daybook but they lead to the following essay, written rather quickly when I got home. I remember how it started. I was driving along, and thought that taxes deserved a good word and was surprised. I knew I had a feeling to explore.

Incidentally, I expected to be attacked and I did get more mail than usual but it was all favorable—and most readers indicated they were retired, well-to-do, and usually voted Republican.

Please Raise My Taxes

1　　TEMPE, Arizona—Out here and over sixty I'm supposed to be a grump, fearful of the young, opposed to change, and dead set against taxes. Any taxes for any purpose in any form.

2　　Well, after a few weeks in the sunbelt I guess the unusual amount of sun for this time of year has affected my brain, because it seems to this old-timer that it's time to say a good word for taxes.

3　　Taxes haven't gotten equal time. Politicians, even those who vote for them, are against 'em. And voters, even those farmers and businessmen who benefit from them, smile and nod as they read the President's lips.

4　　I never felt the urge to speak up for taxes before, even though I live in New Hampshire where it's against the law to tax sales or income and, apparently, give appropriate support to those who care for the ill or attempt to educate the ignorant.

5　　What got my attention was all the retirees out here hiding behind the walls of their moneyed ghettos, crouched in dark houses, trying to escape clouds, rain, snow, ice, and responsibility.

6　　The smug is so thick out here you can taste it. (The smog is often that thick as well, with radio stations in the Phoenix area issuing warnings not to jog and breathe deeply.) The retired will tell you, tell you, tell you how hard they worked, but they've got it made, and if the world is going to hell, it's somebody else's responsibility.

7　　Nobody ever mentions luck or inheritance or the golden handshake given when the corporation decided it was good business to pay Elmer to go to Scottsdale just to keep him from screwing up the Midwest territory.

8　　Now New Hampshire has Christians, too, but most of them aren't bumper sticker Christians. In the sunbelt, and this part of Arizona is Southern California East, Christians are Orange County aggressive. They wear their church going on their hip and expect you to get in line, right now. The Republican Party out here is debating a resolution to declare the U.S. of A. "a Christian nation."

9   I respect the beliefs and commitment of sincere members of all religions, but the theology of economic conservatism in the land of retirement gives sanctimoniousness a bad name.

10   You don't have to leave your neighborhood to see plenty of work for Christians to do, [and many Christians do it, quietly and effectively] but I have been traveling the country a great deal in the past year, and it is obvious we have enormous national problems. Not deficit, balance of trade problems only somebody with a Harvard degree can understand. I mean right-in-front-of-your-eyes everyday human problems.

11   We have people living on the street. Scenes that look like photos from Calcutta. Families living on the street. Children with families and without. There are homeless people who work and still live on the street.

12   And they aren't just in the evil eastern cities of New York and Washington and Boston, they keep sweeping the homeless out of the desert and back to the city streets of the sunbelt.

13   Many of the people are sick, mentally and physically, but we will not, do not care for them. We turn them out to fend for themselves.

14   We have an epidemic of drugs with elementary school children working the trade. They have fine qualifications. My Manhattan daughter's apartment and studio were both just burglarized by children who can crawl between window bars and unlock the doors for their elders, the junior high thieves who are robbing and dealing.

15   We have an epidemic of AIDS that has devastated the gay community and is increasingly affecting the heterosexual community. Some who had cast the first stone should get ready to duck.

16   We have acid rain and a 1100 other forms of pollution that are despoiling our nests because of products that answer our greed and stimulate the greed of those who sell to us. In the land of the sun, we buy our drinking water and haul it home by the gallon.

17   Health costs are multiplying and fewer people are covered in an aging society. When I had my heart attack, they took my blood pressure and my insurance card at the same time. Millions of Americans who have worked all their life have no private insurance cards and we chip away at Medicare and Medicaid. No socialism here—and no need for it in Sun City.

18   Our educational system is increasingly better—a computer at every desk—for the haves who need it less than the have nots who need it more. The have nots have their status confirmed by schools that deny them—in elementary school—any chance of making it in our technical society.

19   I'm just getting warmed up, but let me put myself on the line. I want to pay more taxes. In fact, President Bush, for starters I think my taxes should be doubled.

20   It is the obligation and responsibility of the government to care for those who can not care for themselves, to provide homes for the homeless,

doctors and care for the ill who cannot pay for it, to seek a cure for AIDS and other diseases, to provide education for all citizens—especially those who cannot afford it.

21   Of course there will be graft and mismanagement as there is in the private sector, in savings and loan institutions, on Wall Street, in the Aerospace industry, but tax money may create programs such as the GI Bill, which made it possible for me to go to college and make enough money so I can retire and call for higher taxes.

22   It is the job of our elected representatives to identify the problems facing our society that are not being solved by private interests, establish programs to attack those problems, and to bill us.

23   Will increased taxes guarantee solutions? Will we wipe out mental and physical illness, turn every student into an intellectual (let's hope not), house everyone in a mansion, make every citizen happy? Of course not, but we will make progress.

24   People will be helped, society will be made better, we will be functioning as a responsible democracy.

25   And even if taxes were doubled, most over sixties who have fled to the Sun Belt will still be able to hide behind a wall, fuel up the old golf cart, finish off the day at the 19th hole, grumping about the lazy young and the funny skin tones of many new Americans.

Now let's walk through that piece together. Before writing it I was aware of several problems.

First, I wanted to write in such a way that I would reach those who do not agree with me and would not normally read a "liberal" opinion. I wanted to avoid a sermon as much as possible. Well, let's be honest. I wanted to give a sermon but not have the audience feel they were suffering a sermon.

I needed to fill the piece with specifics that would cause the reader to remember evidence supporting my position from their own world and it had to be lively—specifics will help this—so they would read to the end. And I didn't want the voice of the text to drive readers away.

In all, a big order that I'm not sure I achieved.

Please Raise My Taxes

1 TEMPE, Arizona—Out here and over sixty I'm supposed to be a grump, fearful of the young, opposed to change, and dead set against taxes. Any taxes for any purpose in any form.

> I'm setting up a straw person, an argumentative trick that is dangerous, a position that I can easily knock down. It isn't a great opening, but I hope it has some tension in it: If you're supposed to be that and aren't, what are you?

2 Well, after a few weeks in the sunbelt I guess the unusual amount of sun for this time of year has affected my brain, because it seems to this old-timer that it's time to say a good word for taxes.

This is the true opening and has the tension that I hope will drive the reader through the argument. What? A good word for taxes? Why? And the tone tries to say that although I'm serious about the subject, I don't take myself too seriously.

3 Taxes haven't gotten equal time. Politicians, even those who vote for them, are against 'em. And voters, even those farmers and businessmen who benefit from them, smile and nod as they read the President's lips.

Lips. A dated reference from the presidential campaign. OK for a newspaper but dangerous in a piece meant to be read years later.

4 I never felt the urge to speak up for taxes before, even though I live in New Hampshire where it's against the law to tax sales or income and, apparently, give appropriate support to those who care for the ill or attempt to educate the ignorant.

5 What got my attention was all the retirees out here hiding behind the walls of their moneyed ghettos, crouched in dark houses, trying to escape clouds, rain, snow, ice and responsibility.

The greatest point of emphasis is at the end of a paragraph, and in re-reading this essay, I realized I often used that device instinctively. Here I put a twist on it to catch the reader unexpectedly.

6 The smug is so thick out here you can taste it. (The smog is often that thick as well, with radio stations in the Phoenix area issuing warnings not to jog and breathe deeply.) The retired will tell you, tell you, tell you how hard they worked, but they've got it made, and if the world is going to hell, it's somebody else's responsibility.

I find I used a lot of tricks in this piece to make it lively. "The smug is so thick. . . .", 'tell you, tell you, tell you. . . ." I'm a little embarrassed in reading it over now. I didn't calculate them but I used them. You'll have to decide if the writing is too gimmicky.

7   Nobody ever mentions luck or inheritance or the golden handshake given when the corporation decided it was good business to pay Elmer to go to Scottsdale just to keep him from screwing up the Midwest territory.

I'm fed up with those who were born to wealth, lucked into it, or received it as a reward for incompetence and feel superior to those who are poor and I show it—but, I hope, in a lively, entertaining way.

8   Now New Hampshire has Christians, too, but most of them aren't bumper sticker Christians. In the sunbelt, and this part of Arizona is Southern California East, Christians are Orange County aggressive. They wear their church going on their hip and expect you to get in line, right now. The Republican Party out here is debating a resolution to declare the U.S. of A. "a Christian nation."

9   I respect the beliefs and commitment of sincere members of all religions, but the theology of economic conservatism in the land of retirement gives sanctimoniousness a bad name.

I am into dangerous territory in these two paragraphs and the one following, but I see the Bible as a radical social document and am shocked at how people use religion to support materialism and a lack of social responsibility. Yet I try to be fair. My editor and I talked these paragraphs over carefully and decided to let them stay. No critical letters from Christians were received.

10   You don't have to leave your neighborhood to see plenty of work for Christians to do, [and many Christians do it, quietly and effectively] but I have been traveling the country a great deal in the past year, and it is obvious we have enormous national problems. Not deficit, balance of trade problems only somebody with a Harvard degree can understand. I mean right-in-front-of-your-eyes everyday human problems.

The reader, quite properly, should be demanding evidence. I try to provide it below.

11   We have people living on the street. Scenes that look like photos from Calcutta. Families living on the street. Children with families and without. There are homeless people who work and still live on the street.

12 And they aren't just in the evil eastern cities of New York and Washington and Boston, they keep sweeping the homeless out of the desert and back to the city streets of the sunbelt.

And now I try to anticipate the readers who will say, as one President did, that they want to be on the street and point out why they are on the street.

13 Many of the people are sick, mentally and physically, but we will not, do not care for them. We turn them out to fend for themselves.

14 We have an epidemic of drugs with elementary school children working the trade. They have fine qualifications. My Manhattan daughter's apartment and studio were both just burglarized by children who can crawl between window bars and unlock the doors for their elders, the junior high thieves who are robbing and dealing.

Yes my argument is impassioned, emotional. I let my caring show. And I use my daughter's experience and later my own, knowing that the more specific I am, the more universal I will be. If I am specific, my readers will think of anecdotes, scenes, experiences they have lived or been told.

15 We have an epidemic of AIDS that has devastated the gay community and is increasingly affecting the heterosexual community. Some who had cast the first stone should get ready to duck.

The last sentence tries to preach in a lively way. An effective piece should have little surprises for the reader—unexpected words, phases, details—that surprise with insight. They are not there just to surprise but to clarify.

16 We have acid rain and a 1100 other forms of pollution that are despoiling our nests because of products that answer our greed and stimulate the greed of those who sell to us. In the land of the sun, we buy our drinking water and haul it home by the gallon.

I move from the general to the specific.

17 Health costs are multiplying and fewer people are covered in an aging society. When I had my heart attack, they took my blood pressure and my insurance card at the same time. Millions of Americans who have worked all their life have no private insurance cards and we chip away at Medicare and Medicaid. No socialism here—and no need for it in Sun City.

18 Our educational system is increasingly better—a computer at every desk—for the haves who need it less than the have nots who need it more. The have nots have their status confirmed by schools that deny them—in elementary school—any chance of making it in our technical society.

Maybe I needed to clarify this a bit.

19 I'm just getting warmed up, but let me put myself on the line. I want to pay more taxes. In fact, President Bush, for starters I think my taxes should be doubled.

Now I hope I have earned the right by the evidence I have supplied to present my thesis: We should pay more taxes.
Why?
Will more taxes help?
Keep reading.
Every writer, but especially the writer of argument must "read" the reader, anticipate the readers' response and react to it.

20 It is the obligation and responsibility of the government to care for those who can not care for themselves, to provide homes for the homeless, doctors and care for the ill who cannot pay for it, to seek a cure for AIDS and other diseases, to provide education for all citizens—especially those who cannot afford it.

I start the paragraph with high-flown goals and end with a snapper.

21 Of course there will be graft and mismanagement as there is in the private sector, in savings and loan institutions, on Wall Street, in the Aerospace industry, but tax money may create programs such as the GI Bill, which made it possible for me to go to college and make enough money so I can retire and call for higher taxes.

Again I anticipate the reader's skeptical attitude and try to deal with it.

22 It is the job of our elected representatives to identify the problems facing our society that are not being solved by private interests, establish programs to attack those problems, and to bill us.

A strong restatement for emphasis of what I have said. A restatement. I hope, that carries my argument a bit forward.

23 Will increased taxes guarantee solutions? Will we wipe out mental and physical illness, turn every student into an intellectual (let's hope not), house everyone in a mansion, make every citizen happy? Of course not, but we will make progress.

More anticipation and response.

24 People will be helped, society will be made better, we will be functioning as a responsible democracy.

25 And even if taxes were doubled, most over sixties who have
fled to the Sun Belt will still be able to hide behind a wall, fuel
up the old golf cart, finish off the day at the 19th hole,
grumping about the lazy young and the funny skin tones of
many new Americans.

Perhaps a bit much but I want to state that they won't be hurt too much if taxes are doubled—fat chance—and I guess I wanted to zing them again. I hope it wasn't a cheap shot, "Christian nation" indeed.

A Student's Case History: Debbie Carson-Elwood _____

This student has written on a similar topic to mine but she has done it in an
entirely different way. My appeal is to the emotions, hers to the intellect.

Debbie Carson-Elwood has, by far, the most difficult task. She has to handle
extremely complex material, the kind of material most readers are not interested
in. She has to understand her subject, simplify it—but not too much—and make
the material lively and persuasive. I think she does a magnificent job and we
can all learn from her.

The Instructor's Account by Robert Yagelski

1   Imagine sitting in a workshop group in your freshman English class
and being handed a student paper on tax reform. Would you be excited by
the topic? If you're like most students, probably not. Now think of writing
a paper on that very topic, one you know your classmates probably won't
be interested in. That's the task Deb Carson-Elwood gave herself when she
began writing "Flat Tax—The Sensible Future."

2   It was a risk. Deb couldn't be sure that it would pay off. No writer ever
is. And you've probably heard your writing teacher say on occasion that
good writing involves taking risks. Think of it in mathematical terms: the
potential success of a piece of writing is directly proportional to the risks
the writer took in creating that piece of writing. It's not always so simple,
of course. But if from time to time you leave the security of what you know
well and venture into the unknown, you may find rewards along the way.
That happened to Deb Carson-Elwood.

3   Most interesting to me among Deb's notes on "Flat Tax—The Sensible
Future" are her brief comments on how she came to the topic. Tax reform
was an unknown for her. That didn't deter her, though. Her decision to
plunge ahead despite the unknown reminds me of a writing teacher I had
in college. He used to tell his classes that the essential characteristic of a
writer is curiosity: a writer must want to learn, about the world, about life,
about herself. Curiosity might kill the cat, but it keeps a writer alive.

4   Beginning writers often have a hard time recognizing that. They some-

times think that teachers want them only to stay close to home. They don't know that you can stay close to home and still make a fantastic journey. "Write about what you know," is a favorite aphorism. Your dorm, your friends, your high school football team. Those can all be fine topics, but not if you have no real desire to investigate them—if you have no curiosity about them. So I amend the advice a bit: "Write about what you want to know."

5   Deb took my advice, risks and all. She knew well that tax reform may be a difficult, complex, and perhaps even tedious topic. But she was curious. And that enabled her to overcome any apprehension about tackling such a topic. She was discovering an interest she had, and learning how much she still needed to learn about it. On top of all that, she chose to argue for a flat tax; that is, she chose perhaps the hardest type of paper for a freshman to write; an argument. That required her to think in new and unfamiliar ways.

6   But if you look at Deb's notes and drafts, you'll notice that the process by which Deb constructed her argument is not much different from the process you go through to narrate a story or analyze a work of literature. Deb continually circled back—planning, writing and revising as she went—until she was satisfied that her argument was sound and that her essay was as good as she could make it. Like any competent writer, Deb planned and replanned, wrote and revised, then revised some more.

7   According to Deb's writing schedule, she spent much more time revising than she did writing. Writing teachers often complain that getting students to understand the importance of revision is one of their hardest tasks. Deb learned the lesson well. But something even more difficult for students to learn is hidden in Deb's notes: the importance of planning. Look at the amount of time she spent reading the newspaper index and newspaper articles about tax reform. Look also at her notes from those articles. It's clear that Deb was thinking of her topic and planning as she read; she was reading as a writer reads. Planning made her first draft easier. Of course, the reading and planning didn't end there. Deb says in her notes that she "re-researched" the problem of bracket creep. She learned that revising often means going back to the researching or "collecting" stage to fill in gaps or clarify issues. In the end, going back made going forward possible. The result was a stronger argument.

8   It's clear, too, that Deb never forgot about her readers. You may have a good argument but a weak essay if you lose your readers, and Deb was aware of that. Her suspicion that her readers may not follow her discussion of bracket creep prompted her to "re-research." If she had not thought about her readers as she constructed her argument, she may never have tried to clarify that issue.

9   Most important of all, though, is that Deb cared enough about her writing to take risks, to write about something she didn't "know a whole lot" about, and to stay with it through all the researching and writing and rewriting. She invested a lot of herself in the topic and she was rewarded with a greater understanding of an issue she cares about—not to mention

the satisfaction of producing a fine essay. Deb learned something about her opinions and attitudes—something about herself—through writing an argument about the reform. That, I think, is the real attraction—and reward—of writing.

The Student's Account by Debbie Carson-Elwood

1   The idea of writing about a flat tax came to me during one of my classes. It's a subject that I'm interested in and an argument that I thought I could pose. This is one of the most important points when I'm writing an argument paper, I have to care about my topic. If I don't believe what I'm writing, the paper will be twice as hard. It's difficult to sound convincing when you're not convinced yourself.

2   I went into this project not knowing a whole lot about the flat tax proposal. I understood the basic concept and agreed with it but I didn't have any concrete facts to back my argument. I learned more about the proposal by reading numerous newspaper articles. I made sure to read up on both sides of the issue so I'd know the negative as well as the positive aspects. By being aware of the problems in the proposal, I was able to avoid those areas.

3   There was one part of the paper that I had to change. I originally wanted to strengthen my point on "bracket creep" and I found from re-researching that my concept of it was incorrect. Only minor changes were needed but those small changes made a big difference. If a reader had picked up a false statement, my credibility would have been lost and the rest of the paper would be doubted. An argument paper cannot be successful unless the reader believes that you're a reliable source.

4   Most of the revisions that I made were minor, a lot of restating and strenghtening. My main goal was to get the reader from beginning to end and to seriously consider my argument.

We can all learn lessons in organizing our work from Debbie's schedule.

Writing Schedule			
April	13	45 minutes	newspaper index
April	17	1½ hours	reading newspaper articles
April	17	85 minutes	writing
April	18	3½ hours	writing / re-working first written draft
April	19	1½ hours	typing 1st draft + making more revisions
May	3	15 minutes	revising 1st typed draft
May	7	1 hour 20 min.	typing 2nd draft revising
May	13	10 minutes	making suggestions on draft
May	13	2½ hours	typing 3rd draft revising
May	20	15 minutes	revising
May	21	2 hours	typing + revising 4th draft

Here are some of her notes:

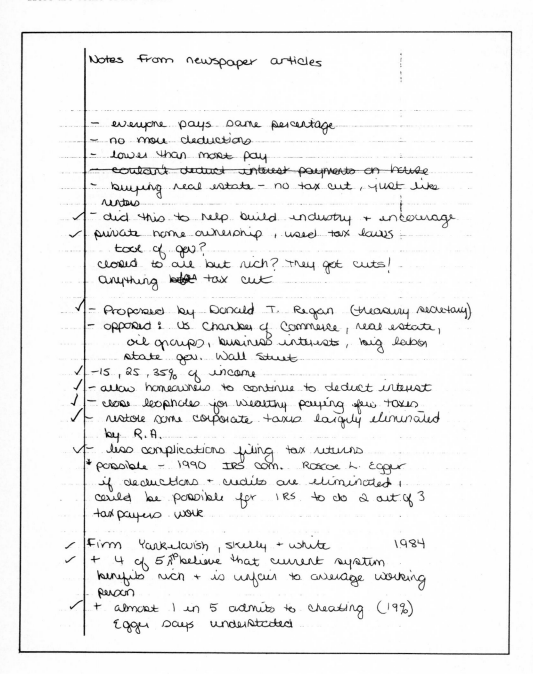

Notes from newspaper articles

- everyone pays same percentage
- no more deductions
- lower than most pay
- ~~couldn't deduct interest payments on house~~
- buying real estate - no tax cut, just like renters
✓ - did this to help build industry + encourage
✓ private home ownership, used tax laws -
    tool of gov?
    closed to all but rich? They got cuts!
    anything but tax cut

✓ - Proposed by Donald T. Regan (treasury secretary)
  - opposed: US Chamber of Commerce, real estate,
    oil groups, business interests, big labor
    state gov. Wall Street
✓ - 15, 25, 35% of income
✓ - allow homeowners to continue to deduct interest
✓ - close loopholes for wealthy paying few taxes
✓ - restore some corporate taxes largely eliminated
    by R.A.
✓ - less complications filing tax returns
* possible - 1990 IRS com. Roscoe L. Egger
  if deductions + credits are eliminated,
  could be possible for IRS to do 2 out of 3
  tax payers work

✓ Firm Yankelovich, Skelly + White   1984
✓ + 4 of 5 believe that current system
    benefits rich + is unfair to average working
    person
✓ + almost 1 in 5 admits to cheating (19%)
    Egger says understated

Her first draft, which shows a highly organized person going through the messy process of discovering what to say and how to say it.

First Draft

In 1984, the Yankelovich, Skelly & White firm conducted a survey ~~to discover~~ in order to find out what taxpayers thought of ~~the~~ tax ~~system~~. The results ~~say little for the direct~~ concluded that four out of five taxpayers ~~believe that~~ the present tax system ~~is beneficial to the~~ the rich and ~~is~~ unfair ~~to the~~ average working person. ~~Nineteen percent~~ 19% of those surveyed (almost one in five) admitted to cheating on their taxes. ~~with the primary reason for this~~ justification ~~cheating is because people believe that the~~ system is unfair. ~~and~~ They ~~feel must~~ believe that ~~that by~~ altering ~~things~~ the taxes ~~themselves to even out the~~ they are just equaling out the burden,

→ Secretary of the Treasury, Donald T. Regan, in a report to ~~the~~ President, ~~Reagan~~ stated ~~the following fact~~ that further discredited our current tax system. According to treasury estimates, in 1983, 9,000 people who earned $250,000 or more paid no taxes due to tax shelters. An additional 59,000 people at the same income level managed through loopholes to reduce their tax payments by half.

Throughout the US, The government has ~~used~~ managed to use the progressive tax as a ~~tool~~ to help build industry and to promote private home ownership. An individual renting ~~there are no~~ ~~home receives no tax breaks~~ receives no tax breaks; however, if you buy a home you qualify for tax deductions. The government allows *homeowners* ~~renters~~ to deduct ~~this interest payments on~~ interest payments on mortgages. ~~of a house.~~ (So in order to receive any breaks, a person must take out a loan. ~~How much of a~~ It's ironic that the one who needs the TB the most is also the one who can't afford ~~shelter~~. The only way to lessen taxes is tax shelters *to buy in the first place* and expensive lawyers to seek out loopholes.) Unfortunately, the only taxpayers who can afford such measures are the wealthy.

The current system also has the problem of "bracket creep". Often times workers will receive

(margin notes: Thro out the US?; rephrase strengthen point; CIRCLE? CATCH 22?; shelters R.H. Lawyers)

Here are the teacher's notes on one page for the conference and the student's notes.

applies to ~~all~~ taxpayers✗ oF all income levels.

There are two main variations of this proposal: a tax simplification proposal by Donald Regan and a Fair tax (also known
as the Bradley-Gephardt proposal) by Senator Bill Bradley and
Representative Richard Gephardt. Both of these taxes would reduce
the tax bracket to three (for instance, 15%, 25% and 35%), ⌐lower
taxes for the poor,⌐ increase the amount of personal exemption
elaborate and keep deductions for interest on home mortgages (the Treasury
on advantages Department would not, however, allow interest deductions on
second homes.)

The flat tax, or a variation of, would close most loopholes
and shelters available to the wealthy. The Treasury Secretary
also claims that the tax would restore some corporate taxes that
have been largely eliminated by the Reagan Administration. It
would do away with all discrimination inlvolved with the distribution of taxes, creating a fair system. Cheating on taxes would
                                              or possible
Argue ✓ no longer be necessary and people of the lower and middle class
why would be unable to label the system as "unfair".
no listing   *to such a degree*
deductions The complicated tax system would simplify (so much) that many
no way,
around it wouldn't even have to do their own returns. IRS commissioner,
Roscoe L. Egger, believes that the elimination of most deductions
and credits would allow the IRS to do two out of every three tax
returns. A bill or refund could be sent solely on information
received from the IRS by employers, banks, stockbro∫kers, etc.

With a relatively low rate, the government would be collecting
about the same amount of revenue that it is now. The primary
difference is that the source of revenue would be economically
neutral, coming from all income✗ levels.

The seventy-one year old system is outdated and it's time

3

Now there's a later draft and with further clarifications.

2nd Draft revisions

transition suggests that

more
↓ back it without numbers

* first 7 lines of p. 2 + 3 cut off. Refer to unrevised second draft

Flat Tax - The Sensible Future

In 1984, the Yankelovish, Skelley & White firm conducted a survey in order to find out what taxpayers thought of our tax system. The results (concluded) that four out of five taxpayers believe the present tax system to be beneficial to the rich and unfair to the average working person. Nineteen percent of those surveyed, almost one in five, admitted to cheating on their taxes with the justification that the system is unfair. The belief is that by altering the taxes, they are doing their part to equal out the burden.

survey suggests

The present tax system is biased, inefficient and in dire need of reform. In a report to the President, Donald T. Regan, Secretary of the Treasury, stated facts that futher discredit our current tax system. According to Treasury Department estimates, in 1983, 9,000 people who earned $250,000 or more paid no taxes due to tax shelters. An additional 59,000 people at the same income level managed through loopholes to reduce their taxes by half.

Through out the years, the government has used the progressive tax as a tool to help build industry and to promote private home ownership. An individual renting a home receives no tax breaks; however, if you buy a home you qualify for deductions. The government allows homeowners to deduct the interest payments on their mortgage. Another words to receive a tax break, you must take out a loan and spend money. It appears to be a vicious circle, the people who are needy of the tax break are the same people who can't afford to buy a house in the first place. In order to save money they must spend money they don't have. One might question if they're really saving any money at all. The only way around heavy taxes are through legal loopholes and expensive lawyers who

The student needs, at this late date, to make further notes to clarify the subject for herself and then her reader.

Figures to explain "bracket creep"

To TAX INC

~~GROSS INC~~	TAX INC	TAX	% TAX	% of TAX INC
	24,600	3465	14%	
	27,000	4065	15%	17%
	29,900	4790	16%	38% (A)
	35,200	6274	17%	31% (A)

(A) $4790 \div 3465 = 38\%$ OR $(4790 - 3465 \div 3465)$
$6274 \div 4790 = 31\%$ OR $(6274 - 4790 \div 4790)$

FLAT TAX of 14%

TAX INC		FLAT TAX %	TAX	$ INC	% INC (A)
24,600	X	14	= 3444		
29,900	X	14	= 4186	742	21%
35,200	X	14	= 4928	738	17%

(A) $4186 \div 3444$ & $4928 \div 4186$

The next to last draft and the writer is still working to clarify what she has to say.

Final Draft
with revisions

Debbie Carson-Elwood
English 401
Bob Yagelski
May 13, 1985

Flat Tax--The Sensible Future

In 1984, the Yankelovish, Skelly & White firm conducted a
survey in order to find out what taxpayers thought of our tax
system. The results showed that four out of five taxpayers
believe the present tax system to be beneficial to the rich and
unfair to the average working person. Nineteen percent of those
surveyed, almost one in five, admitted to cheating on their taxes
with the justification that the system is unfair. The belief is
that by altering the taxes, they are doing their part to ~~equal~~ *even*
out the burden.

This survey suggests that the present tax system is biased
and in need of reform. In a report to the President, Donald T.
Regan, Secretary of the Treasury, [stated facts that further discredit our current tax system. According to Treasury Department
estimates, in 1983, 9,000 people who earned $250,000 or more paid
no taxes due to tax shelters. An additional 59,000 people at the
same income level managed through loopholes to reduce their taxes
by half. These figures illustrate the ~~bias in our~~ tax system.

Those with the largest incomes are the ones escaping taxes because
they can afford to put their money into shelters.) Most people in
the middle class ~~cannot afford to invest money; they need their
cash readily available to pay expenses.~~

Now, the final draft:

Flat Tax—The Sensible Future
Debbie Carson-Elwood

1   In 1984, the Yankelovish, Skelly & White firm conducted a survey in order to find out what taxpayers thought of our tax system. The results showed that four out of five taxpayers believe the present tax system to be beneficial to the rich and unfair to the average working person. Nineteen percent of those surveyed, almost one in five, admitted to cheating on their taxes with the justification that the system is unfair. The belief is that by altering the taxes, they are doing their part to even out the burden.

2   This survey suggests that the present tax system is biased and in need of reform. In a report to the President, Donald T. Regan, Secretary of the Treasury, further discredited our current tax system. According to Treasury Department estimates, in 1983, 9,000 people who earned $250,000 or more paid no taxes due to tax shelters. An additional 59,000 people at the same income level managed through loopholes to reduce their taxes by half. These figures clearly illustrate one of the reasons our tax system is in need of reorganization. Those with the largest incomes are the ones escaping taxes because of the tax breaks and shelters. Most people in the middle class do not have these outlets available to them and therefore are unable to reduce their taxes.

3   Throughout the years, the government has used the progressive tax as a tool to help build industry and promote private home ownership. An individual renting a home receives no tax breaks; however, if you buy a home you qualify for deductions. The government allows homeowners to deduct the interest payments on their mortgage. To receive a tax break, you must take out a loan and spend money. It appears to be a vicious circle, the people who are needy of the tax break are the same people who can't afford to buy a house in the first place. In order to save money they must spend money they don't have. One might question if they're really saving any money at all. The only way around heavy taxes are through legal loopholes and expensive lawyers or accountants who can find them. But if the poor and middle class could afford such measures, they most likely could afford the taxes as well.

4   The current system also has the problem of "bracket creep." Often workers will receive a cost of living raise to help them adjust to the changing economy. But sometimes the workers end up being pushed into a higher tax bracket. The extra money they're making goes toward the higher taxes they're paying. For instance, consider a worker with a taxable income of $24,600. In the current system he pays a tax of $3465 which is

14% of his salary. Now suppose this worker received a $5300 cost of living raise. His taxable income becomes $29,900 and he is now in a higher tax bracket. His new tax will be $4790—16% of his salary. This is a 38% tax increase. If another $5300 was added on to his salary, he would jump into the next bracket and pay 17% of his income in taxes which would be a 31% tax increase. That is the creep. The higher your salary goes, the more of it you pay in taxes. In a sense, this policy is taking away the incentive to work harder and earn more. The more you work, the more you earn and the more you earn, the more you're taxed. The only way to escape this is if you work your way above the brackets. However, this means you must earn $162,000— not an easy goal to attain. The tax system even goes as far as discouraging saving. Money in savings accounts is taxed twice—once as income and again as returns on investment.

5　　　There is a great deal of controversy over what should be done and there have been several proposals for reform. The most sensible proposal is that of a flat tax. A flat tax would eliminate all deductions and credits and replace the progressive tax with a single rate (for example 25%) that applies to all taxpayers at all income levels.

6　　　There are two main variations of this proposal: a tax simplification proposal by Donald Regan and a Fair Tax (also known as the Bradley–Gephardt proposal) by Senator Bill Bradley and Representative Richard Gephardt. Both of these proposals would reduce the tax brackets from fifteen to three (for instance, 15%, 25% and 35%), increase the amount for personal exemption and keep deductions for interest on home mortgages (the Treasury Department would not, however, allow interest deductions on second homes).

7　　　Both proposals would not only lower the taxes themselves but also lower the percentage of tax increase. The burden of taxes would be reduced, enabling people to pay a smaller percentage of their salary in taxes. The wealthy would no longer have the advantage of being "above" taxes, they would be required to pay their fair share along with everyone else.

8　　　The flat tax, or variation of, would close most loopholes and shelters available to the rich. The Treasury Secretary also claims that the tax would restore some corporate taxes that have been largely eliminated by the Reagan Administration. It would do away with all discrimination involved with the distribution of taxes, creating a fair system. The problem of cheating would be greatly reduced because the tax would be a straight percentage of your income with no deductions except mortgage interest and personal exemptions. The IRS has records of incomes and interest payments and the exemption would be a straight $2000 per person. A false tax return would be detected immediately.

9　　　The complicated tax system would be simplified to such a degree that many wouldn't even have to do their own returns. IRS Commissioner, Roscoe L. Egger, believes that the elimination of most deductions and credits would allow the IRS to do two out of every three tax returns. A bill of refund could be sent solely on information received from the IRS by employers, banks, stock brokers, etc. This would save the taxpayer time, effort and money. They wouldn't have to spend hours filling out lengthy returns or figuring out the confusing process. It also would save money for those who have their taxes done by tax accountants.

10   With a relatively low rate, the government would be collecting the same amount of revenue that it is now, if not more. The primary difference is that the source of revenue would be economically neutral, coming from all income levels.

11   The seventy-one-year-old system is outdated and it's time for something new. The majority sees problems and the taxpayers of this country certainly deserve a change. It's time for the government to stop wasting time and money and start reforming our taxes to provide us with a future that makes economical sense.

Developing for the Reader _____

Never underestimate the hunger of the reader. We read, above all, for information, and the business memo, the poem, the engineering report, the essay, the letter, the examination answer are all more effective if the writer anticipates the reader's hunger and satisfies it.

The form of that satisfaction depends on the purpose of the writing and the particular reader you are serving. Sometimes fast foods are just what the reader needs, and lists, indented paragraphs, lines capitalized or underlined, tables of statistics are just right. Other times the reader wants to eat a leisurely meal, to taste and chew over what is served. Then the writer can proceed in a more discursive manner, documenting a point in a thoughtful manner, giving the reader adequate time to think over each piece of evidence and its relationship to other points in the text.

The writer you enjoy reading is generally sneaky. Information may be delivered in large hunks of description, thought, evidence, or documentation, but it is often slid into a paragraph or a sentence so that the reader is not even aware of swallowing information.

Some of the tricks of the sneaky writer:
- *The verb.* "He walked into the room." Marched, strode, stumbled will deliver more information to the reader.
- *The noun.* "He carried a weapon." Rifle, slingshot, bow and arrow, hand grenade, broken beer bottle, hunting knife tells us more.
- *The clause.* "He carried a broken beer bottle, already caked with blood, in his right hand as if he were ready to use it."
- *The immediate definition.* "He carried a cross-bow, a Medieval weapon that shot an arrow with terrifying force, when he came to the reading of the will."
- *The immediate documentation.* "He was a cross-bow marksman, each Sunday morning he shot at the cat, always clipping a few hairs from her tail, never drawing blood."

• ***The specific.*** "The cat hid in the back of the Mercedes sportscar he drove with the top down every Sunday afternoon. When old cross-bow got to Hitchin's curve, the cat leapt on his head and scratched at his eyes. As the car sailed off the cliff, the cat jumped free, shook himself, and strolled home without a backward glance."

The more you write and study the most effective writers in your class and the writers you read in magazines and books, the more ways you will find to sneak information into your writing, line by line.

Questions about Developing _____

• *What if the writing doesn't come? What if there's absolutely nothing in my head when I start to write?*

I always feel that way—and many times it's true, there's nothing but space between my ears.

I don't try to force the writing. I back up, stop, do something else, and try again, perhaps in ten minutes, perhaps the next morning. I'm a morning writer, and I find that if the writing doesn't come one time it will come the next.

• *But what if it doesn't?*

Then I haven't planned well enough. I go back and wallow about the information, mess around with focusing activities, or do some ordering or outlining. If the writing isn't ready to come, then I haven't prepared it well.

• *But won't I get writer's block?*

Few students have writer's block. Some writers do, but not enough that they're filling the back wards of institutions. Writer's block is a convenient thing to say to someone who wouldn't understand planning activities or the necessary rehearsal that precedes writing. It's also a convenient term to use when you haven't gotten yourself into the chair and waited for writing. John McPhee used to tie himself into the chair the first thing in the morning with his bathrobe cord. Getting into the chair and waiting for writing is the hardest thing to do.

Stick some mottoes or quotations from writers above your writing desk. A few of mine:

> I have to write every day because, the way I work, the writing generates the writing.
>
> E. L. DOCTOROW

> Two simple rules. (A) You don't have to write. (B) You can't do anything else. The rest comes of itself.
>
> RAYMOND CHANDLER

If you keep working, inspiration comes.

ALEXANDER CALDER

Most cases of writer's block are the direct result of inappropriate standards. The writer is trying to write better than is possible for this writer to write at this particular time. Just write; worry about how well it works after you have finished the draft.

- *My writing changes. I mean, I have all these outlines and stuff, and then it takes off and goes on its own.*

Good. Writing is thinking, not just reporting what you've thought. Writing is a dynamic, forward-moving force, and when the writing is going well most writers feel they are following the writing. E. M. Forster advised, "Think before you speak, is criticism's motto; speak before you think, is creation's."

- *But what if it's really out of control, I mean, doesn't make any sense at all?*

You have two choices: go back and start over again, or edit with a firm hand and get it under control.

- *My piece doesn't so much get out of control as run off in a dozen directions, like when I take my beagle for a walk and she follows her nose, chases cats, investigates garbage pails, chases shadows, keeps circling around. She isn't out of control—we get home—but she walks ten miles more than I do.*

I used to write like a beagle myself. Then the late Hannah Lees suggested I write each paragraph on a separate page. For years I did just that, using half pieces of paper—8 by 5. When I got the piece done I spread all the paragraphs on a large table or on the floor and rearranged them into an efficient pattern. Some of the trails I had followed belonged in the piece; others didn't, and they had to go.

- *But sometimes I have to write right on deadline.*

So do I, and for years, I was a newspaper rewrite person spending five nights a week writing fifteen to fifty stories a night, on deadline. When you write under that pressure you have to follow the patterns of writing laid down in long-term memory. The experience of writing when you had time—the lessons you learned—is on call when you have to write in a hurry.

- *How do I know what the reader knows? I know the subject so well, I can't tell what someone else needs to know.*

Role-play that reader, make yourself become a particular person you know and respect but who doesn't know the subject and read as that person would read. Show the draft to test readers, asking them to tell you places where they would like more information.

• *Can I give the reader too much stuff?*

Sure, but it's unlikely. Reading a flood of students' papers every year, I see 99 percent that are underdeveloped. The writer knows the subject so well that he or she underestimates the reader's need for more information.

Developing Activities _____

1. Try a different tool. If you usually write by hand, write directly on the typewriter, or dictate into a tape recorder, and then copy down what you've said. Different ways of writing can help capture a working draft.
2. Write a discovery draft, writing as fast as you can to find out what you're going to say.
3. Tell the story to someone else to hear what you say when you have an audience; read the person's reactions by paying attention to body language, interest, and so forth. Don't do this if you think you'll lose the piece. Some writers find this very helpful, but others find that once they have told the piece to someone, they won't write it.
4. Write one paragraph each describing a place, defining an idea, introducing a person, presenting an argument, revealing a process; then write a second paragraph for each one in which you show instead of tell.
5. List the questions the reader will ask about your piece of writing and put them in the order the reader will ask them.
6. Read aloud something you've written before and make notes about what reading aloud reveals to you. One significant thing it may reveal is that it's hard to make notes—you hear the flow of the piece of writing and want to be carried on by that flow; in other words, reading aloud is the best way of testing to see if a piece of writing flows.
7. Take a significant piece of information from the writing you're working on and list all of the ways it can be documented—quotation, statistic, description, anecdote, and so on.
8. Write a draft.
9. Go back and use one of the techniques of collecting, focusing, or ordering to see if it will help you get a draft flowing.
10. Imagine a person you feel comfortable with and write the draft to that person, speaking as you would in a conversation. You may even want to start the draft as a letter to that person.
11. Imagine that you are a ghostwriter writing the piece for someone else. Put your "client's" name at the top to see how the piece would go if you were writing it in that voice. Make believe you're James Baldwin, Joan Didion, George Orwell. Try on another style as a way of seeing how that style works and as a way of getting into a text that you can make your own.
12. Write the draft backward, writing the end first, the next to the end next, until you've worked your way back to the beginning.

13. Write the section that is easiest for you to write, then the next easiest, and so forth until you get all of the parts written and can fit it together into a working draft.
14. Give yourself a quota of time (an hour, an hour and a half, two hours) or of pages (one page, or three, or five), and then write to fill the time or the number of pages. Don't worry for the moment about the whole piece and its final quality; just deal with the chunk of writing time or the number of pages you have assigned yourself.
15. Revise the student's draft, developing it for a different audience or in a different way.

Chapter 7

℞ Explore Your Subject: CLARIFY

I work with language. I love the flowers of afterthought.

BERNARD MALAMUD

What makes me happy is rewriting. In the first draft you get your ideas and your theme clear, if you are using some kind of metaphor you get that established, and certainly you have to know where you're coming out. But the next time through it's like cleaning house, getting rid of all the junk, getting things in the right order, tightening things up. I like the process of making writing neat.

ELLEN GOODMAN

When I see a paragraph shrinking under my eyes like a strip of bacon in a skillet, I know I'm on the right track.

PETER DE VRIES

Listen to Your Text to Revise and Edit: Revit _____

Revit.

What?

Revit. Revise and edit. We keep trying to separate those activities, but they can't be separated so we should combine the word.

We need to resee the text—revision—making major changes in topic, focus, order, pace, even changing the genre and often doing new research, and we need to edit each potential text, working with word, phrase, line, sentence, fact, tone, checking spelling, grammar, and mechanics, working to paragraph, page, section, entire text. Each process runs into the other.

When you change one word, it may lead to a new focus and more research; a different topic may mean extensive changes in language.

Revit.

Once we have a text we have something to work on. I enjoy the terror and excitement of creating a text but I also delight in the satisfaction of practicing the writer's craft, revising and editing: taking out, putting in, moving around.

Your attitude determines how well you help the text evolve. Many writers fall in love with their first drafts. They did it. It is beautiful, wonderful, lovely, true, and untouchable.

Ridiculous. That attitude is silly. The first time is rarely the best time in love, baseball, tap dancing, or writing. There are first drafts that are pretty good but most of the time an effective piece of writing has to be cultivated. A good first draft has potential and it is the job of the writer to develop that potential.

When I wrote my first magazine articles I kept careful records. It took me about two hours to produce the first draft, two weeks to turn that into a final draft. I averaged 30 revisions. Now I am experienced, I revise less, but my most spontaneous drafts are often worried into being, reading after reading, draft after draft.

Listen to the Text

I start by listening to the text, not to what you expected, but what is. I read the text as a stranger, sometimes even role-playing a person I know who does not know my subject and is not interested in it.

I hear the text and ask two questions:

▶ What works?
▶ What needs work?

The first question is as important as the second. I do not know what is right when I finish a draft any more than I know what is wrong. I am too close to it.

The biggest problem I have in reading my first draft is that I think everything is wrong. It stinks. All of it: subject, form, voice. I can't write this piece. I can't write. I wallow in despair, boring those around me—and boring myself. I have to know what works, where the potential in the draft lies.

Then I need to know—in light of what works, in the light of the potential—what needs work.

I find the answer to both questions by listening to the text. I mean the heard quality of good writing, the voice of the text, and more. I do hear the text, and if I listen carefully—craftily—I believe the text will tell me what to do.

The draft will tell me when to speed up and slow down, which words to define, what facts to add or cut, when an anecdote is needed or a quotation, when a paragraph should be added, developed, or cut.

I have to follow the evolving text the way a handler has to follow a tracking dog—with respect. I have to let the text have its head, see where it wants to go and help it get there.

I cannot force effective writing anymore than I can or should force my daughters to choose a career that would be good for my ego, anymore than I can choose or reject whom they decide to live with. I can respect, love, support, help, but never lead.

I have the same relationship with the evolving text: I listen, respect, encourage, respond, support the writing that needs to be heard. This is the attitude that allows me to be instructed by the text.

Is this possible for beginning writers? Yes, we work with first-graders, even kindergartners, with students at every level of education. The person who can produce a text, can read that text and, if invited patiently, can suggest what the text needs: a bit more description here, a slowing down there so the reader has time to absorb that surprising information, a speeding up later when the same thing is said over and over again.

This isn't quantum physics. Every college writer has been using language long before first grade. All of us have been speaking and changing what we say when the message doesn't get through. We try again in a different way. We send the message over, making it clear. We are all experienced at revising and editing. We know how to revit.

Primary Technique to Clarify Your Draft: The Checklist _____

I have worked for the past few years with editors on some of the best newspapers in the country, and I have found these editors make the same mistake most teachers—and their students—make. It is the mistake that every one of us, as writers, will make unless we have trained ourselves to be effective editors. The mistake is to plunge in and start editing language first, working from the written line back to form and then to meaning. It is the backward way of editing, and it simply doesn't work.

You choose one word and reject another word in relation to meaning. If the meaning isn't clear, the choice will be arbitrary and often wrong. There are no rules for word choice unrelated to meaning. And when you choose to write a short sentence or a short paragraph, it is usually for emphasis, and unless you know what you want to emphasize, you won't know whether to make the sentence or the paragraph short.

When most drafts are edited, the meaning isn't yet clear—that's the primary purpose of editing. A careful line-by-line editing before the meaning is clear is a waste of time.

Three Readings

Effective editing is usually the result of three separate and distinct readings, each with its own pace, strategies, and techniques.

The highly skillful editor or writer may be able to perform all three readings simultaneously, moving from the large global questions of meaning to structural questions of order, and to line-by-line questions of voice. But those interrelated skills are best developed by separating the reading—reading first for meaning, next for order, and third for voice.

And of course, in each case, the writer has to keep an eye cocked for the audience, standing back and making sure that what is being said and resaid on the page is clear to the reader.

This seems a slow process, but *the first reading* is usually a very fast reading— a quick flyover of the territory to make sure that there is a single dominant meaning and an abundant inventory of information to support that meaning.

If there is no subject, no dominant meaning, no inventory of information, it is a waste of time to do more revising and editing. Stop immediately. Find a subject. Find its meaning. Find the facts to support that meaning.

The second reading is for form and structure. It is a bit slower, but not much. The piece is still read in chunks to see if the sections support the main point and appear when the reader needs them.

If there is no form to the writing, no order within that form that leads the reader to meaning, read no further. It will be a waste of time. Stop. Choose a form and establish an order within that form.

At the end there is *the third reading*, a slow, careful, line-by-line editing of the text to make sure that it is ready for a final proofreading. Here the reader cuts, adds, and reorders, paragraph by paragraph, sentence by sentence, word by word.

The process of three readings may sound tedious and boring, but it shouldn't be. In each case, there should be the excitement of discovery, of finding a meaning that you did not expect to find and having a chance to make it come clear. Writing gives us the satisfaction of craft, the feeling we have when we lean our weight into the corner and make our bicycle swing gracefully where we want it to go. Writing is similar to stroking a tennis ball, baking bread, building a sturdy shelf, sewing a dress, planting a garden. It is a process of making, and it is fun to make something well, to handcraft a piece of prose that will carry meaning and feeling to another person.

Editing Marks

On a computer, most editing is invisible, but those who work with typewriter and pen or pencil, will find it helpful to mark up the copy according to the traditions of the editor's trade.

> During the first two readings, I sit away from the desk if I am not using a
>
> computer, in an easy chair and use a clipboard or a bean-bag lap desk. I
>
> ✓ read the draft quickly, as a reader will, and I do not mark anything within
>
> ✱ the text. I do not correct spelling, typos, change words, revise, or edit. In-
>
> C stead, I make marks in the left margin. A check for something that works, a
>
> ⇡ star for something that works well, a C for something that needs cutting, an
>
> ⇕ arrow that suggests movement, a two-headed arrow to indicate the need for
>
> → ← expansion, two arrows pointing at each other to show what needs to be
>
> ? tightened, and a question mark for further consideration. These marks al-
>
> low me to move through the text quickly.

Here are some of the most helpful editing marks for the third, careful line-by-line reading:

Editing Marks

If you are not using a computer and reading "hard copy," you will find these marks helpful in editing your drafts or the drafts of a classmate in a peer editing session:

paragraph	The craft of editing depends on reading aloud.
capital	the craft of editing depends on reading aloud.
lower case	The craft of editing depends on reading aloud.
close	The craft of edit ing depends on reading aloud.
separate	The craft of editing depends on reading aloud.
transpose	The craft of editing depends on reading aloud its
punctuate	The craft of editing depends on reading aloud

insert   The craft of editing ~~depends on~~ *is* reading aloud.

take out   The craft of editing, ∧ is reading aloud.

cut   ~~The craft of~~ editing depends on reading aloud.

restore   ~~The craft of~~ editing depends on reading aloud.

move   *insert A*   The craft of editing depends on reading aloud.

large inserts should be numbered or lettered and an arrow

should be marked in the margin of the text where it is to be

more # → *Insert A* → placed.

The following checklists are built on the topic to language principles that uses the three readings. Of course, the process of reviting—revising and editing—will not be so neatly contained. Change of focus leads to change of language and change of language can change the topic, but the master list is a way of proceeding logically and efficiently through a series of confusing writing problems.

Each of us, of course, has our own writing strengths and weaknesses. Eventually, you should adapt my checklist to your own style and your own problems and solutions.

Many times we write on deadline. There is no time to do a careful job of revising and editing. Remember that you have to deal with the first item before going on to the second and the second before the third. Here is a checklist for that situation:

The Quick Checklist
▶ State the single, most important message you have for the reader in one sentence.
▶ List the points that support that message in the order the reader needs to receive them.
▶ Read the draft aloud to make sure the text is accurate, fair, and that the music of the language supports the message you are sending to the reader.

When you learn that the first draft is not at the end of the writing process, you will plan so that there is time—at least as much as comes before the first draft—for reading, revision, and editing. The checklist is designed to help in the three readings for subject, structure, and language. But don't be surprised when you have to move back and forth through the checklist as solutions breed problems and new problems demand new solutions.

The Master Checklist
▶ *State the single, most important message you have for the reader in one sentence.*
—Does the text deliver on the promise of the title and lead?

—Does your message have significant meaning you can make clear to the reader?

—Is the message important, worth the reader's time?

—Does your message contain the tension that will provide the energy to drive the reader forward?

—Is your message focused? Do you have a clear point of view toward the subject?

—Is the message placed in a significant context? Will that context be clear to the reader?

—Does the message have limitations that help you control and deliver the information?

—Do you have an abundance of information from which to build the text? Can you answer the questions the reader will certainly ask?

—Is that information accurate—and fair?

▶ *List the points that support that message in the order the reader needs to receive them.*

—Is the form, the genre, of the text appropriate to deliver the message to the reader? Will it contain and support the meaning of the text?

—Does the structure within the text support and advance the principal message?

—Does the order in the piece make the reader move forward, anticipating and answering the reader's questions?

—Is the structure logical? Does each point lead to the next in a sensible sequence? Is there a narrative thread that carries the reader forward? Will the sequence or narrative stand up to a doubting reader?

—Is the text too long? Too short?

—Are the proportions within the text appropriate to the information they deliver? Are there sections that are too long? Too short?

—Is the text effectively paced? Does the text move fast enough to keep the reader reading, slow enough to allow the reader to absorb what is being read?

—Does the text go off on tangents that take the reader away from the principal message of the text? Are there good pieces of writing that do not support this message but may be developed on their own later?

—Is each point supported with evidence that will convince the reader?

—Is the text at a distance that will involve the reader but also allow the reader to consider the significance of the message?

▶ *Read the draft aloud to make sure the text is accurate, fair, and that the music of the language supports the message you are sending to the reader.*

—Does the title catch the reader's attention and does it make a promise to the reader that can be delivered by the text?

—Does the opening do the same thing?

—Is each piece of information accurate and fair and in context?

—Does the reader need more information? Less? Can anything be cut? Must anything be added?

—Does the reader finish each sentence with more information than when the reader started?

—Can the text be heard by the reader? Does the music of the text support and advance the meaning of the message?

—Does the text reveal rather than tell whenever possible? Does the text call attention to the message rather than the reader?

—Does each paragraph and each sentence have the appropriate information emphasized?

—Does the sentence length vary in relation to the meaning being communicated with shorter sentences at the most important points?

—Does the text depend, at important points, on the subject-verb-object sentence?

—Is the text written in the active voice whenever possible?

—Is each word the right word?

—Has all sexist and racist language been eliminated?

—Has private language—jargon—been replaced with public language the reader can understand?

—Has worn-out language—clichés and stereotypes—been replaced with language that carries specific meaning to the reader?

—Is the text primarily constructed with verbs and nouns rather than adverbs and adjectives?

—Has the verb "to be" in all its forms been eliminated whenever possible? And excess "woulds," "thats," and "ings"?

—Is the simplest tense possible used?

—Are the tenses consistent?

—Are any words misspelled?

—Are the traditions of language and mechanics followed except when they are ungraceful or change the meaning of the text?

—Is the text attractively presented so that nothing gets between the reader and the message?

—Does the closing give the reader a feeling of closure and completeness yet stimulate the reader to continue to think about the message that has been delivered?

As I said before, develop your own list built on your own strengths and weaknesses. And do not forget that this final stage of making should be satisfying as you make further discoveries in clarifying meaning. And it should be fun as you exercise your draft and see meaning come clear under your hand.

Additional Techniques to Clarify Your Draft: Read Outloud

Read aloud, for your ear is a better editor than your eye, and it will catch the break in rhythm, the awkward phrase, the clumsy pacing that will confuse the reader and if continued make the reader turn from the text.

It is also important to hear the text, because that is how the reader receives the text, at least the most effective texts. The reader listens to the writing, receiving the message as a private conversation with the writer.

Read as a Writer

The woman who plays basketball watches the game differently from the people around her in the bleachers. And in the same way, the person who writes reads differently from other readers.

The biggest difference for the writing reader is that every text is dynamic, capable of change, full of possibility. The writer sees choice on every page, in every line. The writer appreciates and applauds when the text represents a good choice, hisses and boos when it doesn't. The reader who writes becomes involved in the text.

The effective writer—and the effective editor or teacher—has to learn to read unwritten texts. This means that the writer has to be able to sift through random words, phrases, sentences that half work, scribbled outlines, telegraphic notes, incomplete paragraphs, false starts, the way an archeologist has to sift through the excavated refuse of an ancient civilization. The archeologist has to be able to read these fragments to recreate what was; the writer has to read the fragments to create what may be.

It's easy to read a text after it has been drafted, but the writer has to develop the skill to read a text when there is no text. The writer has to see which words are code words, words that have special meaning for the writer when they appear in the notebook. The writer has to pick the phrase that gives the hint of a special meaning or an effective voice. The writer has to see how a fragment can be developed and to spot the meaningful connections that may be made between specific details.

The writer reads texts that haven't yet been written. This is a strange form of misty reading in which the reader has to spot meaning before it is clear. It is anything but careful reading. The writer squints ahead to see or hear what may become a draft. The writer can train himself or herself to this form of reading by looking always for the potential in the notes that keep appearing on the drafts that seem to go nowhere, drafts that fall apart, drafts that turn around and destroy themselves, drafts that trail off—all drafts that can have possibility within them.

It is just as important to recognize what isn't on the page as what is. Most of us underwrite; since we know the context and the connotation of what we have written, we think the reader will too. This is understandable. We spend most of our time speaking to those who are familiar with us and with whom we share a common world. Science fiction fans talk about science fiction to others who read it. Scientists talk about their experiments to those who work in the lab with them. Soldiers discuss tactics with other soldiers. Writing takes us out of our world and allows us to speak to those who need to know much more than those with whom we usually converse.

We have to know what isn't on the page; we have to define terms. We have to put details in context. We have to make the significance clear. We have to spell out connections and implications. We have to be able to stand back and see how the text needs to be developed. It is normal for my writing and the writing of students to increase in length by a third between the first and second drafts. We read what isn't there, and then make sure it is.

Read as a Reader

One of the hardest tasks of the writer is to read what is on the page, not what the writer hoped would be on the page. We all, in reading our text, hear what we intended to say when we see the words on our own pages. The difficulty is to read those words without our intent getting in the way.

To do this, I have to give myself a bit of time—sometimes only ten minutes—and I usually have to move to a different chair or place or table, and often I have to arm myself with a different colored pen. Then I am ready to look at the words on the page to discover what I have actually said, what those words I chose with hope and with imagination actually say when my intentions are removed from them.

This is reading with a cold eye, but it is necessary and it is fun. It fascinates me to see what language has done on its own. Sometimes it has done less than I intended, but other times it has done more. Words can conceive their own meanings when placed together on the page. It is my job to make sure I know what is there so I can decide what should be there.

The writer has to become the representative of the reader. This usually means role-playing a specific reader, and therefore coming to the text as a stranger.

The reader will read the text fast. The text must be clear in a relatively superficial reading. The text must carry the reader along: It must be slow enough so the reader can absorb each point, but fast enough so the reader will not put it down. The text must answer the reader's questions—when they are asked. The text must have the music of an individual voice, so that the prose moves pleasingly and gracefully in the reader's ear and eye.

How do you do all those things? Follow the golden rule: Write as you would have others write unto you.

Build on Strength

The focus should be on the positive as much as the negative. Of course, the editing writer solves problems and corrects mistakes. But most of all, the writer builds on strengths. It is important to be able to identify what works well in the text so it can be extended throughout the text. For example, if the voice is strong and appropriate in one part of the text, that voice can be taken and applied to the rest of the text.

A few years ago, I copied my early draft on large pieces of paper so I could keep a record of what I was doing as I practiced the craft of revit—revising and editing.

I thought I corrected error, made failure work, and I did. But, more than that, I developed what worked and extended it so that it eliminated many of the weaknesses of the text. I did not so much correct error as I built up success.

Use Test Readers

First we write, then we step back and read as a reader. But before we know whether to present our manuscript for publication we need test readers. And it may be easier to choose a husband or a wife than to choose a test reader. At the moment in the writing process when we have completed a draft, we are especially vulnerable. We fear criticism, for it may confirm our worst secret anxieties that we have little that is worth saying and that we have said it badly. The writer is exposed by the writing, and none of us wants to be exposed to a critical eye. But we do have defenses against criticism. As John Osborne says, "Asking a working writer what he thinks about critics is like asking a lamp-post what it feels about dogs." The reader is a bad reader; the reader is stupid; the reader is prejudiced; the reader is vicious.

We may know how to protect ourselves against criticism, but many of us never survive praise. We need it, want it, love it, and never get enough of it, and the person who praises our work is wise, fair, just, insightful, understanding, and perceptive. But we have to protect ourselves against the "like wow" critics who give us bland, general, delightful, but meaningless praise. Those readers do not help us resee our text; in fact, they may even prevent us from seeing it at an effective distance.

The writer has to search for those few special readers with whom we can share work in progress, and from whom we can receive reactions that help us when the helping really counts—before publication, when the text can be improved. These test readers may be teachers, editors, or colleagues, but they usually share similar qualities:

- *They Write Themselves.* They know the territory emotionally and mentally and can have an appreciation of how we are thinking and how we are feeling. They understand where we are in the writing process.
- *They Listen to What the Text Is Saying without Preconception of What We Should Say and How We Should Say It.* I once had a well-known poet read my short poems and tell me that since I was a big guy I should write big poems. He didn't seem to understand that the poet in me is a short, secretive little guy. The criticism wasn't helpful. The effective test reader is a colleague who helps you, the writer, see what is evolving that is unexpected and worth keeping. This reader delights in surprises, in variation, in diversity, and helps evaluate the text on its own terms.
- *The Reader Is Honest.* The effective test reader is able, because of the reader's own accomplishments, to admit to envy and admiration and to deliver disagreement and doubt. The critic does not withhold comments from both ends of the spectrum, but tries to deal not so much in praise or criticism as in specific comments on what works, and why; what doesn't work, and why; what may work, and why.

• **MOST IMPORTANT, *the Test Reader Makes You Want to Write*.** The test reader may deliver bad news, but you should always leave the effective test reader eager to get back to the writing desk, to attack and solve the writing problems. Cultivate this kind of test reader.

How do you find such readers? By sticking your neck out. You show your drafts to those who you think will help you, and you return to those who do.

But you say you have to deal with a teacher—or an editor—who isn't helpful. Of course you do; of course I do. So now you know how the world works. But I also have a few test readers from whom I learn. They are my secret editors and teachers. I turn to them to find out how to deal with the others. And some of them actually are editors and teachers, for if you are a writer you never stop going to school.

Experimenting with Form: The Research Paper _____

The research paper is central to the academic world. It allows researchers and scholars to add to the chain of knowledge by which each discipline is extended.

In writing the research paper, we add new knowledge and new understandings of old knowledge to what we know. Because of the nature of this writing task, there are traditions we must all follow in producing a research paper.

The writing must be clear, specific, objective, and accurate in detail and context. The reader who is also building the chain of knowledge needs to know where each fact and opinion comes from, so we write with footnotes. This way, the reader can look behind the text to see what it has used as well as added to the chain of knowledge.

In the same way, the bibliography is vital. The reader who is interested in the content of the research paper needs to know what articles, papers, reports, and books the writer has used because the reader may want to use them as well.

While you are doing your research, notice the way in which research is reported in each field. Each discipline has its own form for the research paper. The clinical psychologist, the social psychologist, the laboratory or rat psychologist, the psychological historian will all have different forms that are traditional in the field because they help deliver the information in the way others can most easily use. Discover the traditions and forms of the research paper appropriate to the discipline in which you write a research paper.

Case History of a Professional Writer: "No! Not Back to High School" _____

I try to make writing a game and so I decided to take myself up on my challenge to see if I could make a column from the examples I produced when demonstrating the process of layering in Chapter 6. I thought it might be a good way to demonstrate both revising and editing—a real-life example.

And that was scary. I was putting myself on the line and it was the scariness that kept me doing it. Fear, terror, anxiety can make the adrenalin pour.

But there is a contradiction. When I start writing I have to be calm, quiet, listening, not making the text but following it.

Last night, while watching a football game on television, I scanned what I had written in the exercise and while getting the paper and making my breakfast in the morning, I half thought about what I might write. This is an interesting process. It's not thinking as much as an awareness, a signal to the memory cells to fire up.

Down in my office at 7:30 A.M., I put the pages from Chapter 6 to the left of the computer and started the draft. I thought I might lead up the section marked 5, that it might be the second half of the piece, but then I told myself not to fool around, to get into the writing, that the text would tell me what it wanted, so I started copying what I had written, knowing it would change within lines.

A few times I looked back at my text but I was really working with the memory of the text. I wanted to use the previous text as a stimulus, a rough first draft that I would revise by developing. I have reproduced this draft as I wrote it, bad typing and all, and I have allowed it to run down at the end, which often happens on an early draft. I just run out of steam. But I know I will revit— revise and edit—later.

No!
Not Back to High School
Donald M. Murray

1   My wife, a daughter and I were talking about high school the other evening—none of us wanted to return—and we laughed at someone who was still angry at being alienated in high school. I heard myself say, "Everyone's alienated in high school."

2   Having zoomed by 65 this month, I am startled by the acceleration of life over 60. I'd like to slow things down a bit—quite a bit—but I don't want to go back. Most of all, I don't want to go back to North Quincy High School.

3   I can still remember what it felt like to be sentenced to those educational cells they call classrooms. Slowly the ceiling lowered, the walls drew in, the air was removed from the room and I concentrated on the huge minute hand on the clock that slowly clicked off each minute.

4   French and Latin were foreign languages, no surprise in that. But so was math and chemistry and physics and even English—I never could figure out those diagrams. I write this in September and I remember that long before that month was over I had sunk for the third time in most classes.

5   Other kids raised their hands, some even seemed to talk back and forth with teachers, laughing at what they thought were jokes.

6   I'd had a good teacher—Bob Hamilton—in the sixth grade and I was to have a good teacher—Mort Howell—in the 13th grade, but I didn't know that. My teachers were angry, angry at the depression, angry at not being able to marry (almost all my teachers were women and they might not have married but they seem angry they couldn't without being fired), angry at the school administration, angry at taxpayers, angry at each other, angry at the class, angry at me.

7   No. No nostalgia. Things were worse outside of the classroom. I was skinny [yes, believe it or not], and my hair wouldn't sttick down in back even when it was weighted with pure grease. I wore glasses, didn't know where to put my hands and they kept knockinmg over things, and laughed at the wrong times.

8   What social life. Once I tried to kiss a girl in east Milton. She pushed me off her back porch into the rose bushes while my "friends" waiting in the fliver turned on the lights and honked the horn.

9   I wrote love letters to a young lady—I have sinking feeling I described how she looked under a street light—and she fead the letters at a party while I smiled as I died.

10   I never dared ask June Miller for a date. She was more beautiful than the movies. later, I heard she never had a date in high school. Everone was afraid to ask her out, sure she alread had a date.

11   Once, knowing everyone would say "no", I asked three girls to the same dance. they all said "yes" compared notes and I stayed home.

12   No! Do not send me back to North Quincy High.

13   Sometimes when i drive by that great curving educational factory, I think I shoudl stop and go in. But so far i haven't had the courage. Yet, in my sixties, I think back and the other day, feklt something close to nostalgia, as I walked again, in memory, the long, empty corridors with the classroom dors closed.

14   I was surprised. I would have expected to remember the classrooms or corridors filled with my classmates or the cafeteria—I thought American Chop Suey exotic and liked it better than the Scottish cuisine at home.

15   Instead I saw darm brown floors gkleaming with wax, dark briown wood work, stucco walls, green metal lockers—all shut—and dim organge celing lights.

16   And it felt good—powerful—to be alone in the corridor. I stopped and the footsterps stopped. I walked and the footseps followed.

17   I remember looking throuigh the glass doors of the classrooms, remeber the weary gestuires of the teachers, their mouths opening and closing, and the numbed faces of the students, drugged with information they did not want to know and would never understand.

18   And I began to understand my high school nostalgia. I was alone in the corrdir. I was outisde. i had escaped. I was free.

19   When we last moved i found styacks of forged corridor passes, stored away in case I goit returned to high school. I never graduated and that is still a real fear.

20   I worked on the newspaper and the Yearbook. I had learned the system and how to work it. I escaped home room aand study hall, gym and sometimes even class.

21   I was an noutsider, a writer before I knew I wpould become a writer. an almost m,an with forged corridior passes, documentation that i muist have felkt predicted i would escape schgpoopl, learn new system and how to beat them—in the same box were Motor Pool trip tickets, also forged—

22   Thoise aged s,lips of paper were, i now realize, my high school dip,.oma. I was [something], proudly alienated, and would choose a liofe of going my own way, firmly alienated and smug.

     [Set a para earlier, tie to over 60 and nostalgia, looking back?]

     I checked the word count on my computer. Eight hundred words is ideal. I had 881. I could cut or add. Seven hundred to one thousand would be O.K.

     Now I will read it aloud, slowly, working with the text to see what needs to be revealed. I feel strongly that the text exists, that it is my job to help it realize itself. When I am finished, I run the spellcheck on my computer and then take the piece to my first reader, my wife, who puts in more commas than I use and catches errors in grammar, voice, or thought.

     Now I will take you backstage and let you see what and how I edited. What I crossed out will be marked through and what I add will be in capital letters. The typos, errors in mechanics, and misspellings I will just correct. I will also share some of my concerns with you in the underlined passages between the paragraphs.

No! Not Back to High School
Donald M. Murray

1   My wife, a daughter and I were talking about high school the other evening—none of us wanted to return—and we laughed at someone who was still angry at being alienated in high school. I heard myself say, "Everyone's alienated in high school."

> I expected to discover a new theme and then would have written a new opening. In this case, the theme has held up.

2   Having zoomed by 65 this month, I am startled by the acceleration of life over 60. I'd like to slow things down a bit—quite a bit—but I don't want to ~~go back~~ SHIFT INTO REVERSE. Most of all, I don't want to go back to North Quincy High School.

3   I can still remember what it felt like to be sentenced to ~~those educational cells they call~~ classrooms. Slowly the ceiling lowered, the walls drew in, AND ALL the air was ~~removed~~ SUCKED from the room. ~~and I concentrated on the huge minute hand on the clock that slowly clicked off each minute.~~

> I was happy in the draft when the text started to take off with a description of what happened to the classroom.

How do I know that happened? I returned in memory and experienced it.

In the editing, I cut myself free of the previous text, striking out things I liked but don't belong in this evolving text. I made the paragraph tighter and more active.

4 French and Latin were foreign languages, no surprise in that. But so ~~was~~ WERE math and chemistry and physics and even English—I never could figure out ~~those~~ SENTENCE diagrams, ALTHOUGH I WAS A READER AND WANTED TO BECOME A WRITER. ~~I write this in September and I remember that long before that month was over I had sunk for the third time in most classes.~~

There's a lot more I'd like to put in about my stupid English classes, but this is enough. Cutting is fun.

5 ~~Other kids raised their hands, some even seemed to talk back and forth with teachers, laughing at what they thought were jokes.~~

I either have to develop this more, putting the reader in the classroom or cut. I decide I have said that before, in another column, and I don't really have the room to develop it here. I cut.

6 I'd had ~~a~~ ONE good teacher—Bob Hamilton— in the sixth grade and I WOULD ~~was to~~ have a good teacher—Mort Howell—in the 13th grade WHEN I WENT TO JUNIOR COLLEGE—ILLEGALLY—TO PLAY FOOTBALL, but I didn't know that.

7 My OTHER teachers were angry, angry at the Depression, angry at not being able to marry (almost all my teachers were women, and they might HAVE CHOSEN not ~~have~~ TO marr~~Yied~~, but they seemED angry they couldn't without being fired). THEY WERE CLEARLY angry at the school administration, angry at taxpayers, angry at each other, angry at the class, angry at me.

Is this off track? No, I guess. It helps explain my alienation. I am surprised in writing this. I had not remembered that anger before. It is this sort of surprising insight that brings me back to the writing desk. I do write to learn, to be surprised, to write what I do not expect to write.

8 No. NoNE OF THE nostalgia I HEAR SOME OVER SIXTY'S DESCRIBE. Things were worse outside of the classroom. I was skinny [WHEN IT WAS FASHIONABLE TO BE BURLY. NOW I AM PLUMP WHEN EMACIATION IS IN yes, believe it or not]. and mMy hair wouldn't LIE sttick down in back even when it was weighted with pure grease. I wore glasses, didn't know where to put my hands and they kept knockinmg over things, and laughed at the wrong times.

> I tie the text in to my readers. The skinny/fat business will also make contact with my readers. They will also remember when men used hair grease and wearing glasses was a major social impediment.

9 What social life.? Once I tried to kiss a girl ON A PORCH in East Milton. She pushed me off her back porch into the rose bushes, while my "friends" waiting in the fliver turned on the lights and honked the horn.

> I don't want to say I was inept and embarrassed. I want to show it and allow the reader to make the conclusions. MY readers will know a fliver was a cheap car. You have to make sure your reader will know the language you use. One of the small joys in this column is to use our outdated language. I imagine I can see my readers smile.

10 I wrote love letters to a young lady—I have a sinking feeling I described how she looked under a street light—and she read the letters at a party while I smiled as I died.

> I could name her but I have grown kind. Well, sort of kind.

11 I never dared ask June Miller for a date. She was more beautiful than the movies. Later, I heard she never had a date in high school. Everyone was afraid to ask her out, sure she already had a date.

> More beautiful than the movies. I think that captures the music of the speech at the time. An editor may talk me out of it. If so, I'll use a name, perhaps June Allyson.

12 Once, knowing everyone would say "no," I asked three girls to the same dance. They all said "yes," compared notes—and I stayed home.

13 No! Do not send me back to North Quincy High.

14 Sometimes when I drive by that great curving educational factory, I think I should stop and go in AS AN ACT OF EXORCISM. But so far I haven't had the courage. Yet, in my sixties, I DO think back TO OLD NORTH QUINCY HIGH, and the other day EVEN felt something close to nostalgia as I

> The transition. I have set the scene, now we will discover a significant meaning, I hope.

walked again, in memory, the long, empty corridors. ~~with the classroom dors closed.~~

15   IT WAS NOT THE IMAGE I WOULD HAVE EXPECTED. ~~I was surprised.~~ I would have expected to remember the ~~classrooms~~ HUMILIATION OF THE GYM, AN ANECDOTE ABOUT MY FRENCH TEACHER'S WIG ~~or corridors filled with my classmates~~ or the cafeteria—I thought American Chop Suey exotic and liked it better than the Scottish cuisine at home.

> I want to stimulate their own memories and surprise and amuse them with my fond memories of the school lunch program.

16   Instead I saw dark brown floors gleaming with wax, dark brownwood work, DARK yellow stucco walls, DARK green metal lockers—all shut—and dim orange ceiling lights.

17   And it felt good—powerful—to be alone in the corridor. I stopped and the footsteps stopped. I walked and the footsteps followed.

> Again, I went back there in memory to discover this. We all remember more than we think we do. Writing retrieves it.

18   I remember looking through the glass doors of the classrooms, remember the weary gestures of the teachers, their mouths opening and closing, and the numbed faces of the students, drugged with information they did not want and would never understand.

19   I WAS OUTSIDE, ALIENATED, AND, ADMIT IT, SMUG.

> Why did I do this now? Instinct, a sense of timing, a feeling it was necessary here.

20   ~~And I began to understand my high school nostalgia. I was alone in the corrdir. I was outisde. I had escaped. I was free.~~

> I've said it. Cut. Move on.

21   When we last moved I found stacks of forged corridor passes, stored away in case ~~I got~~ THE AUTHORITIES returned ME to high school. I never graduated and A MANACLED RETURN ~~that is still~~ a real fear.

22   I worked on the NORTH QUINCY HIGH newspaper and the Yearbook. I HAD CORRIDOR PASSES! I had learned the system and how to work it. I escaped home room aand study hall, gym and sometimes even SUBJECT MATTER classes.

23   I was NOW an AUTHORIZED outsider, ~~a writer before I knew I wpCould become a writer. an almost m,an with forged corridior passes,~~ WITH documentation ~~that~~ that ~~I must have felt~~ predicted I would escape school, learn new systems and how to beat them. (~~—i~~In the same box were Motor Pool trip tickets FROM THE EUROPEAN THEATER OF OPERATIONS DATED 1944, also forged~~=~~.)

24 Those aged ~~s,lips of paper~~ CORRIDOR PASSES were, I now
realize, my high school diploma. I ~~was [something], proudly
alienated, and~~ would choose a life of going my own way, A
WRITER ~~firmly PROUDLY~~ alienated and ~~ETERNALLY~~ smug
~~ABOUT IT~~.

I hate depending on adverbs. And that "about it" is clumsy. What a weak way to end. Let's have respect for the reader who should get it if I go back and kick away the crutches. And I have set it up within the piece after all.

~~[Set a para earlier, tie to over 60 and nostalgia, looking back?]~~

Evelynne Kramer, my editor at the *Globe,* called with a few questions. As always, her reactions to my draft were helpful. We have marked these changes in italic in the version in which it was published in the *Globe.*

Take Me Back, but Not to High School

Donald M. Murray

1   My wife, a daughter and I were talking about high school the other evening—none of us wanted to return—and we laughed at someone who was still angry at *having been* alienated in high school. I heard myself say, "Everyone's alienated in high school."

2   Having zoomed by 65 this month, I am startled by the acceleration of life over 60. I'd like to slow things down a bit—quite a bit—but I don't want to shift into reverse. Most of all, I don't want to go back to North Quincy High School.

3   I can still remember what it felt like to be sentenced to class. Slowly the ceiling lowered, the walls drew in, and all the air was sucked from the room.

4   French and Latin were foreign languages, no surprise in that. But so were math and chemistry and physics and even English—I never could figure out sentence diagrams, although I was a reader and wanted to become a writer.

5   I'd had one good teacher—Bob Hamilton—in the sixth grade and I would have a good teacher—Mort Howell—in the 13th grade when I went to junior college—illegally—to play football.

6   My other teachers were angry, angry at the Depression, angry at not being able to marry (almost all my teachers were women, and they might have chosen not to marry, but they seemed angry they couldn't without being fired). *It seems incredible today, but it was against regulations to be married and teach in the Quincy school system. My teachers also seemed*

angry at the school administration, angry at taxpayers, angry at each other, angry at the class, angry at me.

7   No. None of the nostalgia I hear some over sixty's describe. Things were worse outside of the classroom. I was skinny [when it was fashionable to be burly. Now I am plump when emaciation is in.] My hair wouldn't lie down in back even when weighted with pure grease. I wore glasses, didn't know where to put my hands, and laughed at the wrong times.

8   What social life? Once I tried to kiss a girl on a porch in East Milton. She pushed me into the rose bushes, while my "friends" waiting in the flivver turned on the lights and honked the horn.

9   I wrote love letters to a young lady—I have a sinking feeling I described how she looked under a street light—and she read the letters at a party while I smiled as I died.

10   I never dared ask June Miller for a date. She was more beautiful than the movies. Later, I heard she never had a date in high school. Everyone was afraid to ask her out, sure she already had a date.

11   Once, knowing everyone would say "no," I asked three girls to the same dance. They all said "yes," compared notes—and I stayed home.

12   No! Do not send me back to North Quincy High.

13   Sometimes when I drive by that great curving educational factory, I think I should stop and go in as an act of exorcism. But so far I haven't had the courage. Yet, in my sixties, I do think back to old North Quincy High, and the other day even felt something close to nostalgia as I walked again, in memory, the long, empty corridors.

14   It was not the image I would have expected. I would have expected to remember the humiliation of the gym, an anecdote about my French teacher's wig or the cafeteria—I thought American Chop Suey exotic and liked it better than the Scottish cuisine at home.

15   Instead I saw dark brown floors gleaming with wax, dark brown woodwork, dark yellow stucco walls, dark green metal lockers—all shut—and dim orange ceiling lights.

16   And it felt good—powerful—to be alone in the corridor. I stopped and the footsteps stopped. I walked and the footsteps followed.

17   I remember looking through the glass doors of the classrooms, remember the weary gestures of the teachers, their mouths opening and closing, and the numbed faces of the students, drugged with information they did not want and would never understand.

18   I was outside, alienated, and, admit it, smug.

19   When *my wife and I* last moved I found stacks of forged corridor passes, stored away in case the authorities returned me to high school. I never graduated and a manacled return is a real fear.

20   *On my way to dropping out and flunking out,* I *still* worked on the North Quincy High newspaper and the Yearbook. I learned the system and how to work it. *I learned how to obtain corridor passes.* I escaped homeroom and study hall, gym and sometimes even *chemistry* classes.

21   I *had become* an authorized outsider, with documentation that predicted I would escape school, learn new systems and how to beat them.

(*Further documentation that I had learned about systems are* Motor Pool trip tickets from the European Theater of Operations dated 1944, also forged, *that I still have.*)

22   Those aged corridor passes were, I now realize, my high school diploma. I would choose a life of going my own way, a writer, alienated and smug.

Remember there is no one way to write anything. If I wrote this tomorrow it would probably be different and if I had left the draft overnight I might have edited it differently. Revit—revise and edit—it yourself. See what text comes clear under your hand.

Case History of a Student Writer: Amy Lord _____

The research paper is a rite of passage at different stages in the educational process and Freshman English is often one of them. It is a difficult task for both student and instructor.

The true research paper follows true research in a field in which the student is immersed, but the freshman rarely has a field of interest, and the courses freshmen take are usually introductory. The Freshman English paper becomes an exercise rather than a real experience.

The other problem is that what is a research paper changes according to instructor, discipline, and subdiscipline. When I was Freshman English Director, I conducted a survey of colleges and departments in the university so our research paper assignment would teach the elements common to all departments. I found no elements, even the use of the library, common to all departments. There were, for example, four distinctly different forms of research papers required in various branches of psychology. This was true in all departments including English, where I found radical differences in the requirements for research papers on literature.

There are, however, good reasons to teach the research paper. Most students, properly, I believe, begin to learn to write through the personal-experience paper. There comes a time, however, when it is important to step outside of personal experience and use research and writing skills to learn about subjects on which the student is ignorant and to learn how to evaluate what they have learned.

The student should learn how to use the library and other sources of information; how to evaluate the authority of such sources; how to make use of such raw material to produce clear thinking and graceful, effective communication.

The following student paper is not a document that will change the course of thinking by authorities on terrorism. Of course not. We should not have unrealistic goals for the research paper. The case history reveals a student beginning to learn how to use some essential tools of the academic life.

Instructor's Account by Carol Keyes

1   The poet Richard Hugo talks in *The Triggering Town* about "Writing off the subject," the concept, perhaps the key concept, I like to teach in writing classes. I also like to teach collaboration—the helpfulness of editors and readers, the usefulness of finding people to help you wander off the subject. For her research project, Amy started with the subject of terrorism and arrived at a discussion of "the role negotiation plays in dealing with terrorists" in her research essay. The journey from the "initiating subject" to the "real or generated subject" involved standard academic research— collaboration with the experts—and the collaboration with fellow students in the research process and the writing process.

2   A little past mid-semester Amy and all the other students in her Freshman Comp class came to a class meeting with five subjects they would be interested in researching in detail with two to five other students in the class. Each student wrote five subjects on the blackboard and signed the list. Chaos ensued for awhile as students lobbied for their topics with other students or sought out someone else who had listed a subject they found more interesting. By the end of the eighty minute class, some equilibrium had been established—everyone was in a group and had decided on a specific aspect of the research topic to begin the research with. Some groups had also started discussing how they would present their researched material to the class in the twenty minute presentation required as part of their projects.

3   Amy started out choosing domestic reaction to and public opinion on terrorist violence. For the next four weeks or so she researched material in the library and met with the other three students in her group to exchange information on sources and on the topic of terrorism itself. For the class presentation, Amy's group decided to prepare a mock tv special news report on video, with each student taking on the role of an expert in some aspect of terrorism. Amy's research process had led her to readings on negotiation, and while her reporting on the news show included her original focus on American public reaction to terrorist violence, Amy found that for her the debate on whether or not to negotiate with terrorists was the most compelling part of her research. This led her to her own ideas about the debate. These she decided to explore more specifically in the final part of her research project—the final leg of her journey in writing off the subject, in coming to her true subject—her ideas about negotiation.

4   In her development of her essay, of her ideas on negotiation, Amy did what she had to do in her research process, she had to find better sources— better readers and editors. She notes in describing the process of refining her thinking in her writing that the two people she peer conferenced her essay drafts with, (one she chose from her research group and one I had assigned from outside her group), were not very helpful to her. Of course I wish that the two students she conferenced with had been more helpful. Yet I think the fact that they weren't provided just as useful, albeit frus-

trating, experience for Amy. She became resourceful. She found readers outside the class who were helpful.

5   As she had discovered in doing the library research, Amy learned in the process of writing her essay that not all sources help, be they sources necessary to the research process or those necessary to the writing process. During Amy's initial research she found information that made her want to know more about negotiation. As she explored and refined her ideas on negotiation she found that some of that information, most in fact, was not relevant. She needed to go back into the library to look for material more specific to the debate on negotiation. As she began taking preliminary writing on her ideas to classmates, she found that they were not useful. She looked to other people to find the ideas and suggestions that helped her.

6   And of course Amy had the same experience when she was alone at the computer writing. Many of her ideas did not interest her beyond her initial thinking of them and many just did not help her figure out more clearly what she thought and felt about negotiation. Sometimes her mind provided her with the right source, sometimes not. Eventually, by working with her research information, the editors and readers she found for herself, and her own mind, she generated an essay she felt some satisfaction, although not complete contentment, with.

7   Writing off the subject, I remember that Amy decided to get a haircut after seeing herself on video. You really never know where research and writing are going to lead you.

Student's Account by Amy Lord

1   The most difficult aspect of writing is deciding on a topic. For this research essay we were to choose five subjects and find at least three other people to work with. Selecting the five topics was difficult, until I asked several of my friends for possibilities. Because of their suggestions, I decided terrorism would be the most personally interesting subject. Once the group of four was formed, I was able to start research immediately. The gathering process involved reading through many U.S. Document files for information, in the library, but not in the most common sources.

2   Once I had the material, I was able to begin the note taking and writing process. It helps to take notes from each source separately, then integrate the material. This causes the writing to be less repetitive and it saves time. Once the writing had begun, it was very difficult to find reliable, helpful people to peer conference the rough drafts. I encountered several class members who were unwilling to give constructive criticism. Unfortunately, the others in the research group were difficult to work with. They were reluctant to give their opinions, input, and time to the project. Once again I looked to my friends for assistance. They were able to help me with several segments of the paper that I felt were not correct.

3   My suggestion to anyone writing a research essay, is to look in obvious places for assistance. If the suggestions given are not satisfactory, find someone who can be more helpful. Also, if lack of motivation is a major stumbling block, assign several deadlines for various sections of the project. I always seem to wait until the last possible moment to get the work done and I have found that these deadlines make me finish all of the work without the stress of the final deadline.

   Each student in Ms. Keyes' course had to fill out the answers to a series of questions and then to make a written response to what was learned in the peer-conference sessions. These typed answers had to be brought with the paper to conference each week. Here are the questions:

BEFORE writing please answer the following questions:
► What is your topic?
► What one specific idea would you like to explore in this paper? What questions will you try to answer in this paper?
► Why did you choose this topic? (Or choose to write on this topic again, if this is a revision.) I'd like you to answer this question in terms of what the topic means to you or what you expect to get from the writing process involved in writing about this topic.

AFTER writing please answer the following questions:
► What did you like best about the way your writing turned out this week? (A few examples of what I want you to consider here are: how you organize material, focus, use details, develop a strong voice, found a successful form, wrote the lead, worked out the answer to a complex question, or discovered ideas new to you.)
► What was your biggest problem with this paper? HOW AND WHY was it a problem? How do you imagine you might have solved that problem if you had more time?
► In what other directions do you think you could have taken your writing? (Here you could answer in terms of ideas or writing style or both.) Do you think any of those other directions are worth exploring? Why or why not?
► What do you think was the most worthwhile thing you learned or generated from your writing this week? (Please try to respond in terms of both your writing process and the ideas you were working with in your writing.)

   Too often, teachers expect peer conferences to work without instruction. Students do not know how to read and criticize a draft constructively. Although Amy Lord did not feel she was helped by the peer conferences, Ms. Keyes had given instruction to the group and then followed the peer conferences with a conference with her based on the student's written evaluation of the peer conferences. I think it is important for students to have a structure that helps them realize what they have learned or what they wish they had learned from their conferences. Here are Ms. Keyes' instructions for the student's questionnaire on the peer conferences.

After the conference I want you to write out (need not be typewritten but must be legible if handwritten):

1. What you learned about writing from reading the paper(s) you read and conferenced for your partner(s).
2. What you learned about writing and your paper from the person(s) who conferenced you.
3. Whether or not the conference was fruitful for you, and why or why not, in specific detail and explanation.
4. Specific questions you want me to consider when I read your paper. If you do not have any specific questions, I will not read your paper. And if you do not have any specific questions, you need to write out a detailed explanation of why your paper is one that requires no further feedback beyond the peer conferencing.
5. A brief but precise analysis of what you would do in the next draft of your paper, and why; and a statement regarding why exactly you will or will not work further on this particular writing.

Here is an example of Amy Lord's notes for her bibliography.

1. Reagan, Ronald. <u>International Terrorism:</u> <u>Proposed Legislation</u>. Washington, D.C. April 26, 1984

Will Reagan follow through with his proposed legislation? Looking back at his two terms, did Reagan follow any of this legislation and if so, how?

This source describes the guidelines that should be followed by all members of the government during Reagan's two terms.

The national policy on terrorism is contained within this source.

It is very formal because it is a proposed legislation. Reagan's point of view is being directed to the Congress of the United States.

This is very credible source because it was the legislation proposed by President Reagan and put before the Congress.

This source will be quite helpful as a insight into national policy on terrorism and it will be interesting to compare Reagan's ideas to Bush's current policy. Will Bush change anything or will he keep and follow Reagan's legislation?

This is a page from Lord's notes:

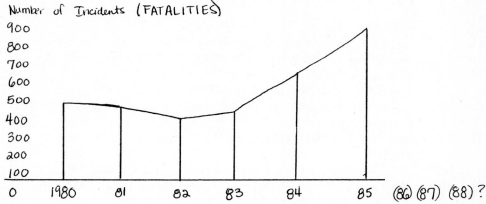

In the 1980's ⅓ of total terrorist acts were aimed
directly at the U.S.
Since 1968 (when statistics were first compiled) terrorist
actions have become bloodier with more fatalities.
There were 20 fatalities caused by terrorism in 1968
compared to 926 fatalities in 1985
Most terrorism is directed at Western democracies.
June 14, 1985 — TWA Flight 847 was hijacked after it
left Athens. — the 1st hijacking of a U.S. airliner in
the Middle East since 1970.
Hijacking of Egyptair Flight 648 + Achille Lauro
Bombing of restaurant on outskirts of Madrid - aimed
at American servicemen and women.
Shooting of off-duty Marine Corps personnel in El
Salvador
All of these show how the U.S. is being targeted
specifically.
During last decade U.S. officals or installations have
been attacked abroad on an average of once
every seventeen days.
In the past 17 years (dating from '85) terrorists have killed as

Another page of her notes and the draft of some of her questions as she prepares for her interviews:

Amy Lord

Source
#4

"Hostage-taking is defined under international law (International Convention Against the Taking of Hostages, Adopted December 17, 1979) as the seizing or detaining and threatening to kill, injure, or continue to detain a person in order to compel a third party to do or abstain from doing any act as an explicit or implicit condition for the release of the seized or detained person."

This statement can be very contradictory—just use Arms-For-Hostages as an example!

The U.S. will not pay ransom, release prisoners, change policies or agree to any demands. This action would cause other terrorists acts.

"The U.S. will use every available resource to gain the safe return of American citizens who are held hostage by terrorists."

What is the prosecution + punishment for these acts?

QUESTIONS FOR INTERVIEWS:
1. What is your definition of a terrorist act?
2. Do you feel safe when you travel within the U.S.? Outside of it's borders?
3. What do you feel should be done when a terrorist is captured?
4. What safety precautions should be made in order to protect U.S. citizens?
5. Do you feel that U.S. citizen's travel should be restricted? Or should citizen's be informed of the dangers and taught how to react if ever in a hostage situation?
6. Do you believe the United States should deal in hostage exchanges like the recent "Iran-Scam"?
7. Do you think the policies stated in U.S. laws, are followed, to the letter, in every situation? Do you feel they should be or should compromises be made in certain circumstances?

Here we see the writer in action selecting and eliminating pieces of information from which she will construct her paper.

I. Intro.

Contradictions between policy & action:

$60 million in military aid to Iran for help in releasing 3 American hostages in Lebanon. (*)

In any terrorist dealings, the written policies should be followed. If not then tell the public what the plans are. A government run by the people for the people should be trustworthy. Telling U.S. citizens selective aspects of their operations is not right. The policies that they are going to follow should be written down for everyone to see. This of course would first be approved by Congress so everything has to be covert. If the written policy is no concessions then it should be adhered to.

Even though politicians call for "sanctions, censorship and regional compacts" to prevent or discourage further terrorism, nothing happens. The public "waits for the next bomb to go off." (#3)

Terrorism is not a "thing", it is a concept. It cannot be fought as a "thing". #5

Some people say actions speak louder than words but not with terrorism.

U.S. policy on dealing with terrorists is: "The U.S. will not pay ransom, release prisoners, change policies, or agree to any demands." "The U.S. will use every available resource to gain the safe return of American citizens who are held hostage by terrorists." (#4)

Because of high technology and mass communications, terrorism is an easy and cheap way to get media exposure. The public reaction to the bombing of the Pan Am flight over Lockerbie, Scotland would not have served the terrorists as well if Newsweek hadn't shown dead people victims littering a field and a dead man hanging from a roof. These pictures have left an indelible mark on many people about terrorists and the policies toward them. Since nothing seems to have improved on the airlines — we can all be terrified of flying because we can't stop it.

Improvements in security have prevented casualties, but it is not the only solution. "U.S. policy is direct. We will make no concessions to terrorists. We pay no ransoms, nor do we permit the release of prisoners or agree to other acts which might encourage additional terrorism. We make no changes in U.S. policy because of terrorist threats or acts. If U.S. personnel are taken hostage or endangered, we are prepared to consider a broad range of actions appropriate to the threat... we are determined to act in a strong manner against terrorists without surrendering our basic freedoms or endangering our democratic principles." (#9)

Ms. Lord's first draft:

"Terrorists feed on instability;
they are the scavengers of strife and
conflict. No moderate state or individual
is safe from them. No change in policy
will appease them. Only an implacable
desire for peace ~~will~~ can stop them.
... Those who seek a ... solution must
seek it ... not through terror, but at the
negotiating table."[1]

    This quote expresses the one and only way to
effectively deal with the rising tide of terrorism. A
decisive step must be taken ~~to eradicate or eliminate~~
~~the~~ prevent the threat of political violence and to
dispel the ~~atmosphere of~~ fear created by terrorist
acts. This step must be negotiation.
    The time to take action against political violence
has long since passed. Terrorism is not a new
tactic in creating and perpetuating political strife.
What is new is the increasing violence and incidence
of this ~~particular act of~~ anti-government action. Each
attack is bloodier than the last and this progression
will not cease until those involved sit at a negotiating
table and resolve their major conflicts.
    Some people say actions speak louder than words,
but this idea is not effective against terrorism. Violence
through military force only perpetuates and escalates the
cycle of political incidents. With each ~~anti~~ retaliation
attack the U.S. makes, the opposing force has ~~maybe~~ another
reason to ~~f~~ either take more hostages or injure those
already held. Each response the U.S. makes further
justifies the terrorists' actions, in their minds and in
those of some citizens. The United States needs to organize
and institute peaceful measures of prevention to
circumvent terrorist acts.

Terrorism:
Negotiating an Answer
Amy Lord

Terrorists feed on instability, they are the scavengers of strife and conflict. No moderate state or individual is safe from them. No change in policy will appease them. Only an implacable desire for peace can stop them. Those who seek a solution must seek it not through terror, but at the negotiation table.[1]

1   This quote expresses the one and only way to effectively deal with the rising tide of terrorism. A decisive step must be taken to prevent the threat of political violence and to dispel the fear created by terrorist acts. This step must be negotiation.

2   The time to take action against political violence has long since passed. Terrorism is not a new tactic in creating and perpetuating political strife. What is new is the increasing violence and incidence of this anti-governmental action. Each attack is bloodier than the last and this progression will not cease until those involved sit at a negotiating table and resolve their major conflicts.

3   Some people say actions speak louder than words, but this idea is not effective against terrorism. Violence through military force only perpetuates and escalates the cycle of political incidents. With each retaliation attack the U.S. makes, the opposing force has another reason to either take more hostages or injure those already held. Each response the U.S. makes further justifies the terrorists' actions, in their minds and in those of some citizens. The United States needs to organize and institute peaceful measures of prevention to circumvent terrorist acts.

4   Even though politicians and public call for sanctions to prevent or discourage further terrorism, nothing happens. The people just wait for the next bomb to go off. This fear has been used by the press and has been expanded to near hysteria. Because of high technology and mass communications, terrorism is an easy and cheap way to get media exposure. The public reaction to the bombing of the Pan Am flight over Lockerbie, Scotland would not have served the terrorists as well if *Newsweek* had not shown victims littering a field alongside debris and the unnecessary photo of a dead man hanging from a roof. These pictures have left a definite mark on many people about terrorists and the U.S. policies.

> U.S. policy is direct. We will make no concessions to terrorists. We will pay no ransoms, nor do we permit the release of prisoners or agree to other acts which might encourage additional terrorism. We make no changes in U.S. policy because of terrorists' threats or acts. If U.S. personnel are taken hostage or endangered, we are prepared to consider a broad range of actions

appropriate to the threat. We are determined to act in a strong manner against terrorists without surrendering our basic freedoms or endangering our democratic principles.[2]

5   This policy seems to imply that we either bargain with terrorists or we use force. These ideas are too simplistic and are therefore unrealistic. The U.S. needs to develop this policy into one that is not lenient but merely has more options. Because this current policy has a very narrow scope of acceptable actions, nothing has improved on the airlines causing passenger fear to rise. Also, special agencies have been formed to deal with terrorism in an illegal manner. If there are going to be more incidents similar to Reagan's "Iran-Scam," then the policy should be altered to include these covert actions. Unfortunately, this idea is unrealistic, as Congress would never approve of these operations. If the U.S. policy was altered to give importance to negotiation, thus causing it to be more effective, covert operations would be unnecessary.

6   Negotiation does not mean concessions. It means the best possible solution to a difficult situation. Negotiation is the willingness to talk to terrorists or even among ourselves, so that options can be considered and the reactions determined. American policy specifically states that there will be no concessions, but it will talk to anyone. This means that the U.S. will take time to better comprehend the motive behind terrorism. If we take this time to understand, we will be better equipped to deal with the problem at hand.

7   While the U.S. is talking, they can also arrange international cooperation to implement economic, diplomatic, legal or military measures. This, along with preemption (prevention), gives more of an advantage than brute force alone. While force may work in some situations as retaliation, it does not deter future terrorism like negotiation.

8   Many people argue that negotiation is ineffective and that terrorists will just take more hostages. This is true, but at least those hostages, who are released due to discussions, have their lives, something which does not always happen when force is utilized. Negotiation also allows both sides to calm down. It gives the time needed to organize thoughts and think about the consequences of any further action.

9   Terrorism is a catch-22 situation, but more killing is obviously unnecessary. It is not effective to just "look the other way" while innocent people are sacrificed, but even when precautions are taken there is no guarantee of success. Negotiation can be done without conceding arms, principles, policies, or prisoners and it should be the first step when dealing with a terrorist situation.

End Notes

1. Dam, Kenneth W. *Terrorism in the Middle East,* U.S. Department of State, Bureau of Public Affairs, Office of Public Communications, Editorial Division. Current Policy No. 618. Washington, D.C. 1 Oct. 1984.

2. Oakley, Robert B. *International Terrorism: Current Trends and the U.S. Response.* U.S. Department of State, Bureau of Public Affairs, Office of Public Communications, Editorial Division. Current Policy No. 706. Washington, D.C. 15 May 1985. p. 3.

Clarifying for the Reader

There you are, a writer, on stage, trying to hold the attention of the audience. If you make things too complicated, far more complicated than the subject deserves, the audience nods, then starts to snore. If you make things too simple, the audience is insulted, stands up and walks out.

Clarity is the result of a balance between complexity and simplicity and there is no absolute scale with which to measure it. The forces involved change with the subject and the audience. What is simplistic for an audience of automotive engineers, or even hobbyists, may be far too complicated for the average auto owner.

Since we are authorities on what we write—or should be—it is usually a good idea to err on the side of simplification. Test this by playing the role of an intelligent reader who does not know the subject. Imagine what you need to know, presented in a way you would understand it.

We always have to be careful of our assumptions. One famous British historian I read when I was young would say, "As every schoolboy knows. . ." and then reel off complicated information I did not understand or know. We need, in clarifying, to see our assumptions and make sure they are the reader's assumptions. If not, we need to give the reader more specific information.

The more complicated and unfamiliar the subject, the more likely you should use short words, short sentences, short paragraphs. But there are exceptions. Some writers can use long words and long constructions with utter clarity. Others could confuse a shopping list.

There are times when you want to confuse the reader, to give the reader the experience of confusion so they may, for a moment, feel the way an immigrant to this country feels when Americans say, for example, "Drop by," or "I'll be seeing you" without meaning either statement literally.

All confusion must be purposeful—and the reader must understand that and not think that the writer is just lazy. It's usually a good idea to give readers signals in the title or subheads, in lead sentences or paragraphs, so the reader knows what the writer is attempting to do. All art imposes an order on chaos; it is our responsibility to make sure the particular order we use is appropriate.

Questions about Clarifying

• *My classmates don't edit my copy the way I would. Who's right?*

Many times no one's right. Except for the most explicit rules of usage, it isn't a question of right or wrong; it's a question of what works—what makes the meaning clear. Your classmates edit with their language, as they should. You should listen to them, because they may have some good suggestions, but you shouldn't follow them blindly. It's your voice that should appear on the page, not theirs.

- *How will reading aloud help me? I don't talk too good.*

You probably talk better than you write, but you should watch out for the slang, the clichés, and the local dialect that may be appropriate in casual talk, but may not be appropriate in the writing you're doing in school.

- *Won't editing ruin my spontaneity?*

Not in my experience. I've heard of editing making a piece of writing go stale, but I've never actually seen it happen. The most spontaneous one-liners by Johnny Carson, hook shots by Kareem, and pistol shots by Billy the Kid came after long practice. John Kenneth Galbraith says, "When I'm greatly inspired, only four revisions are needed before, as I've often said, I put in that note of spontaneity which even my meanest critics concede." I agree.

But if your first draft is clean and clear and does the job, don't mess with it. We don't mess with our copy just to be messing, but to make it work.

- *Do you have to do three readings?*

No, sometimes you have to do seven or thirteen, or one. As I said, when you get experience you may be able to read in the three ways at the same time, but in the beginning you usually have to read separately for meaning, order, and voice. And that may not be enough to make your meaning clear.

- *Doesn't it get bo-o-o-o-o-o-ring to edit so much?*

It seems boring when you look at it from a distance, but it's actually fun when you are in there messing around with meaning and language. Each change—what is taken out, what is put in, what is reordered—is a new experiment in meaning. You keep running into surprises, finding out things that you didn't know you knew, making connections and building new meanings.

"Nothing is more satisfying than to write a good sentence," says Barbara Tuchman. "It is no fun to write lumpishly, dully, in prose the reader must plod through like wet sand. But it is a pleasure to achieve, if one can, a clear running prose that is simple yet full of surprises. This does not just happen. It requires skill, hard work, a good ear and continued practice, as much as it takes Heifetz to play the violin." There's nothing quite so satisfying as making a sentence run clear, carrying a meaning to the reader in a well-crafted way that seems spontaneous.

- *Can't you learn to write so you don't have to edit?*

You can't learn to write; that's one of the great things about being a writer, and one of the not-so-great things. You keep on learning to write. There are always new opportunities and new challenges. Each morning when you sit at your writing desk you start at zero point. You have to prove you can write, and the fact you have written, published, or even won awards doesn't seem to help.

- *I seem to be reading published writers differently. I like some of them better than I did before, but some of them are trying to row without an oar. Does this make sense?*

It certainly does. You are a writer now, and you have an insider's view of the game of writing. You will begin to understand how some easy writing wasn't so easy to make, and how some other writing doesn't work at all. The person who is writing becomes a far different and better reader than the person who does not write.

- *When do I know when I am done editing?*

When the deadline arrives. I once took a survey of all the people in my department at the university who had written books. They had all revised or edited their books *after* their books had been accepted. There is no natural end to the editing process. As Paul Valery said, "Writing is never finished, only abandoned."

Clarifying Activities

1. Read your draft as fast as you can without making notes. Write down what works best and anything that might need to be added or cut. Then use the quick checklist. Do the same thing with several classmates' papers and have them do yours.
2. Read your draft again, more slowly, to see if there are any sections of the piece that need to be cut or expanded and any new ones that need to be added. Then use the master checklist. Do the same thing with several classmates' papers and have them do yours.
3. Read your draft line by line, making the changes necessary to make your meaning come clear. Make the changes right on the text. If you can't read the text after you've made a number of changes, retype it, incorporating the editing you've done, and then attack it again. Have some of your classmates edit your paper while you edit theirs.
4. Proofread your final text. Ask some classmates to check your proofing while you check theirs.
5. Take a published piece of writing and give it the three readings. It may be helpful to photocopy the text so that there are wide margins you can use for editing.
6. Make your own editing checklist of the problems you see in your writing. Go back through your writing folder and identify those writing habits that interfere with communication. Ask your teacher and the classmates who have been editing your copy to suggest other items for your checklist. Keep your checklist where you can use it when you're editing.
7. Take a paragraph or a page by a successful writer and edit it from a different point of view, for a different audience or publication, from a different set of facts or assumptions, to make it have a different voice. Play with it, editing it five, ten, or fifteen different ways. Do the same thing to one of your own paragraphs or pages.

8. Take a piece of your writing, or someone else's, and paste it on the right-hand side of the page; then on the left-hand side of the page write down what each paragraph did to contribute to the overall success of the piece.
9. Take a piece of your writing, or someone else's, and cut it by 75 percent.
10. Take an example of bad writing, your own or someone else's (perhaps a textbook; perhaps *this* textbook), writing that is obscure, confused, unclear, in bad taste, pompous, clumsy, silly, trite, vague, jargony, overwritten, any or all of the above, and edit it so it is clear and graceful.

Chapter 8

𝕸 Put Your Writing Process to Work

The lyf so short, the craft so long to lerne.

GEOFFREY CHAUCER

The first discipline is the realization that there is a discipline—that all art begins and ends with discipline—that any art is first and foremost a craft. We have gone far enough on the road to self-indulgence now to know that. The man who announces to the world that he is going to "do his thing" is like the amateur on the high diving platform who flings himself into the void shouting at the judges that he is going to do whatever comes naturally. He will land on his ass. Naturally.

ARCHIBALD MACLEISH

The form of the poem should seem, when the poem is finished, as inevitable—and invisible—as a man's skeleton.

CHAD WALSH

Develop Your Own Writing Processes

Yes, Processes.

Not one, but many. Not someone else's, but yours: designed to fit your thinking, working style. Not the same for you as you grow in experience with writing and with different writing assignments. Not the same for every writing task, but processes adapted to the demands of each writing task.

But the book is built on one writing process. Yes. I felt that was necessary to introduce the concept of process and to provide readers with a basic process from which they could all grow and learn as they began to grow as writers.

Sometimes you will find yourself writing so easily and effectively that you will not be aware of any process at all. Those are the golden days. They are the days that are possible because you have internalized a writing process and made it your own.

Other days you will start the writing process in a different place from that with collecting. Often you will have an assignment or a hint of a subject that will give you a focus, and you will begin with that focus. If you have your facts in hand you will move ahead, or you may find that you have to go back and collect information so that you can develop the focus.

Poets see the world as poems; novelists as novels; journalists as news stories. And you too may have times when you see the form or order of a piece of writing right away. You may want to go with it and move ahead to drafting, or move back to collect more material and then skip focusing.

The experienced writer often hears writing in his or her head; language leads the writer to a piece of writing. Sometimes a phrase ignites a draft. This morning, my wife, just returned from the small city in Kentucky that she left when she was a teenager, said she felt she had visited an "alien homeland." That might be enough for her to plunge into a piece of writing. There's a nice tension between the comfortable, rooted belonging of "homeland" and the detached unbelonging of "alien." Many of us in a mobile society feel such tensions. And once she has that indication of voice she may be able to write a draft.

If she starts that draft, she may be able to complete it and move ahead, or she may find that the draft runs dry and she has to go back to collect, focus, order, and then draft again.

It may be that the piece of writing will begin during the editing process, when you decide to polish an earlier draft and find that it has a new potential.

All of these approaches are correct. There is no one right way to write. Writing starts in the middle or the end or the beginning of the process. It starts where it starts. And you use the process in whatever way it can to help you make an effective piece of writing.

It is perfectly appropriate to jump around in the process, like a kangaroo with a typewriter, drafting, collecting, and fitting in what you've collected during the editing process. You may write a draft to discover the focus or to discover what you have to collect.

And the dividing lines between the stages of the process will become blurred. Most of the time, you will not be aware that you have passed from collecting to focusing, or focusing to ordering. You may edit as you draft. The parts of the process are not separate nations kept apart by barbed wire, soldiers, and guard dogs. The parts of the process overlap.

The writing process is recursive. You do not march through it as much as keep circling back through it, taking a step or two back whenever you need to make the writing go.

I hope, however, that you have discovered that writing is a craft before it is an art, that it may appear to be magic when it is finished, but that the most magical writing was built in a logical, understandable fashion.

When You Face a New Writing Task _____

We all panic when we face a new writing task. We feel we have to learn to write all over again. The task does not seem to fit our writing methods. We do not believe it will fit our knowledge, our way of solving problems, our way of using the language.

Nonsense. We have a way of writing, now we have to see how to adapt it to the new writing task. I have a checklist I follow when I have a new writing task—my first newspaper column, a ghosted article for a member of the President's cabinet, a type of poem I've never written before, an annual report of a corporation, a review of a manuscript for a publisher, a textbook, a ghost-written draft for a fund-raising letter, a eulogy at a funeral, a newsletter on writing for a newspaper, an academic article. You cannot know now what you will be required to write in the years ahead. One study revealed that ten years after graduation, engineers do more writing than any other university graduates. I am astonished at the many different writing tasks I have faced.

What I need to know:

• *The Purpose.* My purpose may be purposefully vague as I write a poem to capture a hint of a feeling of sadness on a porch on a Sunday morning just before another birthday and try to find out through writing what it means. It may be precise: to convince a specific dean to give an exact number of dollars for a particular program in the English department. I need to know the purpose of the writing before I begin.

• *The Audience.* Again the audience may be personal: myself. I may write to discover how I feel or think. Or the reader may be that specific dean—or readers of the *Boston Globe* who are over sixty. Others may read what I have to say but I need to target the primary audience.

• *My Resources.* I need to know if I have an abundant inventory of information on hand or sources—libraries, research centers, places I can observe, authori-

ties—that will provide me with the specific, accurate details from which I will
be able to construct my writing.

• *Traditions.* Many writing tasks involve strict traditions. A government agency,
an academic discipline, a research lab, a corporation may require a specific form
into which your writing is to be poured. Find out what the tradition is before
you start so that you know what material you have to collect to complete the
form. You may, and often should, adapt the formula when your purpose, information, and audience require it, but you cannot adapt traditions you don't know.
It may be helpful to read models, examples of the traditions readers have found
effective.

When you know these four conditions of the new writing task, you can
build a strategy, adapting one of your writing processes to the job at hand.

Remember to look back to the times when the writing has gone well. You
may even want to describe the writing process in a list:

▶ thought
▶ made notes
▶ picked one element
▶ wrote fast
▶ used test readers
▶ rewrote slowly

or

▶ wrote free association draft from what I knew
▶ picked out issues to be researched
▶ researched 'em
▶ talked through ideas with test readers
▶ wrote slow, careful first/final draft

or

▶ made notes from what I remembered
▶ did field research
▶ wrote up results as final copy
▶ wrote opening, turning pts., closing
▶ fitted field results into slots
▶ edited whole thing

I think it is also important to be aware of the attitudes you held, the
environment in which you worked, all the conditions that made the writing go
well. Feelings often rule our thoughts; the heart controls the mind. Note your
tools, your workplace, the time of day when the writing went well.

▶ thought   In daybook, in car
                                           at park. no phones.
                                           Sun. afternoon.

▶ made notes   Next morning, in
                                           lib. between classes.

▶ picked one element

      Big panic. Joan said go with No. 1 issue. I did.

▶ wrote fast

      At computer center, late at night.

▶ used test readers

      Watch out. Not Joe. Bill, Hugh, especially Joan.

▶ rewrote slowly.

      Edited hard copy with pen, small chunks of time, between classes, at work, retyped making more changes at comp. ctr.

or

▶ wrote free association draft from what I knew

      Easy. On typwrtr. Got up early Sun. 6 AM. Surprised how much I knew.

▶ picked out issues to be researched

      That first draft made clear what they were. Picked too many at first.

▶ researched 'em

      Slow work. START EARLY!!!

▶ talked through ideas with test readers

      Really helped to talk BEFORE I wrote.

▶ wrote slow, careful first/final draft

      By hand. Fountain pen—black in, legal pad, double-space so room for changes as I wrote. "Revited" one para. at a time. Paid Amy to type it.

or

▶ made notes from what I remembered

      On cards. 4 X 6. diff. color for each possible topic. At desk at work, between crises.

▶ did field research

      Wrote five questions readers would ask first from class exercises. It worked, but had to change questions a bit in process. Later, numbered questions in order reader would ask them—had draft outlined.

▶ wrote up results as final copy

Each night before going to bed. On 5 X 8 cards. Calligraphy. Neat. Gave me a good feeling. Reward: choc chip mint i.c. Gained an A and 5 lbs. try dried fruit this time, yck.

▶ wrote opening, turning pts., closing

White 5 X 8s. Really helped me pattern. One sitting. Weekend at home, at dining-room table.

▶ fitted field results into slots

Click, click. All fell into place. 15 mins!!! Then typed up in one night. Couple of hours.

▶ edited whole thing

Just spelling, typos, small stuff. One more night to type final.

Keep track of your writing processes *when you write effectively* and you will build up a writer's toolbox you will be able to call on when you need it. When fighting a writing task you will be able to study the requirements—purpose, audience, resources, traditions—and adapt a writing process that has worked for you to that task—or construct a new one, confident it will work because you have made the writing-process approach work for you before.

Experiment with Genre _____

Most beginning writers—and many experienced ones—are timid. They write the genres or forms of writing with which they are familiar—the academic essay, the book review, the lab report, perhaps a letter—and never experiment with many other forms of writing that might be more fun—or might better deliver their message.

The academic world tends to isolate the forms of writing. Poetry and fiction are insulated from other English department courses as if they might be contagious. [Of course they are, but I don't see how you can appreciate literature unless you have tried to make literature.)

Nonfiction narratives, even descriptions, are often discouraged in composition courses although they are essential to most nonfiction tasks. Drama and film writing are segregated in the theater and film departments; journalism, business, scientific, and technical writing all have their own ghettos. Yet the techniques of each genre may contribute to other genres.

As an undergraduate, I wrote nothing but poetry. I wanted to be a poet who, every five years or so, wrote a great novel. But those jobs were filled when I was graduated and, liking to eat, I tried journalism. Through the years, I have written for newspapers, radio, and magazines; ghost written for politicians and corporations; published a ghost-written business book, two juvenile nonfiction books, two novels, a pile of academic books and texts. I write a newspaper column, publish a newsletter as a writing coach, and have returned to my first delight, poetry.

Each has its particular challenges and satisfactions, but the similarities in all these tasks are far greater than the differences. Writing is writing.

I hope you will try different forms of writing as a way of having fun. I am going to offer a few words about each of the genres from my experience that may help you get started.

Nonfiction

Barbara Tuchman once said that nonfiction was a terrible name for the most popular and largest genre. It implies everything left over after the good stuff. She said we should use the term *realtors*, but it was taken.

There are more forms with the genre of nonfiction than any other form: biography and autobiography, how-to books, nature essays, magazine and newspaper articles, humor, letters, scholarly studies, the list goes on and on and on. Try some of them. You may surprise yourself.

Fiction

Storytelling is the genre central to human civilization. This summer, I stood at the ocean's edge in the Norwegian arctic, studying the stories carved in rock 6,000 years ago. They told the story of their survival. Man is the story-telling animal.

We experience an elemental satisfaction when we hear a story from another person, from film, from the pages of a newspaper, magazine, or book. And we feel an enormous satisfaction—joy—when we tell our stories. And we all have many stories to tell.

The trick of narrative writing is to escape from the habit of telling *about* the story and let the story tell itself. Start with one character. Have that *character* say something significant to someone else in *dialogue* and reveal the *conflict* in the answer. Put them in a *setting* and you have created a *scene*, the basic unit of narrative. The story moves forward from the energy released from the conflict between the characters.

Drama

See above. The great difference is that *everything* has to be done through dialogue.

Poetry

Don't worry about rhyme and meter. Most poetry today is not rhymed. The basic unit of contemporary poetry is the line.

Again, as in fiction, don't tell *about* what you are writing and don't tell the reader how to feel, just give the essential experience in images that will make the reader see, feel, think. Write in lines, not sentences, and play with the line breaks—the lengths of the lines—and verses, if any, the groupings of lines that deliver your message to the reader.

Experiment with genre. The exercise will sharpen and extend your writing skills and, even more, you may experience the joys and satisfactions of the writing art.

A Writer's Case History: "I Still Wait for the Sheets to Move"

This personal essay was written in a most unusual manner. In writing the first edition of *Write to Learn*, I decided to demonstrate *all* the techniques I introduced by working on one piece of writing. This was the result.

The first and second editions of this book showed one writer working on the same material and anyone who wants to know all that went into this essay can examine either edition. Many readers, however, grew tired of grandmother or were concerned with the focus on just one form of writing, the personal essay. And so was I. This edition is the result.

To demonstrate how the writing process I have described comes together, I am going to review what I did at the various stages of the writing process while producing "I Still Wait for the Sheets to Move."

Finding This Subject

When I first decided to use one piece of writing to demonstrate many writing techniques throughout a book I realized I had to have a subject that would maintain my interest through the writing and that would interest students. I brainstormed in my head those subjects that itched, and kept coming back to my grandmother, the most powerful figure of my childhood.

I had not written about her, although she was the dominant figure in my family. She lived with us, but we lived in *her* house. I sensed how much she had marked me, but had never dealt with it. I had to write about her, but I didn't know what I would hear myself writing. I had rebelled against her as much as I loved her, and I was critical of what she had done to her children, and did not share, entirely their admiration for her. It would be a complicated personal and perhaps painful subject, but since all of us have to deal with powerful family members who were present or not, I thought readers would be interested—and stimulated to "write" their own essays in their heads as they read mine.

I began by brainstorming in my daybook and found there was an abundant amount of material and that the material began to connect and relate. I did other activities similar to brainstorming, and they all revealed that I had a rich subject, full of tension, with the possibility of surprise if I pursued it.

Collect

I did formal library research about the period in which my grandmother lived and the country in which she grew up. I also had the results of genealogy that gave me some information, but the first big surprise came when I interviewed her remaining child, and discovered that my grandfather was not the business success he had been built up to be, but a failure. My grandmother had to bake bread to support the family, and he didn't die at home in Boston, where the family lived, but in Philadelphia, where he was working as a clerk. He had always been held up to me as a mill owner, evidence that although we lived in a working-class neighborhood, we belonged in at least the upper middle class.

I had a deeper appreciation for the fact that my grandmother had to be strong, and began to have a bit more compassion for the controlling strength that had seemed to weaken each of her children. And I also understood, more clearly than before, the family's desperate need to hang on to the middle class, not to sink down economically and socially.

Focus

All the focusing activities made me realize that I had to concentrate on my memories of my grandmother. I couldn't write about my grandmother from the family's point of view, or society's, or the point of view of Scottish immigration, or from the point of view of her children, or her other grandchildren; it had to be from my point of view. And if I pursued this topic I would discover something more than I now knew about my grandmother and, perhaps, about her influence on me.

Order

In outlining and writing draft openings, I began to hear the voice that would be appropriate to the piece. It was the voice of a mature person looking back on a childhood. I could not write it as a child, but I could write from where I now am, thinking back to my childhood. I felt and heard a music that I can't really describe in other words, but that kept coming alive in the fragments and in the draft beginnings I wrote. That voice seemed to have enough distance to be able to put our relationship into perspective, so that readers could discover something about their own families as they read me discovering something about mine. And there was warmth in the voice. It could be critical, but it was not the voice of revenge. I heard a loving and compassionate voice.

And the beginning grew clear to me. I had to open by describing my first morning chore, an experience so natural and so much a part of my childhood that I did not think it was unusual and that it had influenced my life, until I told my wife about it. She saw its importance, and then I discovered it.

Develop

I wrote the draft fast. I was full of my subject, and I wanted to let it come as naturally as it would. I didn't fear overwriting; I knew that I would read and cut and add and reorder.

I can remember, although I wrote this essay years ago, hearing the text. I was led by the sound of what I was saying almost as much as by what I was saying. This sort of personal essay is, of course, a matter of tone. It is the tone of voice that leads the writer and, if the writer is lucky, leads and captures the reader.

Clarify

I did the three readings, first for content, then for order, and finally for language. I know that some of the people who read the previous text were surprised at how critical I was. My draft looked very good to them and they didn't believe how harshly I read my text. I am flattered they liked my draft, but I am a professional, and I suppose my first draft seems more complete to the non-professional than it does to me. I have taught myself to stand back and be critical and, in fact, my danger is that I may be too critical and that I will not see what works because of my concern with what does not work.

The first reading did show me that I had a piece, and the second reading helped me to cut, focus, and shape it. And then, in the third reading, I went to work on the language. Now the computer makes all this struggle for spontaneity invisible. Here is how I edited the first two pages of text with pen and ink.

The Final Draft

The difficulty in writing the personal essay is that it may be too personal, an autobiographical listing that has no meaning, or that only has a private meaning for the writer. The effective personal essay takes human experience and gives it a meaning that causes readers to reflect on their own personal experiences. I hope I have accomplished that. You can read the draft and decide.

~~Waiting~~ I Still Wait for the Sheets to Move

~~When~~ I woke in the black New England *a family*
mornings to ~~do~~ my paper route, ~~I had a~~ chore
that came before *and stood*
~~to perform first. I had to~~ go ~~and stand~~ in the
my grandmother's *to*
pale orange of ~~her~~ night-light ~~and~~ watch ~~to see~~
if the sheets rose and fell.

This tall authority of my childhood, ~~who~~
a personal ~~friend of~~
~~was more powerful than~~ God, ~~and was loved with~~
acquaintance of
ed
fear~~)~~ by all the uncles and her daughter, my
now *her breathing barely*
mother, was so frail ~~now she hardly had to~~ move
d
the sheets ~~to breathe~~. I tried not to look at the
black hole of her mouth—her teeth grinned in
a glass on the night table—and studied the top
sheet. It did not move. This was the night
before I decided
Grandma ~~had~~ died. Just ~~as I was ready~~ to go
~~and~~ wake my parents, the sheet suddenly fluttered and fell.

~~(Death had always seemed to live~~ in our
~~dark house, not in the shadows~~ but sitting right
there, his legs crossed, wearing his terrible smile,
just seated in the living room chair, waiting.
The sermons talked of a real life hereafter. There
were houses in Heaven and a universal broiler

Margin notes:

Problem—how to work in my age? Necessary?

Made more active, immediate.

Forgot to introduce "her."

In each line there are a hundred possibilities considered and reconsidered. I considered and reconsidered "authority of my childhood" a dozen times.

This is the fun of editing—I have a piece of writing now that I can work on. It's meaning may come clear to me.

It was important to write this, and important to cut it.

down below. Grandma lived with Morison, who

had gone before, and she was glad that Helen,

her daughter, had died in the flu epidemic, be-

cause she went with a man who drank beer.

Every night I got down on my knees in my dark

bedroom and prayed " ... if I should die before

I wake.... "

I remember ~~?~~ as
~~My~~ first ~~memories of~~ Grandma ~~must have~~ ~~are~~

~~been when I was seated or crawling on the floor.~~

A great column of skirts ~~that rose to the vast~~

~~swellings, and above them~~ her face looking down,

was
disapproving, ~~and~~ her hair gathered ~~into~~ a top-

the   on   is head
knot like ~~a~~ crown, Queen Mary, whose picture

the Bible's and the gilt-framed steel
was in the living room with King George, ~~were~~

engraving crated from Scotland and always hung in the front room.
~~her hair the same way.~~

H   taught me her
~~I knew the legends of~~ Grandma ~~from my~~

own legends. How
~~mother, from the uncles, and from herself. She~~

~~would tell me, to teach me~~ I should never dis-

as
obey, ~~that~~ she had disobeyed when she was a

schoolgirl on Islay, an island in the Hebrides

led her friends through
off Scotland, She had ~~taken~~ the shortcut across

Margin notes:

I thought "swelling" was clever when I wrote it. That should have told me. It wasn't—a distraction.

I hope these details establish the atmosphere of British lower-middle-class respectability.

How hard it is to fight that weed, the verb "to be."

Changed punctuation for emphasis.

I hope there's a little surprise in this.

I Still Wait for the Sheets to Move

1   I woke in the black New England mornings to a family chore that came before my paper route, and stood in the pale orange of my grandmother's night-light to watch if the sheets rose and fell.

2   This tall authority of my childhood—a personal acquaintance of God—feared by all the uncles and her daughter, my mother, was so frail her breathing barely moved the sheets. I tried not to look at the black hole of her mouth—her teeth grinned in a glass on the night table—and studied the top sheet. It did not move. This was the night Grandma died. Just before I decided to wake my parents, the sheet suddenly fluttered and fell.

3   I first remember Grandma as a great column of skirts and her face looking down, disapproving. Her hair was gathered in a topknot like the crown on Queen Mary, whose picture was in the living room with King George, the Bible, and the gilt-framed steel engravings crated from Scotland and always hung in the front room.

4   Grandma taught me her own legends. How when she was a schoolgirl in Islay, an island in the Hebrides off Scotland, she had led her friends through the shortcut across the forbidden pasture. I should never disobey as she had disobeyed. Grandma had looked for the bull, but hadn't seen him, and had taken the chance he was not there, as if she had known better than her parents. Then the bull charged.

5   She shoved her friends behind her, pulled her huge sewing scissors from her schoolbag, and rammed them up the nostrils of the bull.

6   At the end of the story, she always reminded me to obey my parents, but, of course, I started looking for shortcuts, hoping for bulls.

7   When I was a child, still living in a single-family house, there was a great porcelain jar in the front hall and, in it, a bouquet of umbrellas and canes. It reminded me of what happened to the robber. It was after Grandmother sailed to America from Scotland for the first time, and when the grandfather I never knew still owned the mill. The payroll was in the safe at the house, and Grandfather was away on business, when Grandma heard someone downstairs.

8   She found the robber in the kitchen, and he pointed a six-gun at her. She said, "Wait right there." Anyone who knew Grandmother knew he waited. She went to the front hall, selected a heavy cane from the same porcelain jar, returned to the kitchen, broke the robber's wrist with one stroke. Then Grandmother called my Uncle Alec, her oldest son, and told him to fetch the constable.

9   I never really began to understand why the uncles and my mother were so tied to Grandmother for direction and approval. She certainly gave them direction, but precious little approval. Scots felt duty, obligation, and

guilt were better motivators than praise and earthly reward. While researching this paper I found that Grandma's husband, Morison Smith, whose face looked so sure of itself in the brown photograph on the wall of Grandma's bedroom, had died a failure. Mother and Grandma never let on about that. I was told he had been a mill owner, and he was held up to me as a standard of achievement and proof I belonged in the middle class. But Grandfather, it turns out, lost the mill and lost many other positions. Grandma baked bread to keep the family going. The farm girl from Islay had been a servant girl in London on the command of the absentee landlord, but she escaped that life a decade later by marrying a widower as he left for America to manage a linen mill. Eventually he started his own mill, and she had servants of her own as a mill owner's wife. But he had a "fiddle foot." He was always looking for a better position, a quicker way to become rich. Once he made Grandma cook chocolates on a kitchen stove and he sold them door to door, dreaming he was a Cadbury. Their children saw it was Mother who kept them together as Father failed in America, in England, in Scotland, and then back in America again, where he died, his youngest son still in school.

10   I despised her pretensions when I was young. We lived in a working class neighborhood and I could not understand how important it was that we believed we were middle class. She was obsessed with what the neighbors thought. The shades had to be drawn just so, and she changed her clothes every afternoon. We never ate in the kitchen until she was paralyzed and didn't know. Her Sunday dinners were ceremonies, and the family came back for every holiday. She sat at the head of the table.

11   My mother, my father, my uncle, and I all lived in Grandmother's house, all children always. My mother did not cook, for it was Grandma's kitchen and Grandma's special wood stove; my father, who wore his salesman's smile to work or church, always kept his distance from my grandmother, as if he were still my mother's suitor; my spinster uncle, the accountant, ate his meals quickly, then returned to his account books on the oak desk in the corner of his bedroom; and I took to the streets.

12   They feared Grandma too much to leave. Our home seemed glued together by fear: fear of God, whose lightning-fast rod was held by Grandma; fear of the neighbors, especially those who were Irish Catholic; fear of drink, the curse of Scotland; fear of Roosevelt; fear of smoking; fear of sex; fear of failure; fear of having dirty underwear when they take you to the hospital after the accident; fear of being hit by lightning; fear of irregularity and perpetual constipation; fear of food that might poison; fear of the flu that had killed Aunt Helen in 1917; fear of rust that could cause blood poisoning that left Uncle Alec with a bent finger; fear of the bruise that would become the lump that would become cancer; fear of what you might say and fear of what you might not say; and the greatest fear of all, Grandma.

13   But she did not entirely terrify me and I don't know why. When I said "darn" she scrubbed out my mouth with laundry soap, and when I tanned in the summer she took the same brown soap and the scrubbing brush she used on the linoleum in the kitchen to scrub the tan away. She believed that

"to spare the rod was to harm the child." I was not harmed; her rod was not spared. I was spanked with a shaving strap, with the back of a hairbrush soaked to make it hurt the more, and with my father's hand on my grandmother's command. But I also knew her in a way that her own children did not seem to know her.

14   When I was young, my mother, not allowed to cook or clean in Grandma's house, spent her days with friends, shopping in Boston as if my father owned a mill instead of selling ladies' hosiery. I was alone with Grandma, I sang hymns with her as she did the housework and kept quiet when I heard her talking, casually, with God.

15   Grandmother was the only one who knew my friends who lived in the walls. She did not talk at them, smiling knowingly and winking over my head; she visited with them. She always remembered the imaginary cake in the invisible pan, and when I painted and repainted the back steps with water, she always knew to step over the wood where the paint had not yet dried. When I tipped over the woven cane living room chairs and covered them with a blanket, she would visit me in the igloo, the cave, the tent. When I lined up the dining room chairs she would sit in the bow and paddle the war canoe, and when I put the fan in front she would fly with me to Paris, as Lindbergh had just done. At the end of the day, when all her chores were done and it was too early to light the lamps and start supper, yet too dark to read, she would let me sit with her in the gloaming, sharing her quiet.

16   Then one Saturday night I rushed up to bed, leaping two steps at a time, and found Grandmother collapsed on the stairs. Her dress moved at last, but she only grunted and could not seem to make sounds with her mouth, now strangely lopsided, and I can still hear myself scream for help.

17   Late that night, after they had told me time and time again to go to bed and I had paid no attention, long after Dr. Bartlett had gone, we all stood around her bed, where she lay propped halfway up on pillows. I was closest to her on her right side, and when she grew agitated, trying to speak with a terrible animal sound and flailing wildly with her one good arm, I brought her a pad of paper, and I translated the meaning that lay between the scrawled note and the face that was so terribly pulled down on one side. It was I who laughed, and I remember Grandma nodding when I said, "She's telling you when to put the leg of lamb in the oven for Sunday dinner."

18   Grandma might have suffered a stroke—a shock she would call it—but she would survive, and she would tell us what to do. She lived until she was eighty-nine, another eleven years, and she never got out of bed except when we carried her in a special canvas sling to the couch in the living for a few awkward holiday dinners that never went right without Grandma in the kitchen.

19   She grew thin, and her auburn hair that had been gray turned white. Her left arm, which had always been so busy making bread or grape jelly or the thick kidney soup I loved, lay curled and useless outside of the covers, unless we put it in. The skin on that hand grew soft; it was almost transparent, it had the shiny pale colors I saw on the inside of sea shells.

20   In the early mornings when I went out on my paper route, when I returned for breakfast, when I came home from school, when I came in from playing street hockey, I always checked to see if the sheets still moved. I gave my Victorian grandmother the bedpan when it was needed, I wiped her afterwards, I helped lift her up in bed, I put salve on her bedsores, and I fed her who had once fed me.

21   Her physical world shrank to as far as she could reach with her bamboo back-scratcher. She used it to pull up the dark green Black Watch shawl she had brought from Scotland. That back-scratcher is still on my desk. She talked more often with God and lost her sense of time, asking for lunch just after we cleared the luncheon dishes away. But my mother, in her forties and in her fifties, still took daily instruction from Grandma on how to make tea and never felt she did it right.

22   I went away summers to get tans Grandma could no longer scrub off. At home I had a ceiling of maps—Arabia, Antarctica, Africa, China and Japan—and thought I would leave home. I hung out with the Irish. No one in the family smoked, so I learned to let a cigarette hang from the corner of my mouth, and taught myself to squint my eyes against the smoke. I took that first drink and then I took more. I ate strange Mediterranean food—spaghetti and ravioli. I ate the pepper and the salads we never served at home, and went off to college to play football and to think I had left Grandma and my family forever.

23   The last time I saw Grandmother I was a paratrooper going overseas to fight Hitler. I stood by my grandmother's bed and she smiled her crooked smile and held my hand with her good right hand, terribly weak now. She knew I was going off to war, but as we talked I realized I was not this Donald going off to World War II or Donald, her son, who was in the Navy in the First World War, or Donald her father, or Donald her brother, but Donald her great-uncle who had sat around the fire when she was a girl in the 1860's and shown off the bent leg that had taken a ball at Waterloo. And with that bringing together that the elderly can do, spanning centuries in a second, I became that lad going off to fight Napoleon.

24   Grandma died in a letter I received when I was hiding from shellfire in the rubble of a German city, but I knew by then I would never really leave home, that I would never live without the sense of death nearby. Now I have, like Grandma, buried my father, my mother, and a daughter. I live to more of her standards than I like to admit, and when I wake early or come home late it is first with a sense of dread. I stand in the shadows of the upstairs hall, watching the ones I love, to see if the sheets will move.

As I have with my other essays in the book, I am going to invite you to read the text with me, to see what I think my problems were and how I attempted to solve them.

I Still Wait for the Sheets to Move

1 I woke in the black New England mornings to a family chore that came before my paper route, and stood in the pale orange of my grandmother's night-light to watch if the sheets rose and fell.

> I simply want to put the reader in my childhood shoes as quickly and directly as possible. I do NOT want to play on the reader's emotions with language, simply allow the reader to discover the tension in the situation. How did I research it? By becoming that boy again. Reading this over, I am again struck by how much is established in these few lines.

2 This tall authority of my childhood—a personal acquaintance of God—feared by all the uncles and her daughter, my mother, was so frail her breathing barely moved the sheets. I tried not to look at the black hole of her mouth—her teeth grinned in a glass on the night table—and studied the top sheet. It did not move. This was the night Grandma died. Just before I decided to wake my parents, the sheet suddenly fluttered and fell.

> I need to establish how important she was, to make sure the reader knows the implications of the sheets in the first paragraph, and to allow the reader to share what I thought had happened more mornings than not.

3 I first remember Grandma as a great column of skirts and her face looking down, disapproving. Her hair was gathered in a topknot like the crown on Queen Mary, whose picture was in the living room with King George, the Bible, and the gilt-framed steel engravings crated from Scotland and always hung in the front room.

> Now I can go back and describe how grandmother was before she became ill. I went back in my mind's eye and I like "a great column of skirts" and her disapproving look that establishes a key tension in the piece.

4 Grandma taught me her own legends. How when she was a schoolgirl in Islay, an island in the Hebrides off Scotland, she had led her friends through the shortcut across the forbidden pasture. I should never disobey as she had disobeyed. Grandma had looked for the bull, but hadn't seen him, and had taken the chance he was not there, as if she had known better than her parents. Then the bull charged.

> There's a nice tension in that she taught me her own legends. I have to allow the reader to discover the story, the most important grandmother legend to me when I was young. Perhaps I should have gotten out of the way and let her tell the story in a direct quote.

5 She shoved her friends behind her, pulled her huge sewing scissors from her schoolbag, and rammed them up the nostrils of the bull.

6 At the end of the story, she always reminded me to obey my parents, but, of course, I started looking for shortcuts, hoping for bulls.

> I discovered the tension between what she intended to teach and what she taught by writing this piece. I had never realized that before.

7 When I was a child, still living in a single-family house, there was a great porcelain jar in the front hall and, in it, a bouquet of umbrellas and canes. It reminded me of what happened to the robber. It was after Grandmother sailed to America from Scotland for the first time, and when the grandfather I never knew still owned the mill. The payroll was in the safe at the house, and Grandfather was away on business, when Grandma heard someone downstairs.

8 She found the robber in the kitchen, and he pointed a six-gun at her. She said, "Wait right there." Anyone who knew Grandmother knew he waited. She went to the front hall, selected a heavy cane from the same porcelain jar, returned to the kitchen, broke the robber's wrist with one stroke. Then Grandmother called my Uncle Alec, her oldest son, and told him to fetch the constable.

> Another anecdote/legend to demonstrate the importance to me of the person who was dying. I need to establish how important she was to make the reader understand the effect of her lying paralyzed in her bed.

9 I never really began to understand why the uncles and my mother were so tied to Grandmother for direction and approval. She certainly gave them direction, but precious little approval. Scots felt duty, obligation, and guilt were better motivators than praise and earthly reward. While researching this paper I found that Grandma's husband, Morison Smith,

> Now we have the truth behind the legends as I share my discoveries about my grandfather.

whose face looked so sure of itself in the brown photograph on the wall of Grandma's bedroom, had died a failure. Mother and Grandma never let on about that. I was told he had been a mill owner, and he was held up to me as a standard of achievement and proof I belonged in the middle class. But Grandfather, it turns out, lost the mill and lost many other positions. Grandma baked bread to keep the family going. The farm girl from Islay had been a servant girl in London on the command of the absentee landlord, but she escaped that life a decade later by marrying a widower as he left for America to manage a linen mill. Eventually he started his own mill, and she had servants of her own as a mill owner's wife. But he had a "fiddle foot." He was always looking for a better position, a quicker way to become rich. Once he made Grandma cook chocolates on a kitchen stove and he sold them door to door, dreaming he was a Cadbury. Their children saw it was Mother who kept them together as Father failed in America, in England, in Scotland, and then back in America again, where he died, his youngest son still in school.

10 I despised her pretensions when I was young. We lived in a working class neighborhood and I could not understand how important it was that we believed we were middle class. She was obsessed with what the neighbors thought. The shades had to be drawn just so, and she changed her clothes every afternoon. We never ate in the kitchen until she was paralyzed and didn't know. Her Sunday dinners were ceremonies, and the family came back for every holiday. She sat at the head of the table.

Within this new context, I describe how we lived.

11 My mother, my father, my uncle, and I all lived in Grandmother's house, all children always. My mother did not cook, for it was Grandma's kitchen and Grandma's special wood stove; my father, who wore his salesman's smile to work or church, always kept his distance from my grandmother, as if he were still my mother's suitor; my spinster uncle, the accountant, ate his meals quickly, then returned to his account books on the oak desk in the corner of his bedroom; and I took to the streets.

I show the effect of this powerful woman on her children and my father, her son-in-law.

12 They feared Grandma too much to leave. Our home seemed glued together by fear: fear of God, whose lightning-fast rod was held by Grandma; fear of the neighbors, especially those who were Irish Catholic; fear of drink, the curse of Scotland; fear of Roosevelt; fear of smoking; fear of sex; fear of failure; fear of having dirty underwear when they take you to the hospital after the accident; fear of being hit by lightning; fear of irregularity and perpetual constipation; fear of food that might poison; fear of the flu that had killed Aunt Helen in 1917; fear of rust that could cause blood poisoning that left Uncle Alec with a bent finger; fear of the bruise that would

A powerful indictment of my home life. I hope I am being fair. I was astonished as I heard myself writing the litany of fears.

become the lump that would become cancer; fear of what you might say and fear of what you might not say; and the greatest fear of all, Grandma.

13 But she did not entirely terrify me and I don't know why. When I said "darn" she scrubbed out my mouth with laundry soap, and when I tanned in the summer she took the same brown soap and the scrubbing brush she used on the linoleum in the kitchen to scrub the tan away. She believed that "to spare the rod was to harm the child." I was not harmed; her rod was not spared. I was spanked with a shaving strap, with the back of a hairbrush soaked to make it hurt the more, and with my father's hand on my grandmother's command. But I also knew her in a way that her own children did not seem to know her.

Now the reader is asking what my relationship was to my grandmother. I tell them.

14 When I was young, my mother, not allowed to cook or clean in Grandma's house, spent her days with friends, shopping in Boston as if my father owned a mill instead of selling ladies' hosiery. I was alone with Grandma, I sang hymns with her as she did the housework and kept quiet when I heard her talking, casually, with God.

It is a surprising relationship. Not what the reader expects—not what I expected writing this. I try to document that relationship with specific examples. I know the more specific I am, the more I will spark the reader's own memories.

15 Grandmother was the only one who knew my friends who lived in the walls. She did not talk to them, smiling knowingly and winking over my head; she visited with them. She always remembered the imaginary cake in the invisible pan, and when I painted and repainted the back steps with water, she always knew to step over the wood where the paint had not yet dried. When I tipped over the woven cane living room chairs and covered them with a blanket, she would visit me in the igloo, the cave, the tent. When I lined up the dining room chairs she would sit in the bow and paddle the war canoe, and when I put the fan in front she would fly with me to Paris, as Lindbergh had just done. At the end of the day, when all her chores were done and it was too early to light the lamps and start supper, yet too dark to read, she would let me sit with her in the gloaming, sharing her quiet.

Now a transition. The reader probably has forgotten the grandmother who is near death, has concentrated on the powerful grandmother I knew before her collapse. Now a transition, a major turning point in the piece.

16 Then one Saturday night I rushed up to bed, leaping two steps at a time, and found Grandmother collapsed on the stairs. Her dress moved at last, but she only grunted and could not seem to make sounds with her mouth, now strangely lopsided, and I can still hear myself scream for help.

" dress moved at last" ties back to the beginning. I hope the reader shares the horror of this powerful figure struck down and the effect on her young grandson when he finds her.

17   Late that night, after they had told me time and time again to go to bed and I had paid no attention, long after Dr. Bartlett had gone, we all stood around her bed, where she lay propped halfway up on pillows. I was closest to her on her right side, and when she grew agitated, trying to speak with a terrible animal sound and flailing wildly with her one good arm, I brought her a pad of paper, and I translated the meaning that lay between the scrawled note and the face that was so terribly pulled down on one side. It was I who laughed, and I remember Grandma nodding when I said, "She's telling you when to put the leg of lamb in the oven for Sunday dinner."

> The boys's special relationsihp with his grandmother makes this believable. Now we have another grandmother legend: She thought of Sunday dinner at a time like this.

18   Grandma might have suffered a stroke—a shock she would call it—but she would survive, and she would tell us what to do. She lived until she was eighty-nine, another eleven years, and she never got out of bed except when we carried her in a special canvas sling to the couch in the living for a few awkward holiday dinners that never went right without Grandma in the kitchen.

> I cover a lot of material here.

19   She grew thin, and her auburn hair that had been gray turned white. Her left arm, which had always been so busy making bread or grape jelly or the thick kidney soup I loved, lay curled and useless outside of the covers, unless we put it in. The skin on that hand grew soft; it was almost transparent, it had the shiny pale colors I saw on the inside of sea shells.

20   In the early mornings when I went out on my paper route, when I returned for breakfast, when I came home from school, when I came in from playing street hockey, I always checked to see if the sheets still moved. I gave my Victorian grandmother the bedpan when it was needed, I wiped her afterwards, I helped lift her up in bed, I put salve on her bedsores, and I fed her who had once fed me.

> I remind the reader of my early morning chore and extend it to what else I do for her.

21   Her physical world shrank to as far as she could reach with her bamboo back-scratcher. She used it to pull up the dark green Black Watch shawl she had brought from Scotland. That back-scratcher is still on my desk. She talked more often with God and lost her sense of time, asking for lunch just after we cleared the luncheon dishes away. But my mother, in her forties and in her fifties, still took daily instruction from Grandma on how to make tea and never felt she did it right.

> Yet she still controlled the family.

22   I went away summers to get tans Grandma could no longer scrub off. At home I had a ceiling of maps—Arabia, Antarctica, Africa, China and Japan—and thought I would leave home. I hung out with the Irish. No one in the family smoked, so I learned to let a cigarette hang from the corner of my mouth, and taught myself to squint my eyes against the smoke. I took that first drink and then I took more. I ate strange Mediterranean food—spaghetti and ravioli. I ate the pepper and the salads we never served at home, and went off to

> I escape.

college to play football and to think I had left Grandma and
my family forever.

23 The last time I saw Grandmother I was a paratrooper going
    overseas to fight Hitler. I stood by my grandmother's bed and
    she smiled her crooked smile and held my hand with her good
    right hand, terribly weak now. She knew I was going off to
    war, but as we talked I realized I was not this Donald going off
    to World War II or Donald, her son, who was in the Navy in
    the First World War, or Donald her father, or Donald her
    brother, but Donald her great-uncle who had sat around the
    fire when she was a girl in the 1860's and shown off the bent
    leg that had taken a ball at Waterloo. And with that bringing
    together that the elderly can do, spanning centuries in a
    second, I became that lad going off to fight Napoleon.

> A powerful scene—the last time I would see grandmother and she placed my war in a family and an international historical context.

24 Grandma died in a letter I received when I was hiding from
    shellfire in the rubble of a German city, but I knew by then I
    would never really leave home, that I would never live without
    the sense of death nearby. Now I have, like Grandma, buried
    my father, my mother, and a daughter. I live to more of her
    standards than I like to admit, and when I wake early or come
    home late it is first with a sense of dread. I stand in the
    shadows of the upstairs hall, watching the ones I love, to see
    if the sheets will move.

> And we come to what I learned in writing this essay: I did not escape. And, behind that, the larger truth I do not state but I hope will be written in the reader's mind: No-one escapes.

Write to Learn

The more you write, the more you discover your subject, your world, yourself.
I hope through your writing and mine, you have found out that we do not write
what we know as much as *to* know. Writing is exploration. We use language to
combine experience and feelings and thoughts into a meaning that we may share
with a reader.

Why write? I write, above all, to learn. I hope you have learned that you
learn by writing. I write to find out what I have lived, what I have felt, what I
have thought. I use language as a tool of seeing and understanding, and I will
continue to write, for writing increases my living. I hope you will join me as a
writer because I am never bored, and I always have new things that will be
taught me by my own words appearing on my page. As long as I write I will
continue to learn.

But I will never know how to write. The great crafts are never learned. I
take comfort in that. I continue to learn to write each morning at my writing
desk. I sit down empty, drained, without purpose or possibility, and—if I wait
and listen—words start to come. They arrive in awkward clumps. Often I'm not
sure what they mean, but if I'm patient and prepared, if I do not try to force
the writing, some of the clumps may connect, the fragments may start to flow,
and soon I'm not even aware I'm writing.

When I read what I have written, I am often surprised. If I am lucky and have let language lead me toward meaning, it is not what I intended to write. At my desk I keep learning new tricks of trade, new ways to allow language to extend my world, new ways to surprise myself with my writing.

I hope your writing has surprised you while you have written. I hope that you, like me, will never know how to write, but that we will share the challenge, surprise, and excitement of learning to write and being surprised by what we do not expect to write; write to learn.

Have fun.

Index